25/6/2022

FOLLOWING ON

'Emma's memoir somehow manages to be the story of my own youth. It is a touching and funny account of a cricketing era that though recent also feels very long gone.' – Miles Jupp

'A winner – funny, warm, perceptive, and wonderfully evocative. Highly recommended.' – Michael Simkins

'A beautifully constructed and painfully honest memoir of blind loyalty to an unworthy sporting team.' – Lynne Truss

'Wonderful, funny, elegantly turned and strikingly perceptive. Above all it has a warmth you don't often find in cricket writing.' – Marcus Berkmann

'I have read a fair few cricket books but none like this… Consistently witty and full of wonder.' – Arthur Smith

'A fresh and lively read' – *The Observer*

'*Following On* is a delightful book, and I would strongly urge even those who were not cricket obsessives in the 90s to give it a go.' – Tom Holland, *The Guardian*

'Engaging' – *The Sunday Telegraph*

'It is in equal measure funny, insightful, perceptive, illuminating and best of all a jolly good cricket read.' – *Blackpool Gazette*

'A witty and thoughtful recollection of growing up as a sports-mad girl in the Nineties.' – *School Sport*

'*Following On* is the wonderful story of John's rather unhealthy teenage obsession with England's finest set of losers.' – *The Cricket Paper*

'A real treat of a book that will gladden the hearts of any cricket lover over 25, and b⋯ ⋯ *All Out Cricket*

'John met a⋯ ⋯ She recounts their⋯ ⋯ *tesman*

ABOUT THE AUTHOR

Emma John has been a writer and editor for *The Guardian* and *The Observer* for more than ten years. She is a former deputy editor of *Observer Sport Monthly* and *The Wisden Cricketer*, and in 2008 she was the first woman to win a Sports Journalism Award. She lives in north London and has been on the MCC waiting list for 17 years, six months and 21 days. Not that she's counting.

@em_john

FOLLOWING ON

A MEMOIR OF TEENAGE OBSESSION AND TERRIBLE CRICKET

EMMA JOHN

BLOOMSBURY

LONDON · OXFORD · NEW YORK · NEW DELHI · SYDNEY

John Wisden & Co Ltd
An imprint of Bloomsbury Publishing Plc

50 Bedford Square   1385 Broadway
London   New York
WC1B 3DP   NY 10018
UK   USA

www.bloomsbury.com

WISDEN and the wood-engraving device are trademarks of John Wisden &
Company Ltd, a subsidiary of Bloomsbury Publishing Plc

First published 2016
This paperback edition published 2017

© Emma John 2016

Emma John has asserted her right under the Copyright, Designs and Patents Act,
1988, to be identified as Author of this work.

www.wisden.com
www.wisdenrecords.com
Follow Wisden on Twitter @WisdenAlmanack
and on Facebook at Wisden Sports

British Library Cataloguing-in-Publication Data
A catalogue record for this book is available from the British Library.

Library of Congress Cataloguing-in-Publication data has been applied for.

ISBN: PB: 978-1-4729-1689-1
ePub: 978-1-4729-1688-4

2 4 6 8 10 9 7 5 3 1

Typeset in Minion by Deanta Global Publishing Services, Chennai, India
Printed and bound in Great Britain by CPI Group (UK) Ltd, Croydon CR0 4YY

To find out more about our authors and books visit www.wisden.com.
Here you will find extracts, author interviews, details of forthcoming
events and the option to sign up for our newsletters.

To Mum, Dad and Kate

There be some sports are painful, and their labour
Delight in them sets off. Some kinds of baseness
Are nobly undergone; and most poor matters
Point to rich ends.

The Tempest, William Shakespeare

Chapter 1

It all started with the posters.

My sister Kate and I were visiting my parents. It was a sunny summer's day, and we had just eaten one of our mother's over-generous Sunday roasts. These are two-meat, four-veg affairs, generally followed by a choice of three puddings, the choice being how large a piece of each you eat. Now we were outside recovering on their lawn, sprawled in those indecorous post-lunch poses you can only assume in front of immediate family, and making occasional, food-related groans.

At some stage, our father disappeared to the basement. My parents live in a thatched cottage that sits alongside the Grand Union Canal. In the absence of a loft their cold, concreted basement, inconveniently located below the waterline of the canal and thus frequently flooded, has become the repository for all the crap that family life has accumulated. Obsolete electricals, schoolbooks kept for sentimentality's sake, the lampshade that has needed repairing for the last 20 years, and box files of family photos that never made it into albums: they're all condemned to this mouldy oubliette.

The basement is smelly and morbidly damp. It is packed floor to impossibly low ceiling with crates and boxes that are immovable, utterly unidentifiable, and guarded by ferocious spiders. Dad is the only person brave enough to regularly venture into the basement, but even he has given up pretending to know what it contains, or why.

I can't remember why he'd gone down there that day – perhaps to find some garden furniture or a long-lost board game. When he re-emerged into the garden, he was dragging something huge and dusty behind him.

'Look what I found!'

Two gigantic sheets of cardboard were hinged together in imitation of an artist's portfolio and sealed at the edges with parcel tape. The package's contents bulged pregnantly, and I knew what they were. I had made the cardboard folder, just like I'd made everything it contained.

'Oh God,' my sister groaned. 'Is that what I think it is?'

We slit the tape and opened it up on the ground. Dozens of sheets of coloured card spilled out, each covered in clippings from the sports pages and photographs cut out of magazines. Neatly arranged and mounted, the newsprint had been carefully protected with a layer of sticky-back plastic so that the sheets reflected the sun back into our faces. Dry little balls of Blu-Tack, some with flakes of white paint and wallpaper still clinging to them, dotted their reverse sides.

'Oh, it's your cricket posters!' our mother cried. 'You used to sit up in your room for hours making those!' She sighed nostalgically. 'You were such an industrious teenager.'

'She was such a nerd,' snorted my sister.

Looking up at us from the ground were dozens of men, most in their twenties, some a little older. A few wore tracksuits or blazers, but the majority were clothed in the unique and instantly recognisable costume of the cricket field: the long trousers with elasticated waists, the loose-fitting collared shirt, all in an off-white shade last fashionable in the 19th century. Some of the men in the pictures were smiling and punching the air, as if something wonderful had just happened to them. A far greater number looked dejected, weary and worn out.

Their pictures were accompanied by captions and headlines that provided the context for their misery. 'England lose again.' 'England's worst day.' 'Is this the death of English cricket?' Large blocks of newsprint sought to answer this and other questions. In boxes of smaller type, names and figures were laid out in the arcane architecture of the cricket scorecard:

G. A. Gooch	c & b McDermott 4
M. A. Atherton*	c ¹Healy b McGrath 8
M. W. Gatting	b McDermott 8
A. R. C. Fraser	lbw b McGrath 5

If you knew how to decipher the code contained in these boxes, the players' morose expressions made even more sense. All of the above – pictures, match reports, scorecards – were mounted on sheets of A1 card in bright, confectionery colours, which gave a comically cheerful background to their prevailing message of doom.

As a teenage girl, I was in love with the England cricket team, and these homemade posters had covered my bedroom walls. They were the outward expression of my grand passion, and I'd cut and pasted them together with the fastidious care of a *Blue-Peter*-watching Girl Guide, and the commitment of a monomaniac serial killer.

It was the 1990s, a time when the cool girls at school were concerned with whether to follow Blur or Oasis, and the less cool ones were choosing between Brian Harvey and Marti Pellow. The only men in whites considered acceptable crushes were Richard Gere in *An Officer and a Gentleman*, and Kevin Costner in *No Way Out*. Hero-worshipping the national cricket team was, for a girl of 14, bizarre behaviour. Most of my school mates found following sport of any kind a thoroughly unengaging and pointless endeavour, although the term they preferred was 'completely boring'. These included my best friends, who were prepared to tolerate my obsession so long as I never tried to talk to them about it.

To those who had even the slightest acquaintance with sport, however, my teenage obsession made even *less* sense. At that time, England's cricketers were losers. Literally, losers. They got beaten by almost every team they played against, and often in the most depressing and humiliating way possible. Ennobling them, idolising them, and preserving memories of their less than triumphant progress under sticky-back plastic – that was weird.

As we spread the posters out to get a better look, my own creativity surprised me. Among the giant rectangles, smaller, quirky shapes revealed where space had run low, and I'd fashioned pieces of card to utilise every square inch of wall or ceiling, fitting them into a crazy jigsaw. Some contained only a single image – a picture of the England captain training at the gym, or an advert for the beer that sponsored the team's kit. The makeshift cardboard folder itself bore a florid insignia declaring 'Emma's Cricket Posters', along with what I'd clearly thought were witty annotations:

Contents:

44 x Michael Atherton

35 x Angus Fraser

12 x Alec Stewart

1 x Very Angry Illingworth (Ray, not Richard)

Caution: this pack includes 3 Brian Laras. Strictly no wayward bowling.

Look on my works, ye mighty, and despair.

For the first time, I noticed the peculiar and frequently downbeat nature of the images I had spent my teenage years surrounded by. Batsmen contorting themselves to avoid the 90 mile-an-hour missile intended for their body. Grim-faced men sitting on a balcony, or huddled in anxious conference on the field. A man in a suit, on crutches, waiting for his flight home. All these pictures of physical pain and sporting heartbreak. All these epithets of failure in 72-point bold type. These were what I'd chosen to go to sleep and wake up next to. My sister captured the mood with her usual pith. 'You really were a loser,' she observed, safe in the knowledge that none of the Bon Jovi or Cliff Richard posters with which her bedroom had been decorated were down in the basement, awaiting their own moment of revelation.

I didn't respond – I was too caught up in a wave of strange emotion. The eccentric craft projects were stirring memories, yes, but more than that, they were reigniting feelings. My insides seemed to be humming like a computer just warming up. My chest clenched a little. My heart beat a bit faster. My brain had accidentally stumbled across an old piece of programming, and had started to load it up, and here was the rest of my body, running automatically through the old commands.

Initialising > cricket obsession
Heightened emotions . . . running
Unfulfilled longing . . . in progress
Looking for teenage hormones . . .
. . .
. . .
. . . Teenage hormones not found. Try again?

The flash of stored memory receded quickly, but I could just make out a few of its component parts before it disappeared. There was pride and hope and, hidden at the bottom like a carefully wrapped knife, a gentle stab of disappointment and regret. Mostly, it felt like lovesickness. Those moments when you care so much that even the object of your affection can't soften the painful edge of your keening. Those times when being in love feels like doom.

Once they had flown from whatever emotional archive they had been nesting in, those feelings were followed by a kind of heartache. An indecipherable pang squeezed at my insides and I felt sad – not for my teenage self, even if it had just occurred to me for the very first time (which it had) what a dork I had been. No, I felt sorry for myself now, glimpsing a grand passion, and knowing it was lost, and that nothing in my life today could elicit anything like it. When was the last time I cared about anything *that* deeply?

The cuttings went back only to 1993, the year I'd fallen suddenly, heavily, irrevocably in love with cricket. My timing had been poor. England had lost the very first contest I watched: an Ashes series against Australia, which I learned was the pinnacle of cricketing rivalries (according to those two countries, at least). I could not have guessed, when I first applied Pritt-stick to the back of a batsman's head, that England wouldn't revenge that defeat for another 12 years, or that I'd be out of my teens before they won against any major opposition.

From 1993 to 2000, my England team – and yes, they were *my* England team – played 78 Test matches and won only 17 of them. Their best World Cup performance was a quarter-final appearance. To be blunt, the England team I followed with such ardour were one of the worst in the country's history. You could probably argue, if you were so inclined, that they were actually one of the lowest-achieving international sporting teams of all time. What on earth would possess a teenage girl to start – and then keep – following them?

It wasn't like I had any special interest in sport. PE was my least favourite lesson by a considerable margin; I once faked a fainting fit to get out of a lacrosse session. The only sporting event I had previously cared about was the 1990 World Cup semi-final, when England had gone out to West Germany on penalties and Gazza had cried into his shirt. I had tragedised that result for a day then forgotten all about it.

But cricket was different. From the moment I had grasped the basics of the game, I was all in. It's hard to explain, but it was a little like a superhero origin story – the teenager who wakes up one morning to find she has an entirely new identity. Overnight, some biological anomaly, or perhaps a minor cosmic event galaxies away, has rearranged the very atoms of her being and changed her destiny. Her fate is now fused, for ever, with that of the England cricket team.

If anyone could be blamed for the monomania that followed, it was my mother. My mum *loves* watching sport. It doesn't matter whether it involves 11 players, or 15, or 13, or two. It doesn't matter if they're holding bats or clubs, or racquets or javelins or batons, or their opponents' heads between their knees. If you wish to compete physically with someone else, for nothing more profound than a cut-glass trophy and the chance to be sponsored by a brand of fluorescent-coloured energy drinks, my mother will happily spend an afternoon watching you do it.

Cricket has always been her favourite. Mum's father, my granddad Alex, had loved cricket and been the one to teach her about it; she had lost him to cancer when she was 24. Now it was her favourite sport, and she would happily dedicate an entire weekend to watching the middle days of a Test match. Needing an excuse to commandeer the television, Mum would save up our laundry for days, then erect the ironing board in front of the set. In this way she held the living room hostage for hours at a time with some of the slowest ironing known to woman. Botham, Gatting, Gower and Gooch. My mother's heroes read like the opening credits of *Trumpton*, although the names meant nothing to my sister and me; we merely resented the interruption to our usual programming. From Headingley '81 to the Tiger Moth incident, not to mention both blackwashes, Mum could remember where she'd been for them all. Mostly ironing.

My father did not understand her passion, either for the game (he had never played it) or for watching it. He found the idea of wasting a perfectly good afternoon in front of the television provoking: 'Why do you want to sit inside on this gorgeous day?' For nearly 20 years, my mother ploughed her sofa-shaped furrow alone. No wonder that when one of her daughters finally showed an interest in cricket, she indulged that fledgling passion to the hilt. No wonder she didn't complain about all the Blu-Tack on the walls.

Since its sudden, impassioned beginning, my relationship with the England team has endured two decades. That means it has outlasted any romantic relationship in my life by a factor of at least four to one. This is a mere observation, and certainly not a point of pride.

I have devoted an inordinate amount of my time, thought and heart to English cricket. People tend to consider football fans the most passionate and committed consumers of sport on the planet, because they make the most noise and are, at times, frankly scary. But no one stops to think how many hours of the day we cricket lovers have to devote to our sport. Our games are epic in scale. Test matches – the highest, noblest form of the game, played only between a handful of the best teams in the world – can last five days. Even the one-day international, invented in the 1970s to be a faster-paced format, takes seven hours.

There have been 254 England Tests since I started following them. Assuming these managed an average of three days' play – factoring in early finishes and time lost to rain, and erring on the mean side – that's at least 762 days of cricket. Which is a little over two years. That's not even counting England's one-day games, of which there have been more than 400. I have spent more time actively following my cricket team's progress than it took for Francis Drake to circumnavigate the earth.

With BBC, C4 and Sky Sports as our eager go-betweens, the England team and I have shared a great deal of my available leisure time, and a surprising amount of my work time too (thanks, the internet!). Naturally, a 20-year relationship sees good days and bad ones. There have been sulks and ultimatums and cooling-off periods when the team have let me down once too often, and I have sworn it's all over. But those angry outbursts never seemed to last long, and I'd normally be back, repentant, in time for the very next Test series.

For the first decade, the England team I knew and loved led me a not-so-merry dance of false hope and false starts. Their results were woeful, and their performances sometimes staggeringly awful, but they regularly offered hints, to the optimistically inclined, that they were capable of better. A middle-order batsman would score a century full of flair, a fast bowler would magic up a devastating spell, and fans would begin to wonder aloud if, actually, England weren't a bit underrated. They would then disprove the theory by losing the game and, normally, the series. If there was one thing that was consistent about England in the 1990s, it was their ability to snatch defeat from the jaws of victory.

In 1999 England failed to make it past the qualification rounds of a World Cup that they were actually hosting, then lost a Test series to New Zealand to secure their ranking as the worst Test side in the world. In other words, England, the inventor and exporter of the game, was now worse, officially, than Zimbabwe, a country a quarter of its size and with a smidgeon of its resources, who had been playing Test cricket for only seven years. There were other low points that left greater dents in my psyche, but this was, if not the end, then the beginning of the end of one of the worst periods of English cricket's history.

Groggily, awkwardly, and with more than a few backward stumbles, the England team began to haul themselves off the mat. They started to win series at home and – even more shockingly – abroad. (Until I was 22 years old, the only team I had known them beat in an overseas Test series was New Zealand. And they made hard work of that.)

And then came 2005 and . . . well, you know what happened. Even those who had never watched cricket before became aware, that summer, that something incredible and historic and nerve-janglingly thrilling was happening in the Ashes against Australia. England were competing toe-to-toe with their oldest, toughest enemy in one of the closest fought series in decades. Their progress was followed with the collective national breath-holding normally reserved for the country's football team during a penalty shootout. And when England's cricketers finally secured victory, they were so popular that thousands lined the streets, and a two-mile stretch of central London was instantly closed off for an open-top bus parade.

For cricket fans of a particular generation – those like me who are too young to have lived through previous golden eras – the year 2005 was a watershed. Life before it was lived under one certainty: that we were, when it came down to it, losers. That Ashes victory changed our identity. We may have gone on to suffer other defeats, but defeat was no longer what defined us. Beating Australia was our fairytale ending: it was Cinderella at the ball and Brer Rabbit's revenge and Prince Charming's kiss rolled into one.

Like any fairytale ending, it was also a beginning. Over the next few years I watched England achieve heights I could never have imagined as a teenager. They learned to beat teams, not luckily, dicily, or by the skin of their teeth; this England team could thrash you in three days, then repeat the trick a week later. They went into their matches as favourites. By 2011 they were the number-one ranked team in the world. And those Ashes contests that I'd watched them lose again and again and again (and again and again and again) as I grew up? They won three of them back to back. The England team and I had been on a long journey together. I had learned to accept their flaws, and they, in return, had provided me – eventually – with some of the happiest memories of my life.

But something had altered in the process. When England started winning regularly it had felt, for a while, like heaven. I was justified, vindicated, ecstatic . . . all the things a faith fulfilled is supposed to bring. And then, as the winning had continued, and become expected, I'd begun to feel a bit lost. My team had finally climbed the mountain. They were standing on the summit, looking at the meadow grasses and the goats, and then they were marching on, finding new peaks to ascend. My once-teenage self was wheezing behind at the back, possibly suffering from altitude sickness, and watching them leave.

I had struggled to adulthood alongside a team that seemed to understand my experience of overreaching, toiling to prove myself, of being, in my sister's words, a bit of a loser. I had spent 20 years defining myself with individuals who kept promising as they failed – even when, together, they proved less than the sum of their parts. But now they were world-beaters. Did they even need me any more?

Not long after my dad came across the posters, I was at home in London, and England were in India, at the start of their winter tour. The first Test was taking place, somewhere, I wasn't sure where exactly as the build-up had passed me by. I woke up and reached a sleepy arm out to the radio and turned on the news. '. . . And in the cricket, England face an uphill struggle after India declared on 521 and Cheteshwar Pujara scored a double-century . . .' I switched over to *Test Match Special*. There was a distant thonk, the sound of an England batsman losing his bails four thousand miles away. England were 30 for 3, in dire straits, needing 322 to avoid the follow-on. And I felt . . . nothing. I was completely blasé about the result. I turned off the radio with a heart full of blanks.

I thought back to the afternoon on the sun-frazzled lawn of my parents' house, where I had relived the rush of teenage passion. Relationship counsellors say that indifference is the death knell of a marriage. In that case, England and I were in trouble.

The summer after that tour of India, the one I barely followed, England are facing Australia at home. It isn't a vintage Ashes. England play scrappily, and entire days are lost to the kind of squat, malign rainclouds that only the British summer can conjure. During one of these interruptions, Sky Sports run a replay of the 1994–95 Ashes series. This in itself is rather unusual – normally when required to fill hours of airplay with no new content, the broadcaster chooses to focus on England's glory days of the seventies or eighties, or at the very least replay the epic 2005 triumph in full. But perhaps enough time has passed that the 1990s now feel nostalgic. Maybe everyone has finally had enough of watching England win.

I am intrigued. The original took place in the middle of the British night, and I had seen nothing of it on television but the truncated highlights clips shown on the breakfast news each morning, which usually comprised a raft of England wickets strung together at lightning pace.

Sky are showing the second Test, in Melbourne, which England had arrived at 1–0 down. I can't remember the result – it has been a while since I've even thought about this series, and while I tend to assume that England lost all their matches in Australia in the 1990s, I know they won the odd, consolatory game. So I watch with genuine delight as the England bowlers, Darren Gough, Phil DeFreitas and Devon Malcolm, manage to bowl Australia out for 279 – an unusually low score for the Aussies – and when England respond by getting out for 212, I hiss at my screen. This is a classic wasted opportunity, one we are bound to rue.

I could, of course, confirm my hunch with a quick Google. But instead I keep watching as Australia set England a target of 388 to win. Highlights packages can often feel a little abrupt by their very nature, but the speed of the England demise that follows – all out for 92 – was scarcely slower in real time. Wickets tumble like dominoes; batsmen leave the crease almost as soon they have reached it. The moment that strikes me most is the fall of Michael Atherton, England's captain.

Atherton had watched three of his companions depart and ground out 25 runs before edging a catch down the leg-side – the kind of dismissal you're considered to have brought entirely upon yourself. As he turned to head back to the Melbourne pavilion – the longest and loneliest walk of all cricket grounds – he knew that with him went every sliver of English hope. I wonder: what was he thinking?

Ten thousand miles away, there was a teenage girl who would wake up to the news. Atherton was her favourite player; she'd feel devastated, for him, for his team, for herself. And then she'd carry on supporting them. And I wonder: what *the hell* was she thinking?

I have more questions, too. What kept that England team going at all? Why *did* they lose so much? How come their players never seemed to improve at their job, like normal people? How did all that failure feel? Did it hurt them as much as it hurt me? Could they still get excited about the start of a new season, the way I had? And what was it a nerdish teenager needed, that she could only find in a group of perpetually underachieving cricketers?

Over the next few days, a thought begins to form in my mind; a way to find out the answers. Perhaps I could track down the players and ask them. After all, these men had felt as real, as close, as permanent a part of my life as my family and friends. They had influenced me as much as any teacher or mentor; I had fashioned my identity around their exploits, made life choices based on theirs. Wouldn't it be interesting to find out who they really were, in person? Perhaps it might help me understand – and remember – why I had fallen for them in the first place.

I start to consider how I would go about it. The selection policy for the national team in the 1990s being infamously haphazard, there were dozens of players who earned their place on my teenage walls, and I can't meet them all. But if there's one thing being a cricket fan teaches you, it's the art, and sheer joy, of choosing an imaginary XI. Soon my brain is mulling over the candidates, trying to pick a balanced team. I want the players who best represented the struggles and vicissitudes of my youth, but also epitomised their cricketing era in all its hope, folly and occasional Pyrrhic triumph.

I narrow it down, eventually, to six batsmen, an all-rounder, and four bowlers. A captain and a vice-captain. Some of them are still famous names, their voices heard regularly from commentary boxes, their faces glimpsed at presentation ceremonies. Others seem to have disappeared entirely. I wonder whether they will even talk to me: sportsmen do not typically enjoy dwelling on their own failure. The whole idea starts to seem a little dangerous. Everyone knows you shouldn't meet your idols, but this probably counts for double if you want to talk about a time that was pretty inglorious for them personally.

But the more I think about it, the more I want to risk it. I want to know what was so special about this team that the faded newspaper print of their pictures can still cause my heart to race – even when their far more victorious successors cannot.

Chapter 2

Two white helmets. That's the first memory I have of the England cricket team. It hovers in my mind, free-floating. It's not moored to any particular piece of sporting action. It's just there, like an impression from early childhood, formed long before you had the understanding to give it context. The colour of your dad's suit, say, or the smell of your nan's face-powder. The squeak of the springs in your first bed.

These two white helmets were worn by two very different men. Underneath the first helmet was a weathered face, skin somewhat tanned, eyes somewhat small. Its wearer had a neat black moustache that seemed to be issuing a stern statement, one slightly undermined by a soft dimple in the chin below it. He had reached maturity a couple of decades before – in the 1970s, if that moustache was anything to go by. The helmet itself, with its white peak, didn't seem so different from a construction worker's hard hat, except that it extended down further, and had yellow flaps that protected its wearer's ears.

The other man's helmet also had ear-protectors – they were a sky blue – and a grille across the front which partially obscured his features. Still, it was easy to see that this man was much younger: he had a positively boyish look. When he smiled, which he seemed to do more often than the first man, it was the smile of the schoolyard, of someone wrapped up in a fun game at break-time.

The men were called Graham Gooch and Michael Atherton – he was never, in my household, 'Mike' – and they were the first players whose names I knew, and whose features I learned to recognise from the television. For someone who had never watched sport, it was hard to understand how two people of entirely different generations could be in the same team, and perhaps that's why the image of the pair of them stuck in my head. But more likely it was the daft look of those ear-protectors.

Mum – who was no doubt ironing at the time – explained that Gooch was the captain of the England team. What this might actually mean was as unfathomable to me as what was happening on the screen. In close-up, the men in helmets seemed to be doing little but standing around, holding a large hunk of wood at their side. Every so often, the TV camera would show a long brown rectangle on the ground, and someone positioned at the end of it hitting a ball. Was it one of the men in helmets? And, if so, where were the rest of their team?

Sport, with its private jargon, invisible rules and assumed patterns of behaviour, can be impenetrable enough at the best of times. But nothing can appear as confusing on first encounter as cricket, particularly if you're watching it on television. A typical sequence of images will include: men in identical kit lobbing a ball between them; men rubbing that ball on their trousers; men clapping their hands; men pulling up their trousers at the knees and positioning themselves into a crouch. And at semi-regular intervals, someone will sling a ball at a chap in a helmet.

Occasionally, a wider shot of the field will attempt to put this baffling mummery in context. Of course, in a football match, when the camera pulls back to reveal the whole pitch, the purpose of the players' actions becomes instantly clear: they are manoeuvring a ball across the ground towards a target at the other end. The same is true of rugby – and of netball, basketball, ice hockey, lacrosse, NFL and Aussie rules. Even if you don't know the first thing about the sport, you can tell what they're trying to achieve.

Show an overhead shot of a cricket pitch, however, and it looks like you've stumbled on a military exercise from the days of Waterloo. White-clothed men stand across a green field in a curious asymmetric pattern, a giant snake of rope surrounding them. At their centre is a thin strip of discoloured turf with some geometric white markings and a man in thick padding standing sentinel at either end. What the overall purpose might be, other than signalling messages to extraterrestrials, is left to your imagination.

The commentary isn't always going to help either. It certainly didn't when I first stumbled across cricket in the early 1990s. This was a time when the BBC treated Test cricket as something that furnished your living room like gently murmuring wallpaper. The discretion of the commentators was supposed to allow the images to speak for themselves. Which was all well and good if you understood how they related to each other, but for the rest of us, a day of Test match coverage was as mystifying as David Lynch on a particularly obtuse day, and one-third as entertaining.

One afternoon I asked my mum a question about what she was watching. Who knows why I asked it; perhaps I was bored. More likely I was lazy and trying to get out of some chore or other, and thought that engaging her in conversation might distract her from the fact she had asked me to tidy the kitchen or lay the table. On the TV, a man was chasing a red ball across a swathe of green, but in the top-left corner of the screen, a separate box showed two men nonchalantly jogging up and down a brown strip, crossing each other as they ran.

'Mum, why are the men in the box jogging?'

'Because they're trying to score runs.'

'What are runs?'

'They're the things that batsmen get when they run between those two white lines.'

'So why is that other man chasing the ball?'

'Because if he gets it back to one of the ends before the batsman gets home, he'll be out.'

'Like rounders?'

'Yes. But instead of having bases, you have wickets.'

'What's a wicket?'

'*Right*—'

When my mother says '*right*', it is not so much a word as a statement of intent. It is delivered with a downward inflection and a brisk, schoolmarmish tone, followed by a slightly dramatic pause. This is a habit left over from her days as a courtroom lawyer, and it signifies that you – be you plaintiff, judge or daughter – are about to be rendered cognisant of Truths which are Vital, Needful and Incontestable. If my mother says '*right*', you pay attention, and you find a chair. You are about to be schooled.

The education that followed was overwhelming, intriguing, dense, ephemeral and all-consuming. Every new piece of information I processed only prompted more questions. Why did everyone get two goes at batting? Why did some bowlers run up fast, and some slow? What did the two men standing around in white coats actually *do*? And, most confusingly of all, why did the word 'wicket' mean three different things?

My mother answered everything with a patience she had no reputation for. In our house, technical questions were summarily despatched to my father, a details man who has a head for trivia and a preternatural understanding of the workings of things. But here she was, leading me step by step through the ten different ways a batsman could get out, who was who in the batting order, how to read the score, and why the fielders stood where they did; my mum uncovered the cogs of the game, plus the intricate, invisible structure that held them together. She did it with such care, such enthusiasm and such seriousness that I intuited how important these conversations were to her, even while I struggled to understand the game itself.

Cricket is not a game you can learn instinctively; nothing about it is especially natural. Just look at the peculiar way you have to hold the bat: no child, lifting a piece of wood to hit a ball, chooses to hold it side-on and lead with their elbow. A bowler's delivery stride, with its learned mechanics, is utterly contrary to the accepted laws of human anatomy. The complexity of the leg-before-wicket dismissal is so evolved that my teenage self spent as much time figuring it out as she did learning to solve quadratic equations.

It is, therefore, a sport that requires a special form of introduction. You cannot come to cricket on your own: it demands a relationship. I have yet to meet an obsessive like me whose fervour was not stoked by a teacher, a friend or a family member. Up to that point in my life, my father had been the parent my sister and I associated with play, the one who messed around with Lego and took us kite-flying. Mum was at the business end of parenting, checking up on homework and report cards, setting the chores. She often seemed serious, and exhausted. My relationship with her was about to change for ever.

Another thing I've realised only in hindsight: if cricket hadn't been so difficult to understand, I might never have bothered with it at all. The game was constantly raising more questions than it answered. Some of the answers never even made sense – the existence of a fielding position called 'cow corner', for instance, or the fact that the members in the Lord's Pavilion had chosen to wear orange-and-yellow-striped ties of their own free will. You had to work hard for the privilege of understanding what you were watching, and it was impossible to ever feel satisfied that you understood this game in its entirety. But that was a big part of the pleasure.

Back to those white helmets. After Graham Gooch and Michael Atherton, the third cricket player whose name I learned was Alec Stewart. He too had a white helmet – it must have been the fashion that year. There was something about him I found rather daunting. He reminded me of my mum's brothers, not because of any family likeness but because of a certain serious, adult expression that his face settled into.

I hadn't come across many male teachers in my single-sex education so, aside from my dad, my uncles were the only men I knew with the power and the licence to tell me off. I was seriously intimidated by the authority they wielded, and the inscrutability of their moods, especially since they were not easily charmed by my know-it-all behaviour, or my word-perfect performances of the songs from *Cats*. I remember the day my uncle Martyn took my sister and me to the seaside, and I bounded up to deliver some clever insult, clumsily brandishing my candyfloss. Its pink stickiness stained his brand new jacket and his wrath was terrible. And I was stunned: how did he not find me adorable?

Alec Stewart looked like the kind of man who would not find me adorable. His face, his body, his whole personality seemed to have been hewn from granite. He held himself with the open-chested deportment of an off-duty soldier, and at 14 years old I instinctively understood, without even knowing the phrase, that this was a man's man.

There was more about him that I could not relate to. He was, for instance, a player of great personal discipline, whose timekeeping, tidiness and immaculate wardrobe were matters of record – and utterly alien to a teenage girl whose bedroom looked like the aftermath of a burglary. Stewart was the kind of man who initialled his shoes and numbered his gloves. He ironed his playing shirts. He also used moisturiser a good decade before it was fashionable for men to do so. Instead of making him the David Beckham of his day, this grooming habit only seemed to render him more practical and predictable.

Stewart had been England's vice-captain for two years, the willing adjutant to Graham Gooch. Gooch was turning 40, and no one knew how much longer he could feasibly go on playing international cricket – many of the chief companions of his playing days, from Ian Botham to David Gower, had already retired. Some thought Stewart would soon succeed him as captain. But not my mum. She thought it would be the baby-faced batsman with the sky-blue ear-protectors. Michael Atherton.

Do people choose their heroes? I'd argue not. Cultural achievements, covetable style, acts of compassion or derring-do – all of these things can make someone a hero, but they don't determine that they'll be your hero. We can admire an artist because their work moves us, or follow a visionary leader because we believe in the rightness of their cause. None of these things, however, can explain why my best friend at primary school, Philippa, had pictures of Bros on her wall, or why she kissed them goodnight before she turned out the light. (Philippa knows I'm not judging her. I was crushing on William Shatner in *TJ Hooker* around that time.)

We hero-worship people not just because of who they are, but because of who we are, too. In the days before it was chic to be a geek, before nerds became celebrated Silicon Valley billionaires, I was an old-fashioned swot. I loved schoolwork and I was good at it. The fact that doing well at my studies pleased my parents, combined with a natural competitive streak, made me a hard worker, the kind who wasn't embarrassed to win school prizes (and got annoyed when she didn't). On top of this, I was an extrovert – a show-off – who loved to be on stage. My dream was to be an actor, and my role models were Stephen Fry and Hugh Laurie, Emma Thompson and Rowan Atkinson. Their common feature: they had all studied at Cambridge University, a place I desperately wanted to go to.

It was an ambition my parents were proud of; they had got their degrees at the same polytechnic, and no one in either of their families had previously been to university. So I'm pretty sure that Michael Atherton's Cambridge degree was one of the first things my mum told me about him. It was certainly what piqued my interest. It isn't entirely unusual for an England cricketer to have an Oxbridge education; cricket has always been the sport of toffs, after all. But in the professional era, when young athletes like Stewart left school at 16 to sign to a team, Atherton's history degree was unusual enough to be a cause for regular remark and mickey-taking among commentators and teammates, and rare enough for me to confer a special status on him.

The fact he was such a young-looking 24-year-old also appealed to a girl who still found grown men rather daunting. What really won my sympathy, however, was watching him trip over. It was June, and cricket was still an unidentified blip on the very periphery of my radar. England were playing Australia in the Ashes at Lord's, and Atherton was on 97, three runs away from scoring a century. If I had understood what I was watching, I would have known that England were 427 runs behind on first-innings scores, and that this was epically bad. I could have appreciated that Atherton's stand with Mike Gatting, which had lasted almost three hours and yielded more than 100 runs, was a vital and positive contribution to the game. But I didn't know any of this. All I saw was the young man with the white helmet and the blue ear-protectors and the Cambridge degree hit the ball to his left and set off to run.

Twice he and Gatting passed each other, almost brushing shoulders as they crossed. When Atherton started for the third time, he saw the fielder ready to throw the ball and quickly realised it was the wrong call. Turning to cover the short distance back to safety, his body seemed to move in two directions: his legs slid forward under their own momentum while the rest of him, already on its way back, fell abandoned to the ground. Even as Atherton re-gathered and pitched himself desperately forward on his knees, the ball arced into the gloves of Australia's wicketkeeper Ian Healy, who broke the stumps while Atherton was still grubbing on the ground.

Getting out on 99, one short of your century, is the most galling thing that can happen to a batsman. Getting run out on 99 is even worse, because unlike, say, being bested by an unplayable delivery, you have effectively fashioned your own downfall. It's like doing the perfect driving test, then sideswiping the examiner's car as you park up. But back in 1993 centuries were one of the confusing traditions I had yet to understand. The significance of scoring 100 runs left me nonplussed: it wasn't like your team got extra points for it, so why was it so much more important to players and spectators than scoring 99 or 95 or 92?

On the other hand, watching a man humbled to the point where he was literally on his knees, crawling in the dirt in a frantic scramble to save himself – that was almost too real. For the first time, sport had revealed itself as cruel and humiliating. The sight of Atherton's demise touched my sensitive teenage soul as surely as Wilfred Owen's 'Anthem for Doomed Youth'. The unfairness and sheer awfulness of that suspended moment won my sympathy, and from now on I cared what happened to Michael Atherton.

The 1993 Ashes series was not an auspicious time to begin watching cricket – not if you were English, at any rate. England had already lost the first Test at Old Trafford, and after Atherton's run-out at Lord's defeat there became inevitable too. After a draw in the third Test, Australia were 2–0 up with three matches left to play. To salvage the series and regain the Ashes, England would need a fantastical reversal of fortune, the kind that required the imagination of Hans Christian Andersen, Heinrich Hoffmann and the Brothers Grimm combined.

Of course, reality prevailed. In the fourth Test, at Headingley in Leeds, England conceded another gigantic first-innings lead and suffered the ignominy of losing by an innings. I don't remember being particularly interested or depressed by the results – my mum had explained that losing the Ashes was both a formality and a regularity – but I did notice Michael Atherton's scores. He had made two half-centuries in Leeds. And while I was still sceptical about the mathematical significance of scoring 50 simply because it was half of 100, it seemed to me further proof that he was a cut above his teammates.

Half an hour after the Ashes had been lost, Graham Gooch, still at the Headingley ground, resigned as captain. Now things had got really interesting. My mother was convinced that Atherton would be England's next captain, and I discovered that this possibility was really quite appealing.

There was, of course, one man in his way.

It is not hard to track down Alec Stewart these days. He's the director of cricket at Surrey, the county he played for all his life. Gooch's vice-captain is one of the uncontested names on my teamsheet, partly because he was England's leading run-scorer of the 1990s – he, more than anyone, must have been frustrated with the team's performances – and partly because I want to know what he really thought of Atherton.

Stewart agrees to see me during a county game at Surrey's home ground, The Oval. On the day of our meeting I set my alarm early. It isn't just that I dread being late to meet someone whose punctuality is legendary – I also need to try on three different outfits before I settle on one smart enough for the encounter. Even when I do, I change out of it to eat breakfast, because the laws of probabilities, of Murphy and of Sod all agree that if I am wearing the only crisp white shirt I own I will absolutely, definitely drop porridge down it.

Heading south on the Northern Line, I emerge from Oval station 20 minutes early – so early, in fact, I kill time with a cup of tea at a café, and make myself late. The resultant scramble to the ground is neither dignified nor professional and puts paid to the crispness of my shirt. Even with the help of the gatemen, it takes a while to find the right entrance to the team offices, and then I find myself lost in an empty, anonymous corridor, whose doors I am terrified to open in case I find myself surrounded by sweaty men in jockstraps. Eventually I run into a man in a suit who explains I am on the wrong floor. In my hopelessly nervous state it seems I got out of the lift too early.

As I head back, a familiar voice reaches me. 'Emma, there you are!' I've heard Stewart on radio and TV too many times to mistake his tones – and here he is, sauntering down the staircase next to the lift. 'They phoned me and said you were here so I thought I'd do the decent thing and come and meet you, but I've been going up and down the stairs and I couldn't find you . . .' He holds out his hand and smiles. The handshake is much gentler than I expected, but then, so is the smile.

The Alec Stewart of the 1990s had a set expression. There was a hard look in his grey eyes that stayed there even when he smiled. If an England fielder had the temerity to miss a ball, or a journalist asked him an irritating question at a press conference, his cheek muscles lapsed into a headmaster-ish look of disappointment. But age has softened his edges. His face shows a modest amount of wear – he has an embedded tan, his tight, wiry crop of hair is enlivened with grey – and it all suits him. He makes for a particularly handsome 50-year-old. I also realise I needn't have worried about my wardrobe choices. Stewart is in a black tracksuit and white trainers; his watch looks the kind you can drop on the floor and expect to bounce.

He takes me to the 'team room' which doubles as his office; there is a boardroom-style table, large enough to sit a 13-man squad, and, on the back wall, a whiteboard, presumably for illustrating tactics, although today it carries nothing more strategic than a few jokey messages between teammates. A row of enormous sash windows, thrown fully open, faces on to the pitch and floods the room with sunshine. The sounds from the middle are so immediate you feel you are practically in the field yourself.

Stewart pops out to make us tea, and I try to take my mind off my nerves by focusing on the game in front of me. Surrey are in the field, and a young Worcestershire batsman called Moeen Ali, with a black beard that reaches past his collar, is closing in on his century. I've only been watching a few seconds when a mistimed shot loops the ball towards a man standing deep in the leg-side field. It passes clean through his hands, and a ghostly sigh whispers around the almost empty stands.

There is a tut of annoyance as Stewart re-enters the room. 'That's the third he's dropped today. *Jees*—' He stops himself. 'Sorry. Kept my language in check there, didn't I?' Handing me a mug, he settles into the chair behind his desk. There is a stool to his left, and I perch on it awkwardly, now a foot taller than Stewart, and terrified of falling off. I start babbling about how, when I first moved to London, I used to live just up the road in Stockwell, and even became a Surrey member for a year or two before I moved to north London. 'And you still support us . . .' he says, not quite a question. My panicked look must give me away. 'It's all right,' he teases. 'You can just lie.'

He is himself a man of strict loyalties – his father, Micky, was a Surrey and England cricketer, and there was no question, as Alec grew up, that he wanted anything different for himself. Still, it hadn't come quickly, his England career: Stewart started playing professional cricket for Surrey at 16, but it was ten years before he got his first cap. In the meantime, he worked and worked at his game: as soon as the English season finished at the end of the summer, he would fly to Australia and spend the winter playing grade cricket in the kind of tough, uncompromising leagues that promise to make a man of you.

Even when Stewart did make it into the England team – against a fearsome West Indies attack in 1990 – there was no suggestion from his scores that he'd stay there. It took him 14 Tests to register his first Test century, and at one point he was dropped from the team by his own dad, who was manager at the time. But Stewart wasn't just a batsman – he'd taught himself to keep wicket, too. 'And it was being able to do dual roles which may have just given me . . .'

The edge?

'. . . a slightly extended stay of execution,' he smiles.

Within two years, Stewart had been installed as Graham Gooch's vice-captain. It made sense. Gooch was a disciplinarian, and Stewart 'looked up to him more than anyone I've played with or against'. To some, this young batsman–keeper who had grafted harder than anyone to secure his place in the team, this 20-something who didn't touch alcohol because he hated not being in control, seemed like Gooch's mini-me. That's why, when Gooch resigned, the naming of his successor took on an extra significance. What did the England team need: more of the same, or a dramatic change? A battle-ready pro with a safe pair of hands? Or a 24-year-old with an academic mind?

It felt, even to someone with as basic and hasty an understanding as mine, like a crucial moment in English cricket. The simple yin–yang narrative was easy to absorb, and the suggestion in the press that there was 'no love lost' between Atherton and Stewart added piquancy. I ask Stewart if the week before the captaincy announcement was a tense one. 'Yeah, so at the time it was built up as a rivalry with Athers which was never, ever the case. It may sound strange, but I had never had an ambition to captain England. My big ambition was to *play* for England.'

I am sceptical. There must have been rivalry. A year before Gooch resigned, Stewart and Atherton had been batting together in India and managed, somewhat idiotically, to get themselves stranded at the same end of the pitch. One of them would have to be given run-out, but each refused to leave until, in the end, the umpire made the decision for them. Stewart was given out, to his obvious displeasure. Some have even claimed it was the moment the England captaincy was decided.

Stewart rolls his eyes at this. 'Run-outs happen all the time,' he says. 'I was actually *in*—' he coughs, jokily, 'but I promise you, there was never any problem between us at all. Which is probably a bit boring for you to hear.' He sounds genuinely apologetic.

In truth, if Stewart had been made captain, my interest in cricket might have been over as quickly as it had begun. It might have died as a one-month fad, like my equally fleeting enthusiasms for plaid, Nicholas Lyndhurst and the poetry of Elizabeth Barrett Browning. As it was, reading on Ceefax that Atherton had got the job was my first taste of cricketing victory.

My family was on a camping holiday in Somerset during Atherton's first Test in charge. Each morning, I darted to the campsite shop to buy whatever newspapers I could get my hands on. It wasn't very thoughtful of me, hijacking these limited, communal resources, especially since I wasn't going to read anything but the match report and the picture captions.

My parents indulged this peculiar use of my holiday allowance, and I found a kindred spirit in Joe, a friend of my sister's who was also at the campsite. As a 12-year-old boy, Joe knew far more about cricket than me. He even knew how to play it, and had brought his cricket bat and a tennis ball. With the confidence of the truly ignorant, I would bowl at him from about ten yards, and with the humility born of a two-year age-gap, he would grant my lbw appeals. Then we'd pore over the newspapers, and discuss whether Graham Thorpe and John Emburey were going to save the Test match in Birmingham.

They didn't, which was lucky, because if it had looked likely I would probably have forced my parents to drive us home a day early to watch the climax. (The radio in my parents' car did not have longwave, otherwise Joe and I would have spent four days of the holiday holed up in the car.) But I was more frustrated than upset by England's defeat. With Atherton as captain, I had been sure we would instantly start to win. I expressed as much to my mum, who looked at me with interest. 'Oh, it's "we" now, is it?'

Sporting allegiances don't seem to be like other lifelong forms of bond. You don't need to spend a lot of time getting to know each other, or establishing trust. Yes, some football fans will come to support their local team through a process of childhood indoctrination that would shame the Jesuits – give me the child until he is seven, and I will give you the Sheffield Wednesday fan, etc. – but, in my experience, it's more of a done deal. You fall in love with a sporting team the way our grandparents' generation hooked up in wartime – hastily, wholeheartedly, with no thought for the years of conjugal obligation to come. The England cricket team had walked me home from the post office a couple of times, offered their hand in marriage, and I'd said yes at first asking.

After our camping holiday, and just before the last Ashes Test, my family moved house. We had been living in the countryside, exactly halfway between the ludicrously pleasant village of Harpenden and Luton, multiple winner of the Crap Town Award. The recession was biting, and the cottage that my parents had rescued from dereliction and spent three years turning into their perfect home had to be sold. We were swapping life in a tiny hamlet surrounded by acres of fields and common land for a town-centre house a short walk from Luton's Arndale Centre.

I suppose I should have been sad that we'd lost our rural idyll, but I liked the idea of being within walking distance of a cinema, shops and friends. Plus, the TV was the first thing to be unpacked and I was pretty swiftly distracted by England's final game at The Oval. England had batted surprisingly well in their first innings, and that was nothing compared to what came next. I watched open-mouthed as their pace bowlers tore in and tore up Australia's batting. Michael Slater for 4, David Boon for 13, Mark Waugh for 10; to an ingénue like me, every wicket appeared a genuine miracle.

I ran up and down the stairs relaying each new occurrence to my sister Kate, busy decorating her new bedroom, who was by turns baffled, bored and irritated by my excitement. As I was quickly to learn, however, winning a cricket match is rarely simple. Ian Healy helped squeeze another 100 runs out of Australia's last two batting partnerships, almost wiping out the bowlers' good work. And while England's batsmen stood firm in their second innings, a bout of rain blew in from nowhere, eating up the overs needed to bowl Australia out a second time.

In the end, one day remained to take ten wickets. With hindsight, I would back the fielding team's chances in that scenario almost every time. But I was a 14-year-old girl who knew nothing of cricketing probabilities. I found it extremely hard to get to sleep that night, and the entire next day I was locked on the sofa, calling my mum at her office to inform her of each wicket, desperate for her reassurance that victory was still on track.

When England finally did win, they had ended a drought of six years and 240 days since their last Test victory over Australia. Strangely, I don't remember the final wicket falling – perhaps my young mind wasn't yet equipped for such moments of intense pleasure. Instead, it is two newspaper clippings from the following day that have stuck with me. The first was the Matt cartoon from the front page of the *Daily Telegraph*. A man in bed with his sleeping wife is shining a torch at a piece of paper on the wall: it reads, 'England won. It wasn't a dream.' That cartoon summed up the sleepless wonderment I felt for days after. Atherton's England had just given me my first teenage high, and it took me ages to come down.

The other picture I see whenever I think of that match is a photograph of Atherton and Stewart running off the field together, side-hugging as they went, both grinning like nincompoops. The Oval win was the beginning of a relationship between the two men that was to prove as solid and long lasting as it was unsuccessful. For the next eight years, the two of them seemed to come as a pair, whether opening the batting together, consulting in the field, or facing down an increasingly hostile press as England's performances went from bad to worse.

They struck complementary attitudes on the field: Atherton's arms crossed, his brow furrowed; Stewart with his mouth open wide, clapping his gloves together. The thinker and the encourager. The strategist and the enforcer. The officer and the sergeant-major. And

I often wondered, as a teenager, how their conversations went, this student of Magna Carta and his stalwart sidekick.

I mention this to Stewart, who laughs: 'You need to get out more, Emma.' He can't recount particular conversations with Atherton, or even their first impressions of each other – the man with the military bearing seems to have a pragmatic, rather detached, power of recall. He talks about past matches in the manner of a pundit, relaying the essential facts as if he had been a spectator rather than a participant, and his conversation is scattered with observations that sound like coaching mantras: 'You've got to have physical courage . . . I always used adversity to spur me on . . . When you're winning things go your way, and when you're losing they don't.'

Anyone who has spent any time listening to professional sportsmen being interviewed on TV has heard these kinds of phrases. We hear them often in the aftermath of a game, when players unfurl obvious sounding yet supremely meaningless clichés about 'doing what they had to do' or 'soaking up the pressure'. I tend to dismiss them as unthinking, and they often make me roll my eyes and groan with frustration.

For Stewart, they have always been something of a trademark. He actually earned his nickname, 'the Gaffer', because his dressing room colleagues thought he talked like a football manager. But listening to him, I wonder if it isn't unthinking at all, just a very different way of thinking: less contemplative but more disciplined, and far more useful on the frontline when you're getting pummelled by the enemy. 'If everyone walks around looking miserable you'll guarantee everyone is miserable,' he says at one point. 'What can you do about it? Lie down, cry and feel sorry for yourself – and they'll walk all over you. Or front it up, go out there and be brave about it. Sport can be tough, so get on with it. You never gain anything, do you, from feeling sorry for yourself?'

I look around again at the room, and the order he has imposed on it. His large desk is clear but for a computer, a printer, a glass tankard full of highlighter pens. Next to them, lying open, is the notebook they've been used on, its pages full of team lists written in neat capital letters. Beyond where Stewart sits, there is a printed schedule on the wall, and a pile of books stacked carefully on a side table. The top one is called *Cricket on Everest*.

Batting at Base Camp would, I suspect, be a picnic compared to the travails that Stewart had to endure in his 13 years playing for England. He was bruised and battered by the world's most vicious pace attacks. He was asked repeatedly to sacrifice his opening position to keep wicket and bat in the lower order – a job he liked less, but willingly assumed for the sake of the team. When he did finally inherit the captaincy from Atherton, in 1998, his tenure was short-lived, despite managing to win a series against a strong South Africa side. He fell out with management, and was fired after England's humiliatingly brief appearance at their home World Cup in 1999.

And yet Stewart remained, throughout a decade of ordeal, arguably England's most upbeat presence, both on the field and on the balcony. He may not have seemed a reflective kind of guy, but maybe his was the better way. Perhaps the only chance to stay sane in the face of constant defeat is to stop considering it at all. Stewart had created the perfect paradox. He cared deeply, passionately, about his team, even elevating their needs above his own. But he never forgot that he was just playing a game. Losing need not make him miserable.

Or discourteous. As we talk, we've watched Moeen Ali score a hundred, pretty much assuring Surrey of defeat. And when Moeen gets out, Stewart stands and applauds him back to the pavilion. We are in an office, and no one can hear or see Stewart's ovation. But he does it anyway, because he appreciates the performance and because, well, it's the decent thing to do.

Cricket's little civilities have always made me happy. I like the antiquated courtesies that are written into the game – the handshake at the toss, the rustle of applause at the end of an over. They remind me of school, and the way we'd stand up for the teacher when she entered the room. Back then, I was nothing if not respectful of authority. The most rebellious thing I did during my schooldays was to get caught eating a chocolate bar in our form room. It wasn't even during class. But the piercing look of disapproval on my French teacher's face left me with a lasting sense of shame.

My parents weren't especially strict, but they did like manners, and my mum was a strong proponent of Commitment and Follow-through. An agreement to go to a distant cousin's birthday party six months in the future was a binding contract, and nothing short of my own death would release me from it. Perhaps Stewart and his old-fashioned values were as important to my burgeoning love of cricket as any handsome new captain. Loyalty, work ethic, deference to authority, a tendency to over-prepare – these were qualities my teenage self had in spades. Here was a game that prized them, and a player who encapsulated them. No wonder I'd fallen for it so fast.

With a couple of overs to go before lunch, Stewart has to make his way to the Surrey dressing-room. He gives me a kindly farewell and I realise that I am actually sad to say goodbye. There's just something so safe and comforting about his company. I've only spent a couple of hours with him and I already want him as my 'In Case of Emergency' number.

The Tannoy announces that spectators are welcome to wander on to the pitch, and the 100 or so people who have been scattered around the ground are now gently promenading across the Oval turf. It's a funny old tradition. You're never allowed anywhere near the actual wicket, so the whole exercise is, well, just exercise. I sit in the stands, pondering my recent encounter. Before we parted, I asked what Stewart's parents had taught him when he was growing up. 'It was always said to me whatever you do, do it to the best of your ability,' he replied. 'Never look back and say, "what if . . .?", or "if only . . ." and start feeling sorry for yourself.'

Being an England fan was clearly nothing like being an England player. Pretty much 90 per cent of my time as a follower of England has been spent asking 'what if' and sighing 'if only.' The other 10 per cent was devoted to feeling sorry for myself.

But at least I knew that I'd given it the same level of commitment.

Chapter 3

One reason I find it impossible to recreate my original, all-engrossing fervour for cricket is that there is currently so much of it to watch. In these days of multiple sports channels, the men who run cricket (and that's not sexist – it is still men) make most of their money from selling the broadcast rights to international games. In other words, it pays to have your national team playing as much as possible. The channels also expect value for their money, and the upshot is we have lots of tournaments, and plenty of games.

This ought to be a win-win situation for a cricket fan like me. You want to give me more of the thing I love? Yes, please. Dish it out and keep it coming. But with every added fixture, the results become incrementally less significant. You can't keep yourself in a froth of excitement when your team seem to be on the telly as regularly as *The One Show*. And so I've become increasingly blasé about the games; it's hard to keep up with all the action unless you make it your full-time occupation.

Twenty years ago, an English summer comprised six Test matches at most, and a smattering of one-day games. Every game was an event, and every moment that could be spent following the live action was savoured. That's why *Test Match Special*'s promise of 'ball-by-ball coverage' sounded so richly appealing (and not, as one of my teenage friends once told me, like a threat). It's why I would start anticipating a Test match at least a fortnight before. When those games were through you might have to wait half a year to see your team play again. There were no other international games available to watch in the meantime.

Today, I feel guilty every time I see an Indian Premier League game is showing, because I know I'm not going to watch it. Who has the time? Back then, I know I'd have given anything for a Twenty20 all-star league, or the chance to watch highlights from a South Africa v New Zealand Test in Paarl. The longueurs without cricket were excruciating and unfathomable. I'd consider myself in agony, and curse the authorities for their lazy scheduling: more proof that you can never really make a sports fan happy.

In 1993, following England's win in the final Test against Australia, there was . . . nothing. Literally, nothing. It was the end of August, and the England team weren't scheduled to play their next match until February. The cricket season was drawing to a close, so I couldn't even follow domestic games in the newspaper. I'd experienced my first hit of sporting ecstasy, and someone had immediately cut my supply. It only made me think about cricket all the more.

I filled the dead time with imagination and fixation. As a 14-year-old girl, I had accumulated a certain number of soft toys and teddy bears, and these were now named in honour of my new heroes, mostly the bowlers who had taken wickets at The Oval. A tartan Loch Ness monster that my grandmother had bought me on a trip to Scotland was dubbed Angus Fraser, after the bowler who had been drafted into the England team at the last moment then stolen the show. A pale bear with an expression of permanent worry was named for the fragile-looking spin bowler Peter Such. A slightly scruffier, wirier bear was invested with the name of a Welsh player who, as it turned out, never played another Test match. I still have it today, and it makes me happy to think that I am the only person in the world who habitually says goodnight to a teddy called Steve Watkin.

It wasn't all flights of fancy; I also spent those months applying myself rigorously to my education. September marked the start of my GCSE year, and my bookshelf began to swell with new purchases. My favourite was *What is a Googly?*, a helpfully illustrated guide to the laws and the more technical side of the game, which I worked through like a textbook, stopping to quiz myself on each chapter. A book called *If the Cap Fits*, containing short pen portraits of every England player since the Second World War, became my encyclopaedia. If Mum mentioned a name I'd not heard before – Fred Titmus, Tony Greig, M. J. K. Smith – I'd run to pull it down from the shelf and read their entry.

I had always loved the sensation of *knowing* stuff. The pleasure wasn't in the act of learning, but the way a piece of pre-digested knowledge would pop to the front of my mind, unasked for, at the perfect moment, like a magic trick. I put this down to my dad. He was the kind of person who, if he couldn't answer a question, would immediately look up the answer in a book. He couldn't watch a film without pointing out anachronisms and inaccuracies, and he drove my mother to despair derailing conversations with fascinating but entirely tangential facts. I had inherited his hungry brain, and cricket was a sport that seemed to offer infinite new information to hoard.

While learning had always come easily, the social side of my education felt more of a struggle. I went to an academically competitive school and constantly compared myself with others, which made me a bit of a worrier. But I was no introvert – I was, in fact, rather loud and over-eager, and my adolescent hormones unleashed a tendency to intensity. Forget the Hollywood bromance: for hidden affections and tortured emotions, nothing can beat the teen-girl 'best friend' phenomenon, whose politics are byzantine, and whose passions are all-consuming.

I would throw myself, full-hearted, into these exclusive relationships. A best friend was a constant companion; you waited for them before class, and made plans to meet them at the lockers straight after. Leaving for morning assembly with someone else, or failing to save a seat for them at lunch, could lead to violent arguments, deep wounds and social anarchy. When the inevitable break-up came, I would cry for days. A teacher once found me in the locker room, having bawled myself into a state of dehydration. She had to send me to the matron for fluids.

By the time I turned 15 I had burned through a number of best friends. But now that we were living in Luton, I had to start taking the train to school, and that introduced me to a new set of girls: the half-dozen whose parents dropped them off far too early, and who killed time by playing cards until the bell went. They let me join their game, which continued one morning to the next, the scores kept as scrupulously as if we were high rollers in Monte Carlo. My new friends were happy to let me burble about cricket while we studied our hands. They weren't looking for deep emotional chats or everlasting bonds of friendship; they were looking for trumps. So we played cards, and I poured my excess feeling into my newfound love of cricket, which they tolerated and gently ignored.

While I was enjoying this new start, Michael Atherton was overhauling the identity of the England cricket team. Their next challenge was a tour of the West Indies, and a month after the Oval victory the squad that would fly to the Caribbean was announced. It was a team full of fresh young faces. Atherton had insisted on a 'clean break' from the past and the last remnants of my mum's batting heroes – Mike Gatting, David Gower, Allan Lamb – had been told that their services were no longer required. 'We've had some older players in the side in the last few years,' Atherton explained to the gathered press, 'and we haven't been winning.'

As someone with very little sense of cricketing history and no past to be nostalgic about, I was the kind of thoughtless, ruthless kid who cheered their exclusion. Having just turned 15, I knew that youth was better than age. Irvine Welsh had just published *Trainspotting*, there was a 46-year-old president in the White House, and Tupac and the Wu-Tang Clan were cementing arguably the greatest year in hip-hop's history. I noticed none of these things, as I was about as iconoclastic as a Charles & Di wedding mug. But I did know that England's cricket team were embarking on a new era, and it was a privilege to be alive at such a time.

Among the tour party were a number of players I had never heard of before. Some, like Nasser Hussain, would go on to play crucial roles in the development of English cricket. Others, like Alan Igglesden, would disappear into obscurity. Then there was Phil Tufnell, whose every mention tantalised with trouble. 'Often moody' and 'difficult to handle' were typical epithets. Frequent reference was made to his drinking and smoking, and a third bad habit of arguing with umpires. 'Phil Tufnell has been cast as England's *enfant terrible* and at times he appears determined to live up to his reputation,' read his entry in *If the Cap Fits*. It was accompanied by a headshot of a long-haired young man giving the camera a who-do-you-think-you-are? scowl.

I neither drank nor smoked. My family went to church together each Sunday, and I had little interest in the opposite sex unless they were characters in a 19th-century novel. I was not the kind of girl to fall for a bad boy's dubious allure but, as we all know, those are just the girls who do. Tuffers, as he was known, was instantly fascinating to me. I wanted to know more about him, so I asked my mum. Her fondly liberal opinion was that Tufnell had great potential, but had been mishandled and misunderstood by previous England management. 'If anyone can get the best out of him, Atherton can,' she remarked.

In my mind I began to picture Tufnell as an errant older brother (I was too innocent to imagine anyone 12 years older than me as a boyfriend), the kind who needed the help of a loving, patient, ingenious younger sister to get him out of occasionally life-threatening scrapes. I created little fantasies to this effect: in one storyline, he owed money to a mafia gang who were going to cut off his fingers if he didn't pay. I would pull off an audacious rescue, delivering a couple of pithy one-liners along the way, then deliver him back to Atherton in time for the next day's Test match. Atherton, impressed with my resourcefulness, quick-thinking and sense of calm in a crisis, would then ask me to join the team as a personnel manager, a sort of horse whisperer to England's most difficult players. And that is how we would win back the Ashes.

Tufnell's playing career was to be full of incident, much of it off the pitch. He missed curfews, training, and even a couple of matches; there were on-field tantrums, bitter rows with soon-to-be-ex-wives, and a furious father-in-law who hit Tufnell in the face with a brick. And yet his colleagues spoke warmly, if despairingly, of him – his poor behaviour seemed less the result of viciousness than of thoughtlessness or laziness, or both.

These days, Tufnell's roguish appeal extends far beyond fans of nineties cricket. Anyone who has watched a bit of mainstream telly will know him as that cheeky chappy who has flirted with Sue Barker on *A Question of Sport*, danced with Katya on *Strictly Come Dancing*, and been crowned 'king of the jungle' on *I'm a Celebrity . . . Get Me Out of Here!* Like most winners of that show, he triumphed by appearing the most casual and unambitious of the contestants – just a bloke who liked a beer, a nap and a laugh. It's an endearing attitude on reality TV, although you can imagine it being less so in the context of team sport.

He has never, in his new guise as a television personality, been a preserver of reputation – in fact, Tufnell seems to revel in telling stories against himself. So if anyone is going to tell me the truth about what life was like in the England team of the 1990s, I reckon it is him. His colourful private life was well documented, and he never learned to hide his emotions on the pitch. It is easy to feel I know him well already.

I contact his agent and, after some diary wrangling, am told that Tufnell can meet me on a bank holiday Monday in a pub near his home. It turns out to be an old, gabled building, a rambling country pub with timber beams and a plethora of nooks, crannies and snugs. I inveigle myself into one of these, a sort of three-sided booth, and at our scheduled meeting time, around 1 p.m., Tufnell appears in front of it. He is wearing black Nike tracksuit bottoms, a dark T-shirt and a black puffer jacket, and there is a lost look on his face which, taken in combination with his wardrobe, suggests he might only just have rolled out of bed.

This impression grows as he sits down to join me. His greeting is friendly but vague, as if he can't quite remember how he came to be here, and I can hear a couple of pieces of gravel clinking around when he speaks. He stretches and sighs and admits that he has been making the most of the three-day weekend. 'It's just a licence to go and get smashed,' he says. 'Which I suppose is fair enough, innit? Life's too bloody short not to, when you've got Monday off, if you know what I mean.'

I am thrilled. My first encounter with Phil Tufnell, and he has a genuine hangover. He squints at the menu quietly for a long while, then asks for a sausage sandwich. 'And a bottle of Laurent-Perrier!' he giggles, before settling for Peroni. The partying isn't, it turns out, the only reason he seems a bit tender. Tufnell has also burst his eardrum. 'It's like someone's punched me in the ear,' he says. 'I was sitting there filming A Question of Sport and all of a sudden there was all blood coming down the ear. And I went: "Shit! My brain's falling out of my head! I'm dying!" And everyone was very shocked and then they went, "Oh no, you've burst your eardrum." And no one felt sorry for me any more.'

Telling the story seems to wake Tufnell up a bit. He asks which other cricketers I've been speaking to: just Alec Stewart, I reply. 'To be fair to Alec, he was probably the only professional cricketer in the side. Ha, ha, ha! You want to know what was going on in the nineties? Good question. What the hell was going on?' He chuckles, and the pieces of gravel chink together in the back of his throat.

He doesn't want me to get the wrong idea: the team had trained hard, and played hard, and enjoyed each other's company. 'But there was never a feeling of . . . all moving towards a goal. It was just turn up, play, and go home. It was all ad hoc. There were different physios, different players, different people in charge. No one seemed to know where they were.'

The sausage sandwich, when it arrives, proves the stuff of life; Tufnell grows chatty and open. 'I loved playing for England, but when I first got picked, I was disappointed in a funny sort of way. I thought there was going to be this next step in my development . . . I was like a sponge,' he says, lingering on the word, squeezing an imaginary one in his hand. 'I thought: "Right, something's going to happen, someone's going to tell me something that I didn't know and I'm going to become the best bowler in the world." And I sat down and everyone went: "Do you fancy going out to dinner?"' He leaves a beat – he is a practised storyteller. 'And I went, "All right, then." It's a big piss-up, like it is back home. You've just got a different badge on the front of your shirt.'

I think back to the first flush of my romance with the England team. The autumn of 1993 was a honeymoon for both of us. I basked in the glow of England's one recent win, and pictured a happy life together, while they spent a week in the actual sun, doing warm-weather training in the Algarve. With no games being played, my faith in them grew, unfettered by reality.

In December they gathered at the National Sports Centre in Lilleshall, Shropshire, for a two-week boot camp, and were pictured in the papers doing exercises in slightly naff tracksuits. England's cricketers had never prepared so thoroughly for an overseas tour, and even though the bookies were still quoting them at 14/1 to beat West Indies, this newfound professionalism brought with it an overwhelming sense of optimism. For onlookers like me, at any rate. Tufnell's memories of it are rather different.

'It was the worst two weeks of my life.' His lip curls at the memory of cross-country runs, and team-building activities. The players slept in tiny rooms no bigger, says Tufnell, than the booth we are sitting in. 'It was absolutely freezing cold and snowing. What a great preparation that was, to go to the Caribbean. Whoever thought of that idea should be shot.' He sounds surprisingly angry about a fortnight of training that happened 20 years ago. 'All we wanted to do was go down the pub. We were already going to go away for four months. "I know what we'll do, we'll just take them away from their kids and their families for a further two weeks just before they go, to go orienteering in the snow and sit in a cell." How to get 15 guys really pissed off before they go on tour.'

I want to remonstrate. He can't complain about a team's lack of professionalism, then moan that his managers made him go to practice instead of drinking. Then I remember that at the same time that Tufnell was being forced to go on cross-country runs, I was faking period pains to get out of PE. Perhaps we are more alike than I realised.

Either way, faced with playing West Indies, you needed all the practice you could get. Mum had been educating me about the Caribbean's proud and terrifying cricketing heritage and their tradition of bowling so fast that a batsman was lucky if he even saw the ball that cannoned towards his head. She told stories of black eyes and broken ribs that appealed to the love of the physically gruesome that all adolescents possess. When she came to Michael Holding, the man they used to call 'Whispering Death', my first question was: 'Did he actually kill anyone?'

Curtly Ambrose and Courtney Walsh, the giants who would be terrorising England, were left to my imagination. The BBC did not broadcast England matches overseas. There was a way to watch England play during the winter, but it involved paying money to a company called British Sky Broadcasting that people like my parents deeply disapproved of. Plus, it was considered rather vulgar to have a satellite dish installed on the outside of your house. The dishes were indeed large and ugly, but I think my parents' objection was more metaphysical – in their minds, wanting more television than the four channels universally available was a sign of stupidity. (This position has not stopped them, in their later years, becoming slaves to the Alibi channel and ITV Encore.)

So there was no chance of satellite TV, and the only stereo in the house was the apparently lead-lined system installed in our cold, uncomfortable dining room. I chose instead to follow the cricket on Ceefax. This caused problems with my sister, who never seemed to appreciate how suddenly a match might turn, and did not enjoy my need for regular updates. A typical scene would develop:

> Me: (pressing the Ceefax button on the remote control, rendering the screen completely black) 'I just need to check the score.'
>
> Kate: 'Stop it! I'm trying to watch *Byker Grove!*'
>
> Me: (holding remote strategically out of reach) 'But there'll have been another over by now. Someone might have got out.'
>
> Kate: (grabbing at remote) 'But I was here first!'
>
> Me: (refusing to relinquish remote) 'You don't understand. This is a crucial session! I need to see the score!'
>
> (Dialogue becomes wordless grunts as Kate and I wrestle the remote to the floor.)
>
> Kate: 'Mum! She's making me miss the programme!'
>
> Me: 'She's making me miss the cricket!'

Yes, my first England tour was tough.

It began well enough. The first Test started just as my imagination had scripted it, with a century stand from Atherton and Stewart seeing England through the onslaught from Ambrose and Walsh. And then the West Indies went off-script: one of their back-up bowlers, a young guy called Kenny Benjamin, ran through the batting line-up like a knife through Nutella. England never recovered.

On the final morning of the game, I turned on the news to discover that Walsh had bowled a spell so deadly it verged on the psychopathic. The footage showed Devon Malcolm, England's number 11, being hit again and again. Malcolm was no batsman, and Walsh was using him as target practice. Aiming to injure a batsman is not strictly illegal in cricket, but the umpires are expected to protect those like Malcolm who are unable to defend themselves. On this occasion, they had decided to stand back and enjoy the show.

Malcolm was lucky to escape with bruises; the deliveries Walsh was sending down could have broken bone. Mum was shocked by the umpiring; I was just shocked. When I'd read about the danger posed by fast bowling, the word had always sounded largely metaphorical. Watching Malcolm under assault, I saw a new side to the game I'd adopted, one that was brutal, physical and ruthless.

Never underestimate the threat of violence working on a romantic teenage mind. I was your typical teenage pacifist: war poetry made me cry, I was permanently in fear of nuclear Armageddon, and I couldn't understand why political crises couldn't all be resolved with a little chat and a nice cup of tea. But seeing England's players under attack awoke a belligerence I never knew I had.

It is crass, of course, to compare sport to war, and sportsmen to soldiers; we know that their situations and sacrifices do not compare. But the narrative was just too powerful for a girl like me (reader of Byron, watcher of *Sharpe*) to resist. The sports reports spoke of men 'under fire' from a 'blistering barrage'; pictures showed England batsmen contorted at the crease, dodging invisible bullets. I cloaked their deeds in the mantle of heroic warfare, and felt every wicket like a mother reading the lists of casualties from the front. When Atherton scored a century in the second Test, while his comrades fell around him for single-figure scores, it had the doomed valour of a solo cavalry charge. England went 2–0 down.

In our nook in the pub, Tufnell is finding it hard to recall the West Indies tour, probably because he wasn't picked in the first three Test matches. 'That was a mistake,' he says, ''cos that'd mean I'd just go on the piss for three weeks.' In the third Test in Trinidad he was twelfth man, the substitute role that traditionally involves carrying drinks or equipment out to the players, and taking the field in the case of injury. In Tufnell's case, it was a perfect opportunity to indulge in his favourite hobby, sleeping.

While Tufnell catnapped, England did something unexpected – they established a lead. It was the first time on tour that they had managed to outscore the West Indies. They bowled well, too. Not perfectly – West Indies' lower-order batsmen put in a resilient performance – but their final target was perfectly achievable. My thoughts ran to victory, then sprinted on past it. With a win in Trinidad, they would carry their confidence into the next game – and if they won that one, they'd square the series. England had clearly turned the tide.

That's how it seemed, four and a half thousand miles away, in a teenager's bedroom in Bedfordshire. Tufnell, meanwhile, was in the dressing-room, handing out drinks to his friends as they prepared to return to the field. One hundred and ninety four runs was all that was needed. 'I can remember going round, looking at the batters. And their eyes were all like . . .' he makes saucer eyes '. . . and I thought to myself, "Ooh, they don't fancy it." I could just feel something was wrong.'

Still, it was only 194 runs. In a team of 11, that's fewer than 18 runs per player.

It was 4.03 p.m. when England began their final innings in Trinidad – 9.03 p.m. in Luton. I had recently discovered a large and ancient radio that had belonged to my grandmother, the only thing in the house (other than the titanic stereo in the dining room) that received longwave. It was too old to have an earphones socket so, to muffle the sound, this piece of salvage was snuggled in bed next to me, poking me with its sharp corners and importing a great quantity of dust on to my sheets.

Atherton took guard and prepared to face the first ball. Two sounds followed – a giant thud, and a terrifying, collective yell that sprang out of that ancient radio like something from Edgar Allan Poe. I can still feel the adrenalin shock and the despair of knowing, from that sound alone, that Atherton was out. A few minutes later Mark Ramprakash ran himself out, and England were 2 for 1.

As I lay in bed, despair turning to nausea, Tufnell was having a snooze in the St John Ambulance tent beneath the stands. He had heard the roars from the crowd over the music from his headphones, but chosen to ignore it. 'I've thought, "That's two down." But this is one of my favourite tracks, I'm enjoying this. And then two seconds later, there's another "*Yaaaaaaay!*"' England were 5 for 3. 'They just started going down like fucking ninepins.' What followed was one of the most humiliating episodes in England cricketing history. Ambrose, the silent giant of the West Indies team, tore through England's batting in fewer than 20 overs.

Tufnell acts out the scene in the dressing-room with a manic energy, immersed in the memory. 'Everyone's scrambling . . . it's the first time I've seen five England batsmen all padded up, their helmets on, chest pads on, all in a line, like parachutists waiting to get out the fucking aeroplane . . . "C'mon, next one, go!" . . .' He trails off, a look of Kurtzian horror in his eye. 'Chaos . . . chaos . . . chaos . . . chaos . . .'

I had listened to England's implosion, my duvet over my head, my insides clammy. The radio, ugly harbinger of doom, now had complete hold over me: I was paralysed, incapable of switching it off. This, I thought, must have been what it was like for my gran during the Blitz, or for my mum as the Cuban missile crisis unfolded. Or maybe it was just what people experienced when watching scary movies – I'd never tried one – but worse, surely, because this was actually happening.

When the game ended early the next day, England had been bowled out for 46. That wasn't a low score, or even a terrible one: it was shameful and unheard of. Such a result might have been comical in a village match, but here the humiliation was too deep, too raw, for humour. I devoted an entire poster to it – I guess I found the process cathartic, expunging the horror by Pritt-sticking it on to a moody magenta background. 'Requiem for Atherton's Army,' ran one doomy headline; at the time it captured my own elegiac state, although now it just sounds creepy. Underneath, a photograph showed members of the England team lined up at the post-match ceremony, arms uniformly folded, staring at the ground in the manner of chastised schoolboys. I diagnosed the expressions on their faces as shellshock, but it was probably embarrassment.

It said something about the quality of my family life that this Test match was one of the most traumatic experiences of my sheltered life to date. My sister and I were extremely lucky – our home was happy and stable. Even when my parents had money troubles, like the ones that had forced us to move, our own lives continued in blissful ignorance of the fact. It was a marked contrast to Tufnell's tumultuous story, which I watched play out, like a long-running soap, in the years that followed. After the Caribbean tour his partner Jane left him, taking their daughter with her, and Tufnell was fined for slapping her across the face.

I remember his court appearance, because the *Evening Standard* my dad brought home carried a rare picture of Tufnell wearing a suit. The suit was fawn coloured, and he still managed to look slovenly in it, which probably didn't help his case. My mum, probably wanting to shield me from the ugly reality of domestic violence, did not make a fuss about the story. I didn't want to believe that Tufnell had hit his wife, but he had admitted it, and the news left me with a pang of vicarious guilt, which I quickly ignored. The fact that Jane's father had followed up with a brick to Tufnell's face seemed to deliver a cartoonish comeuppance and deposit the affair into the safe realm of farce.

There were plenty more plot twists to come in Tufnell's private life, but none stopped me wanting him in the side. He was an aggressive, wicket-seeking bowler, which marked him out in an era of colourless, unthreatening English spinners. Perversely, for someone whose behaviour was so wild, his deliveries were not. Tufnell's dainty skip to the crease, his long fringe flapping about his forehead, masked his arm's dangerous intention; as his wrist flicked forward, the ball would fly out faster, perhaps, than you expected, yet hanging in the air a little longer than it had a right to.

I was his vehement advocate, and railed with frustration when Peter Such or Ian Salisbury were picked ahead of him. Sure, he added nothing with the bat, and his fielding could actually damage a side's efforts, thanks to the fact he was able to drop the most basic of catches, but these deficiencies only made me like him more. He was unpredictable in every regard, and in an era when England's results were only too foreseeable, that was a big part of his appeal. A bit of mischief-making seemed exactly what you needed in a team looking to turn the tables on its betters.

And when he was good, he was very, very good. For all his wildness off the pitch, Tufnell had the composure and consistency to frustrate batsmen with his left-arm spin, and the wiles to outthink them. There was no better proof than the final Ashes Test of 1997, a series he had been left out of all summer. His fourth ball of the match was to Matthew Elliott, a delivery tossed so provokingly high that Elliott was halfway through a mighty drive, already picturing the boundary boards' tremble, when the ball jumped out of the way of his bat and rattled the stumps behind him.

After that, Tufnell bowled without rest for 34 and a half overs, picking off the Australians one by one. He made the ball turn and bounce and dance in the air, and the ground responded with little puffs of dust each time he worked his magic. By the close of the innings, he had taken seven wickets and got England back into the game; by the end of the match, he had 11 and had won it for them. 'Only about the third time I managed to out-bowl Shane Warne in my fucking career,' he says, with a slightly caustic laugh. 'Pain in the arse he was. Fucking Shane Warne.'

Tufnell was cursed with living in an era when all spin bowlers were measured against Warne. And there *were* comparisons, not in their careers so much as their personal lives. Spinners often have personalities that tend towards the anarchic, the rule-breaking, the occasionally unhinged. And, like Warne, Tufnell has always shrugged his off with a comic turn.

There's no better example than the time he suffered a breakdown during an Ashes tour and trashed a Perth hotel room. The story has been told in the autobiographies of everyone who witnessed it: Atherton was summoned to Tufnell's room to find him sobbing on the edge of his bed amid a carnage of broken furniture, and Tufnell was taken, in the middle of the night, to a psychiatric unit. The version Tufnell tells today has ludicrous embellishments: he escapes from the ward chased by orderlies, hides in bushes and leaps over fences, his hospital gown flapping open to reveal his naked bottom.

Beyond these almost certainly fictional details the tale returns to the verifiable: Tufnell flagged down a passing taxi and got a lift back to his hotel, where the team management were staging a crisis conference. He sauntered in with a can of lager in one hand and a cigarette in the other. 'I'm terribly sorry, I've got it out my system. Can we just forget about all this now? See you at the ground for warm-ups? Thanks very much!' And he walked out. 'Oh, it was funny!' cries Tufnell. I laugh, of course – but was it funny? It sounds uncomfortably close to tragedy to me. 'I thought to myself, "Why am I getting upset about some woman?" And run the risk of not playing for my country? An England cap's worth more than a woman, I'm afraid.'

Just like that, his effervescence vanishes. The suddenness of his mood change throws me; there is something of the Victorian gothic about it. He slumps forward, talking to his beer, as if it isn't a second pint over lunch but the flavourless dregs of closing time, and I am the barman, listening to the late-night complaints of an unhappy husband. Memories, hot and bitter, flood out unchecked. I can't tell if I've touched a nerve, or if his feelings are always this close to the surface. Is this what it was like to share a dressing-room with him?

He says his piece; the episode passes. Awkwardly casting about for something to say, I tell him that, being a teenager, a lot of his off-field scandals were too adult for me to understand. 'Well, there you go,' he says. 'They were quite adult for me at the time as well. All I wanted to do was play cricket but I kept seeming to find myself in all these scrapes.' He looks genuinely bewildered. 'They just kept coming, day after day . . .'

It would seem fair to say that Tufnell struggles to appreciate how his actions affect others. At one point he tells me a story about touring with Atherton. They were good friends, he says, despite their very different characters ('I'd be drinking whisky out of the mini-bar and he'd be reading *War and Peace*') and one night during a Test Tufnell had a party in the room next door to Atherton's. 'About four in the morning we're still making lots of noise, and he knocked on the door in his pyjamas, and said, "Phil, I've got to open the batting for England tomorrow. Can you please turn the music down?"' Tufnell lets rip his infectious cackle; the thing that tickles him most is the thought of Atherton waiting until 4 a.m. to confront him. 'Just come and tell me at half-eleven and I'd have turned the music down then, mate! But perhaps that was my mindlessness. Because I didn't have to open the batting.'

Back in 1994, I was convinced that Atherton was the man to give Tufnell the counselling and direction he needed. After all, the last

Cambridge-educated man to captain England, Mike Brearley, had done the same for another famous bad boy, and look at Ian Botham's legend now. My mother revered Brearley, the first man whose acute understanding of the human mind had earned him both a psychology degree and an Ashes victory. He had known how to handle egos and superegos, and I fully expected Atherton to perform the same Jungian feats on his players.

After the catastrophe in Trinidad, the team might have welcomed a mass lobotomy. Sitting on the sore end of a 3–0 scoreline, the series already lost, England officially had no chance at the Bridgetown Oval. The ground was known as 'Fortress Kensington' because the West Indies had not lost there in 59 years. The England manager, Keith Fletcher, told the press that a draw would count as a victory. And when England's total passed 46 in their first innings, the crowd gave a cheer.

So, how to account for what happened next? How to explain the fact that, whenever I returned to the radio, Alec Stewart was still batting? Why, when I switched on Ceefax, did the scorecard blink with pleasure at the news of another West Indies wicket fallen? With no more dignity to lose, England had finally combined every crumb of grit and flash of flair that they possessed. By the fifth day they had turned the tables on their Trinidad tormentors. It seemed poetic to me, that the wicket which brought them victory should be that of chief torturer Curtly Ambrose.

The next day, adverts for Tetley Bitter, the team's shirt sponsor, showed the England players dowsing Stewart in beer, and I was inebriated by proxy. Tufnell's abiding memories are of the crowd, which was filled with British holidaymakers. He had been standing near the boundary rope, surrounded by supporters, when the final wicket fell. 'The place just went mental,' he said. 'I got scooped up in this surge of people and carried back to the pavilion.'

When Tufnell remembers the games he played in, he often mentions the supporters, but not in the mechanical manner that Wimbledon winners thank the crowd, nor in the disingenuous way footballers talk of their loyalty to the fans. 'I think the crowds realised we were good players but that it was a bit of a shambles,' he says at one point. He loved going out drinking with the fans – both the holidaymakers and the locals – when he was on tour. 'It was like a roadshow!' he said. 'It was like *The X Factor* coming to town!' And it was sometimes like *National Lampoon's Vacation*, too. 'I'd be hysterical at some of the situations we got ourselves in.'

I try to marry the giggling mischief-maker with the tortured soul who had passed under a dark shadow half an hour earlier. And it dawns on me why I was so forgiving of Tufnell throughout his career. He was sulky and moody; he was also subject to uncontainable waves of enthusiasm. He was needy for affection, and desperate to please, but inconsiderate of others; he felt misunderstood. He just wanted to have fun; he just wanted to sleep. I didn't need Mike Brearley to diagnose Tufnell, I could do it myself. He was a teenager.

No captain ever managed to tame Tufnell, and none seemed to fully trust him. He was in and out of the side more times than any other player in the nineties. For all mine and my mother's predictions, nurturing someone like Tufnell didn't come naturally to Atherton, a young man himself, with no immediate desire to raise children. I have always wondered if Tufnell felt any guilt at all for his behaviour and, as it turns out, Atherton is the only man he seems to regret 'sodding about', as he puts it. 'I did give him a hard time, probably. At this point I would perhaps like to apologise to Michael. But I always tried my utmost for him on the field. I never didn't fancy a bowl for him.'

The implication is that, for other captains, he might have refused to bowl at all. Tufnell has managed to turn a moment of contrition into something at once blame-dodging and incriminating. It's infuriating, but it's honest. How honest he is with himself – how much he holds himself to account for the way his life had panned out – isn't for me to divine.

He is happy, that much is clear. He loves his wife Dawn, and I wonder if, as a TV personality, he has found a career that suits him even better than cricket. He doesn't agree. As we leave the pub and he turns to walk up the hill that leads back to his house, he pauses to reiterate how much he has enjoyed his England years. He says he hopes he hasn't sounded bitter, because he loved the camaraderie, and has shared his life with 'a great group of lads'.

I feel like I've already met three Tufnells in the past couple of hours, and here is another – serious and sincere, protective of his friends. His television persona doesn't seem so much a construct now as Tufnell at his best, his most free. And I sense, once again, what my 14-year-old self valued in Tufnell. He made his sport fun. He brought it to life. Whether he was taking wickets or kicking his hat in frustration – whether he was fielding or misfielding – he was incapable of not being himself.

Chapter 4

I never knew my granddad, the one who had introduced my mum to cricket; he died before I was born. When my sister Kate came along, our grandmother moved in and was, for the next ten years, a sort of second mother to us both. Mum, the only female lawyer in her firm, had been told by her bosses when it would be 'convenient' to have her second child; she loyally planned her pregnancy and was back at work two weeks after the birth. Nan was the woman who made that possible.

Nan did the school runs, cooked our meals, washed our clothes, and kept us entertained until our parents got home. She was the lynchpin of our household: a comforter, a peacemaker, a baker of deliciously buttery fairy cakes. She had a separate living room that was her private domain, somewhere the rest of us were only allowed if invited. In reality, this meant that my sister and I were in there constantly, watching the soap operas that Nan enjoyed and our parents wouldn't otherwise let us see.

Nan wasn't interested in cricket, but as well as *Sons and Daughters* and *Crossroads* she did like to watch snooker. Her consumption of the game was entirely passive – I never once remember her remarking on a frame, or explaining the rules to us – and she had a habit of falling asleep during matches ('I'm just resting my eyes,' she would murmur when we accused her of this). But the giant green rectangle in the TV screen and the suited men gliding quietly around it were a constant backdrop. Even today, I find something of the nursery in the soothing clack of snooker balls.

One of the reasons Kate and I loved Nan's living room so much was that it offered complete amnesty from our mother's temper. Our mother was loving, and tender, and self-sacrificing. She also staged outbursts straight out of the Basil Fawlty book of tantrums. The frustrations of having a high-pressure job and a mildly forgetful husband would build unseen until a seemingly trivial incident – a computer failing to work, or an absence of orange juice in the fridge – would trigger an explosion. There wasn't anything violent about them – just a bit of shouting, the slamming of doors, a rare swear word hurled angrily at a piece of uncooperative technology. Full of sound and fury, signifying nothing, as Shakespeare would have said if he'd actually met my mum. On the other hand, their unpredictability, combined with the sheer force of Mum's personality, made them quite terrifying.

My sister and I came to think of them as a sort of Incredible Hulk rage, because Mum seemed such a different person when they happened. At the first sign of trouble we would make for Nan's living room. Its protected status within the house made it a safe haven, a buffer zone over which Nan presided with far greater authority than either Kofi Annan or Ban Ki-moon ever mustered. Only in special circumstances – if we had lied, or broken things, or lied about breaking things – would we be handed over for punishment. Otherwise, we were safe. Nan was our great defender.

We lost her when I was 12, and Kate was ten. Mum tended her through the terminal months of cancer; my parents had moved Nan's bed into the living room when she became too ill to climb the stairs. Nan's final departure was probably less painful than the months before, watching her shrink into a numb silence. I'd never thought of my mum as a nurse before, or seen her as a daughter, and I remember coming home from school once to find her asleep in the armchair next to Nan's bed. We used to laugh at Mum and Nan for their shared habit of falling asleep in the middle of the afternoon. Now it dawned on me how tiring it was to look after other people.

After Nan's death, our family changed. Not dramatically, but perceptibly. Routines and relationships adjusted. After a disastrous experience with a childminder who fed us nothing but Findus crispy pancakes for a month, Mum was suddenly around a bit more. Her bouts of temper, which had already waned, disappeared almost entirely. Nan's living room became the TV room, a place where Mum could switch off from work and relax with her daughters. A place where she watched the sport she loved, and did the ironing.

In the summer of 1994, Mum and I went to our first cricket match together. Despite her great love of the sport, she had never been to a live game, because she never had anyone to go with. She came home from work one day and told me that we were going to a Test match at Lord's. This is the cricketing equivalent of going to see your first ever gig at Glastonbury. My mum had never seemed cooler to me. In truth, I'd never considered my mum cool at all, but her ability to secure us seats to the third day of the Lord's Test was definitely as impressive as the time she'd gone to argue a case in the high court.

I knew that Lord's was the world headquarters of cricket, but I didn't really know what that meant until we arrived there. Cricket had been my solitary obsession, one only my mother could understand; even the other two members of our family rolled their eyes and left the room when we started talking about it. Now I was joining a stream of people with picnic boxes, all vibrating with the same subsonic thrill as we neared the ground. As the crowd thickened at the turnstiles, people all around me were talking about the state of the game. I'd never heard so many conversations about cricket, and I wanted to listen to every one of them.

The walkways inside Lord's were packed and difficult to navigate. Bypassing every instinct of a 15-year-old girl who wants to be taken seriously, I clung tight to Mum's hand for fear of being separated. Sports stadia have one magical attribute in common: they make little sense until you emerge into the stands. And then pop! an impossible space bursts in front of you. 'It's like the Tardis!' I whispered, awestruck. 'It's bigger on the inside!' The stands were blazing white; the greensward in front of me was trimmed and primped; the pavilion looked like a painting on the lid of a tin of shortbread. The whole place seemed primed to host a royal garden party rather than a sporting contest.

My mum's colleague, a very kind man named Robert, had secured us the tickets. England were playing South Africa and were already in a mess, seven wickets down and 200 runs behind. Being a novice at watching live cricket, I missed many of the key events. I found it hard to make out the ball, and every time a wicket fell, I was looking the wrong way or rooting around in the picnic bag for a Jaffa Cake. In the afternoon the South Africa captain, Kepler Wessels, took two hours to score 28 runs, which was every bit as boring as it sounds.

But I was at the spiritual home of cricket, and only a short if illegal sprint across the boundary rope from my real-life heroes. There was an air of celebration; it was South Africa's first tour to England since the end of the sporting boycott, and the rainbow flag flew from their balcony. I, who had learned more about apartheid through reading up on rebel tours than I ever had in history or geography lessons, could feel my nascent social conscience swelling with pride. Nothing could spoil my day.

Then Robert, who had been listening to his pocket radio, leaned over. 'Michael Atherton's been caught cheating,' he said. I assumed he was pulling my leg – he knew that Atherton was my favourite player – so I laughed at him. 'No, really,' he insisted. 'They're saying that he's been tampering with the ball. He's been summoned to explain himself to the match referee.'

I had learned a little about ball-tampering in the books I'd read. I knew two key things about it: it was the worst crime you could commit on a cricket field, and it was done by foreigners. The idea that Atherton, my Atherton, would flirt with such a felony was outrageous, and I told Robert so with feeling. The more details he relayed from the radio, the more stubborn I became. No, no, no. Atherton didn't do anything. Someone had made a mistake.

The next day I discovered that that someone was me. Every newspaper carried close-ups of the moment that Atherton had taken dirt out of his pocket and rubbed it on the ball. He had told the match referee that the dirt was just to keep his hands dry of sweat, but there was no denying those screen-grabs of shame. By the evening, England had lost the game and Atherton had been fined £2,000 by England's chairman of selectors, Ray Illingworth – not for tampering with the ball, but for tinkering with the truth.

That incident should have taught me many lessons. I should have learned that even the best men are fallible. That idols are made of breakable stuff, and that human beings cannot bear the weight of too much hero-worship. I might even have had my eyes opened to the depressing but inevitable machinations of *realpolitik*. But instead, I learned the power of denial. Faced with the damning evidence that my cherub-faced captain had done something wrong, I simply rejected it. The 'dirt in the pocket affair', as the cricket press prosaically named it, was one of the most controversial of Atherton's captaincy, but it was the only major incident of those years that was not recorded anywhere on my walls.

The days immediately following the game were tough for both of us. He was labelled a cheat and a liar. People called for his resignation. The pressure was so great that he was forced to disappear for a few days. And I – well, I was just worried that he'd disappeared. But, like, properly worried. This was the closest my real life had ever got to a Brontë plot, and even the news that Atherton had been spotted in the Lake District couldn't entirely reassure me. What if he'd gone there to throw himself in a lake?

The newspaper writers and the television pundits were not the only ones giving him a hard time. Taxi drivers, radio callers, and friends of mine who had shown no previous interest in cricket all cried shame – and my uncle Martyn took great delight in teasing me with his opinions of 'the great big cheat'. But instead of causing me to doubt Atherton, Pocketgate (as absolutely no one calls it) just made me champion him more fiercely. I was, as far as I was aware, the only person in the world who wanted to take his side. And that was, to me, a prized position. To this day, I can still mount a passionate defence of Atherton's right to carry dirt in his pockets, and to rub it on whatever he damned well pleases.

Atherton refused to resign, just as he had when England were 3–0 down in the Caribbean. His stubbornness was a trait that would come to define him, and it was one he shared with England's new 'supremo', Ray Illingworth, the man now in charge of both selecting and managing the team. England were now led by a flinty Lancastrian and a mulish Yorkshireman, and their northern grit was starting to influence my own, more sensitive, soul.

The fact that I had chosen to follow what was universally considered the most boring of all sports did nothing for my social standing at school. I was generally beneath the notice of the popular crew, a clique of blonde girls who were good at netball and knew how to wear make-up. The crueller ones, who weren't as pretty or athletic, earned their place on their wits and dispensed putdowns that could send their victims running to the bathroom in tears. Sometimes they would pick me out, narrow their eyes, and pronounce their dread judgement: 'You're just *sad*.'

It hurt, the belittling. Each time was a nagging blow landed on that tender spot where you sense you don't belong and you likely never will. But mostly it felt unfair. The feelings I had about cricket were stronger than any I had experienced before; it was a passion that burned so fiercely I was desperate to share it. If I could just explain the game to these girls, I thought, surely they would see that they were the ones in the wrong?

So I became an evangelist, and hid my newfound joy from no one, not even my teachers. Cricket even infiltrated my GCSE assignments. I insisted on writing up a piece of coursework on the Trojan War as a sports report, and accompanied it with a picture I had doctored to show Warwickshire's Dermot Reeve running a quick single with a horse. One of the compositions I submitted in music class was called 'Bridgetown, 8th to 13th April 1994'. And when my English teacher asked us to write an essay entitled 'What I Hope to Be Doing Ten Years from Now', I confidently asserted that I would be joining England's tour of the West Indies as a cricket correspondent and the newly-wed wife of the team captain. I'm not sure I'd thought through the conflict of interest.

The books and stationery I carried between classrooms were, inevitably, decorated with pictures of players I admired. One folder was wrapped in tartan paper in tribute to the emphatically non-Scottish Angus Fraser; another was plastered with Panini stickers of county cricketers. I still struggle to believe that Panini used to make albums for a sport as little followed as county cricket, or indeed that our newsagent carried the stickers. I was certainly the only person I knew who bought them, or who had the grinning mugshots of Ian Austin and Richard Blakey on her chemistry folder. The lever-arch that contained my English notes had just one picture on it – an A4, full-length photo of a man mid-stride, his bat held upright like a light-sabre, his head turned towards the place where an invisible ball was arcing gently over a boundary rope. 'Cricketer of the Month: Graham Thorpe' read the legend in the corner. It wasn't the pose that captured him – one assumes that Thorpe had just lifted the ball leg-side with a typical flick of his wrists – so much as the expression on his face. He looked insouciant, and ever so slightly sceptical.

If you ask a cricket fan to name their favourite England batsman of the 1990s you tend to get one of two answers. You can even tell what kind of person you're talking to by which one they pick. The romantics choose Mark Ramprakash, a man who never fulfilled his talent at international level but whose style and grace achieved, to many, a kind of perfection not seen since David Gower transferred his languid ease from his batting to his broadcasting career. The fact that Ramprakash rarely demonstrated his greatest qualities for England only seems to add to the allure.

The pragmatists, however, choose Graham Thorpe. So do I. Thorpe may not have been England's highest-scoring batsman but he did seem its most dependable. When England's middle order was folding like an origami deckchair, Thorpe was the one man whose appearance I always looked forward to. He strode out to the middle, brooding darkly beneath a pair of Clark Gable eyebrows, a man of action, not words. His face fell naturally into a glower. A white headband was unconsciously echoed by the sunblock that ringed his lips. No one else could have pulled off that kind of minstrel chic, but he made it look badass.

However poor the state of England's innings (and it was generally pretty poor) Thorpe's instinct was to counter-attack. He deserved his number-four spot in the batting order – traditionally reserved for the batsman of greatest flair – but I loved him more for his urgency than his fluency. Where his teammates were cautious or fearful, Thorpe just got on with it. There were dab-handed singles and quick-run twos, and boundaries punched through the gathering field. His pull shot, the last-second swing he took at a ball making a beeline for his body, was the one that brought me most joy. It just looked so damn brave.

And it was effective, too. In my mind, he had always made a gutsy 70 by the time he was out. I used to feel he was one of the most underestimated men in British sport; it was only when I was older that I discovered how many other cricket lovers had the same affection for him. Even sports fans who had taken only a passing interest in cricket during its decade in the doldrums would mention his name, and smile at the memory. During an era when disappointments were frequent, the prospect of a trustworthy half-century from Graham Thorpe had been a special pleasure.

And I want to tell him that. I'm not sure he can know just how much he was loved. At the end of his career, Thorpe revealed that touring had broken his marriage; that while still in the England team, he'd become depressed and had drunk too much. It had made me really sad to hear that someone who had brought me so much hope and joy had been unhappy while he was playing. I want to let him know how important he was to fans like me.

He works for the England and Wales Cricket Board these days, a batting coach to those on the fringes of the international squad.

He tells me a day he's free to meet, and it happens to be my birthday. If you had told my 14-year-old self that one day she'd enjoy a birthday tea with an England batsman who drove her in his Jaguar to a country house hotel, she'd have choked on her Ribena. And yet here we are in a sun-filled conservatory, and Graham Thorpe is drinking a cappuccino.

He is dressed exactly how you'd imagine an off-duty sportsman would be – a Ralph Lauren polo shirt, dark blue jeans, a sports jacket and wraparound sunglasses. What is surprising, however, is his conversation. Ever since he picked me up in his car, he's been lively, positively chatty, and has smiled a lot. He doesn't seem dour at all. The only time I see him lost for words is when a smartly liveried waitress offers us biscuits, and he asks what sort, and she replies that they are 'in the shape of a rabbit'. And then he orders them anyway.

I start by telling him my memories of the South Africa series in 1994, beginning with the disastrous Test at Lord's. 'The dust in the pocket!' Thorpe laughs. 'I think Athers showed his naivety there. "Gardeners' World", he got called in the dressing-room.' (Stewart had said something similar: 'Typical Cambridge University bloke, highly intelligent but you've got no idea what you're doing. It looked hopeless, it looked stupid, but I still to this day don't believe he was ever trying to change the state of the ball.' And that's why I love Alec Stewart.)

Thorpe didn't play in that Test, but he was picked for the next one, at Headingley. He remembers it well – it was, he says, an important match in his career. The previous winter, he had gone to the West Indies as one of Atherton's young guns, and suffered as much as any of them under the humiliation of Ambrose and Walsh. 'That was my first tour,' he says, 'and it was brutal. It was an eye-opener for me.' During the final Test in Antigua, he and the rest of the team had fielded for three days straight as Brian Lara racked up a world record score of 375. It reminded him of what his veteran teammate Robin Smith had said to him in his first ever England game: 'Do you like fielding, China? Because you're going to be doing plenty of it!'

But Thorpe had made the most of the experience. He spent that tour watching Lara carefully, and when he returned to England he reworked his own technique in the nets: 'I had Stewie [Alec Stewart] throw balls at my head for two hours.' He also identified a key failing. 'The English way to play the short ball was the back-foot drive, up and under – I call it "the poke". It's a bullshit shot. It's what those fast bowlers *wanted* you to play.'

Instead, Thorpe developed a way to attack them back: the pull shot that I so admired. At Headingley, against the South African opening bowlers Allan Donald and Fanie de Villiers, he gave it its first major outing. He scored 72 in the first innings, batting alongside his captain (Atherton made 99, the ideal sympathy score after everything he'd been through), and 73 in the second. England drew the match. In the third and final Test of the series, Thorpe scored 79.

I've looked up Thorpe's statistics before we meet, and he didn't actually score as many 70s as I remembered; still, I tell him, it felt like he was often out for those midway scores: an honourable total, but not a big one. He reaches forward for a sip of cappuccino, and nods. 'In those early days I used to get too many 50s, not enough 100s. I used to get through to the second new ball then get out.' The tendency was exacerbated, he says, by the three-day games he used to play at county level. 'I didn't have that mentality that you could bat all day and bat the next day as well. You'd go and get 70 or 80 for your county side, and that was OK.'

Thorpe's 79 is not what people will remember of that last Test against South Africa, however. I was home for the holidays, watching as Devon Malcolm faced his first ball from Fanie de Villiers.

Malcolm's batting hadn't got any better since the winter in the Caribbean, and the head-high delivery hit him flush on his helmet. In the action replay, you could see his England badge break off and tumble poetically to the ground. The physio ran on to check him for concussion, and that interruption took longer than the rest of Malcolm's innings, which lasted another three balls.

From our living room in Luton, I couldn't hear Malcolm's chilling response to South Africa's slip cordon – 'You guys are history' – but I did watch the history unfold. Malcolm had a reputation for his off-days, the times when, whatever he intended, the ball did the opposite and his bowling became an enthusiastic but malfunctioning sprinkler system, spurting erratically in all directions. This, however, was not one of those days. The very first ball he bowled rose up at Gary Kirsten's throat, a faster, meaner version of the delivery that had clocked him ten minutes previously. The next ball did the same. The third reached only Kirsten's waist, but the batsman was so spooked by the first two that he turned away, and the ball ricocheted off his glove. Malcolm hurled himself down the pitch and caught it in his follow-through.

Kirsten's half-brother Peter tried to survive Malcolm's bowling by hooking at it – he was caught on the boundary. When Malcolm despatched Hansie Cronje too, South Africa were 1 for 3, and I was hyperventilating. Such a scoreline couldn't be possible: even at England's worst, in Trinidad, we hadn't lost three wickets for one run. My mum came back from her Saturday shop, and I breathlessly filled her in. She took up residence beside me on the sofa. The minute she went to the kitchen to make a cup of tea, Malcolm struck again.

In fact, my mum missed every one of Malcolm's wickets. After she'd resumed her seat the phone rang in the hall, and the next player was out while she hurried to answer it. Some trifling matter required her presence in another room; the next wicket fell. She soon became convinced that she held South Africa's fate in her hands, and sat out the rest of the innings in the kitchen. My mum missed one of the greatest individual bowling spells of all time in order to keep it happening, and I think Devon Malcolm's match-winning figures of 9 for 57 should carry a footnote in her honour.

Thanks to Malcolm's contribution an important series was drawn, and Atherton's dirty pockets were forgiven, if not forgotten. England had shown improvement and Ray Illingworth's appointment looked like a good idea. As Atherton prepared to lead them to Australia to attempt to regain the Ashes, for the first time in forever you could believe they stood a chance.

In the bright conservatory, I admit to Thorpe that he is not what I expected. 'I always read that you were . . .'

'Surly?'

'Shy. Or poker-faced. Or dour.'

He nods. 'I think on the field of play I was,' he says. 'I never used to take my helmet off, even when I was walking back to the pavilion. "The Man with No Name." That's how I used to view myself. I was quite happy with that.'

And it worked for him. He played his first Test against Australia, under Gooch's captaincy, when the England dressing-room was an intimidating place for a 23-year-old: 'Gooch seemed such a huge bloke. I was in awe of him.' Meanwhile the opposing captain, Allan Border, had confronted the young batsman as he took the crease and told Thorpe in uncomplimentary terms that he didn't expect him to last long. The first three days of that match had gone badly for England and, according to a peculiar tradition of the time, there was a rest day halfway through. 'I went down to London [from Trent Bridge], had a barbecue and a few beers. I realised that you needed to embrace the harshness of that environment, and not be afraid to mess up. You think, "If I'm going to go down, I'm going to at least go down on my own terms."'

The next day, Thorpe scored a century, only the fourteenth Englishman to do so on debut, and Allan Border himself shook his hand. 'So from very early on I understood that's how the game was. There wasn't anywhere to hide. I'd played rough football when I was younger, in a dirty football league, where people used to try to break each other's legs. And that was far worse than a Test match arena. Once you've realised that you start to enjoy playing for England. You realise you can survive in this dog-eat-dog world.'

He might as well have said the last sentence with a cheroot hanging from his lips. No wonder I used to think Thorpe was the coolest of the England cricketers: he refused to be cowed by the opposition, whoever they were. It was a trait he shared with Atherton, and, at the end of Atherton's 54 Tests as captain, Thorpe had played in 48 of them, more than any other player. Maybe that's another reason I liked him so much – Atherton had given him the ultimate stamp of approval.

Thorpe hadn't, he tells me, warmed to his new captain instantly. 'He was a totally different background,' he says, then pauses. 'Well, he seemed a totally different background. He'd been to Cambridge University; mine was a state school education. I could have been a little bit chippy in my early days – not really founded on anything but my own insecurities, to be honest. He might have been guarded around me, too. That's Athers' nature in many ways – don't dive in or reveal too much about yourself. But I had an evening out with him in the West Indies when we got drunk together and I got to know him a bit more. A rum and Coke generally loosens things up.'

And just like Atherton, he loved the fight most when the chips were down. The chips were often down. In an ideal situation, a number four comes in to bat when the top three have seen off the new ball and put some runs on the board – a score of 100 or so provides a safe launch pad for a number four's more expansive style of play. When England went to Australia in the winter of 1994–95, Thorpe played ten Test innings. Only twice did he come in to bat with the score over 60, which must have been frustrating? He shakes his head. 'I generally thrive on a bit of a crisis so I used to love that. At 11.30 a.m. we're 30 for 3 and everyone's jeering at you . . . by lunchtime you're walking off and you're 120 for 3 and they're a bit quieter. That became my role. I was better in that situation than I ever was going in at 300 for 3.

'Even if the team were in a mess there was the enjoyment of going out and doing well, still doing your bit, looking around and thinking, "You're playing Test match cricket, you're learning, and you're going to make it as difficult as it can be for the opposition." I can still remember those feelings.'

I can remember the feelings, too. With its nine-hour time difference, an Ashes tour is the most difficult of propositions for the cricket fan, especially one who has school the next morning, and has just started studying for her A levels. I was still in the habit of taking the radio to bed with me, but to follow the Ashes required a harsh regime. I would listen as long as I could stay awake, which was usually midnight, then set an alarm clock to wake me up midway through the afternoon and evening sessions, at 3 a.m. and 5 a.m. respectively. If England were having a decent spell, it was my duty to listen on as long as it lasted.

This was rarely very long, however. The hope that had built through the summer quickly burst, and England's batting proved just as collapsible as the winter before. They even managed to get beaten by the 19-year-olds in Australia's academy side. In between games, there were constant bulletins of new and inventive injuries to England players: bad backs, broken fingers, torn muscles. Two of the bowlers managed to catch chickenpox. I was studying *Hamlet* in my English lessons, and I remember distinctly reading a scene in which Gertrude told Laertes, 'One woe doth tread upon another's heel, So fast they follow.' 'Gertie,' I thought, 'I know exactly what you mean.'

I could glean a little private joy from the fact that Atherton repeatedly top-scored for England, but even that was limited: one of those high scores was 25. Australia had retained the Ashes by the end of the third Test. England gave them a fight, at least, in Sydney. My walls had long run out of space for more posters, so after that match it was my ceiling that was adorned with pictures of Darren Gough, the sunny young Yorkshireman who hit a hearty half-century, then scuttled the Australians for 116.

His irrepressible confidence inspired England afresh. They actually won the following Test in Adelaide, thanks in no little part to Thorpe, who rescued a teetering second innings with a swashbuckling 83. I looked hungrily at the pictures of the England players celebrating on their balcony, and emptying an ice bucket on their captain's head. It seemed like an important moment, and I'd been asleep when it happened.

But that victory, like the one in Barbados before it, was an early example of the mirage effect that attended England over the next few years. A solitary victory against major opposition, often achieved after the main prize was already lost, would convince me and other gullible fools that England truly were capable of beating anyone, at any time. The occasional, random wins raised my hopes beyond what was remotely reasonable or likely; their mere existence was enough to convince me that our team was on some sort of upward trajectory, however slight. I should have become inured to defeat, but those false glimmers kept the disappointment fresh. After Adelaide, England capitulated again. Thorpe scored 123 in the first innings – he had come to the crease with England 5 for 2 and made nearly half their entire total of runs – but he was out for 0 in the second innings, when only three England players made it out of single figures.

By this stage the regular interruptions to my sleep had become impossible to conceal from my parents. I was a kid who rarely stayed up later than *Have I Got News For You*. Now I was emerging from my room each morning with the drawn look of someone who had discovered a far more serious vice than Mars Bar ice creams. I had neither the energy nor the wish to speak before leaving the house. I was exhausted to the point of mental disintegration. When Darren Gough, the one bright star of the tour, succumbed to injury in the one-day games that followed the Tests, it's possible I suffered some sort of episode – I'm not sure how else to account for the number of pictures I collected of Gough being carried off the field/sitting with his leg on ice/flying home on crutches.

That was the last tour where England kept up their tradition of a fancy dress dinner at Christmas time. There's a photograph of them all: Darren Gough in the most star-spangled of Uncle Sam outfits; Mike Gatting convincing as Henry VIII; Ray Illingworth as a Chinese emperor. Other costume choices seem less obvious: Phil DeFreitas, for instance, is looking off to one side, apparently unsure why he chose the skintight Lycra Batman costume. Atherton, perhaps secretly hankering for a more cavalier style, is Robin Hood. At the back stands a Roman centurion. He's smiling more than you imagine a grim-faced warrior would do, but it's nice to see Graham Thorpe enjoying himself.

That image fitted with the cartoon sketch I had of Thorpe, of his reliability, his battling spirit, his role as a silent but willing protector. The longer Thorpe played, the more essential this presence seemed, and I couldn't fathom Atherton's team without him. But twice, in his later years, he withdrew from England duties because of personal troubles. He wrote in his autobiography that matters away from the pitch – including the break-up of his marriage, but also the deaths of cricketing colleagues Graham Kersey and Ben Hollioake, both killed in car crashes – had caused him great turmoil. At the time, a player choosing not to represent their country made no sense to me at all. It never occurred to me that Thorpe might have more worries than the two-dimensional variety my head could handle.

I'm telling him about Alec Stewart's memories of the nineties, and how he looks back on the games he played with a surprising detachment, almost as if someone else was playing those games. I wonder aloud if it is some sort of protective mechanism. 'I think that's a good way of putting it,' says Thorpe. 'Alec was very good at compartmentalising. Things off the field Alec could deal with really well. Whereas with me . . . I think it's pretty obvious, once something was going on behind the scenes I found it very difficult to stay focused on the job in hand. Al could probably think, "Just another game of cricket." Whereas I was thinking, "What are we doing on this pitch, really?" For periods, cricket just seemed entirely irrelevant.'

As it turned out, Thorpe's England career outlasted that of any of his nineties colleagues. He played his last Test in 2005, just a couple of months before England finally regained the Ashes. By that stage, England were, in his words, 'a tough team to beat'. I agree but I feel I've got to ask, why were they so easy to beat before? 'I'd put a certain amount down to never getting the same bowlers on the park,' Thorpe says. He quickly reels off a list of a dozen bowlers who opened the bowling in the mid-nineties '. . . and I'm not even putting a great deal of thought into it. For me, that was a big reason.'

Later, I'll look up the number of pace bowlers who played in the first 15 months of Atherton's captaincy: 14 bowlers, in 14 Tests. England couldn't seem to find a regular group of players to work in partnership. There were myriad injuries, and sometimes bowlers just didn't perform well enough to justify their place. Thorpe thinks he knows why: their contracts. The county sides they played for week-on-week were the ones who paid their salaries. Playing for England was a reward for doing well, but it had to be fitted around the day job. 'You finished a county game, you drove up, one day's practice, straight into the game,' says Thorpe. 'Everything was in a rush. You'd finish a Test match and go and play for your county the next day. There wasn't always a game, but more often than not there was, and you would pack up your bags and go straight on – which was unhealthy. You couldn't reflect over a few beers with your team – what did we do well? or why weren't we successful? – and going back and playing for your county would take energy from the bowlers. In a Test match, we could have a side 100 for 5, but then our third spells would tire off.' I remember it well, I say. The opposition would rally, and a promising situation would disappear.

Tufnell had brought up the same issue. 'I used to have to try to get Angus Fraser out of bed every morning,' he remembered, and performed a little skit of Fraser – as a zombie with rigor mortis – attempting to get to the bath. 'We'd be playing on a Monday for Middlesex, we'd bowl 40 overs, get in a car, drive up to Old Trafford, lose the toss and be bowling against Australia on Thursday. We'd be absolutely shagged out.'

Many players were advocates of 'central contracts', which would see them reporting directly to the England team, and would require their welfare to be put above the county's pound of flesh. Thorpe remembers a senior cricket official once telling him that they would only consider central contracts when

England started winning some matches. 'I said, "How are we going to win Test matches when we don't get the same bowling attack on the pitch, because they're bloody injured every other week?" The Australian bowling attack hadn't changed for three series, because they got looked after properly.'

When I was lambasting their uselessness from my sofa, I didn't consider that players might just be tired. In fact, when a player did badly for England, people would say that what they needed was to get back to their county and get some more runs/overs/wickets under their belt. I tended to nod along at this sentiment, because it didn't occur to me that the county schedule might be what was wearing them out. Still, I shouldn't beat myself up about it. Apparently it didn't occur to the people who ran cricket either.

It's getting on, and Thorpe will soon be heading home to his two young daughters. I don't want to embarrass him, but I can't leave without telling him what I came here to say. 'You're remembered fondly,' I start. 'Among lots of my friends. Well, not *my* friends, but people I've met. You're their favourite batsman. At least 50 per cent of them.' I realise this sounds like a low figure. 'No, more. Maybe, like, 80 per cent.' Embarrassing Thorpe was never the issue; I was always 100 per cent more likely to embarrass myself. I stumble on. 'I just wondered, well, hoped, really, because we have this perception that perhaps you didn't realise . . . how popular you were. You were very well loved. Did you know that? Did you even know how good you were?'

I can feel my ears turning red, but Thorpe is unruffled. He answers my last question first. 'I felt I was learning on the job,' he says. 'My first 35 Tests were a barrage, so you're constantly just standing up for yourself. You're fighting all the way through it. It wasn't until towards the end of my career that I felt I'd worked the game out, and I knew when I'd done well.' He smiles. 'But it's wonderful when you finish and you meet people and they talk fondly about you. It's really nice to hear.'

He drives me back to the train station, and we chat about his little girls. They have some hobbies – playing piano, riding bikes – but he's worried they don't seem very serious about anything yet. 'Just wait until they're teenagers,' I want to say. 'You'll be begging them not to take everything so seriously.' But I don't, because he's probably seen far enough into the scary mind of an adolescent girl for one day.

Chapter 5

I've always preferred watching my teams bowl to watching them bat. When your team are batting, your instinct is to maintain the status quo, and you don't really want to see anything dramatic happen. At least, I don't. I certainly didn't in the 1990s, when England's middle order carried a hairline fracture that could snap at any second, and I would watch an entire batting session through my fingers, praying desperately for nothing exciting or noteworthy to take place.

When your team are in the field, however, you're willing the action on. Perhaps even more so when things are going badly. Sure, your bowling attack may be getting thrashed around the park right *now*, but it only takes a single ball to get a batsman out. Nothing can rob you of that tiny moment of hope when the ball leaves the bowler's hand. Every delivery is a miniature grenade of possibility.

Bowlers are cricket's demolition artists. The batsmen head out into the field, their hard hats on, to spend minutes, hours, sometimes days carefully constructing the largest and most stable edifice they can. Meanwhile the bowlers do their damnedest to knock it down. It's like reverse Jenga: instead of removing the blocks with surgical care, the bowler is just hurling stuff at the tower from 22 yards away.

Unfortunately, England bowlers did not, at the time, have a great reputation for accuracy. Or pace. Or penetration. Most of the time you wouldn't have backed them to punch their way through a Japanese paper screen.

The motley cast of returning characters seemed to be gathered from a bag of factory misfits: here, a terrifyingly fast but woefully inaccurate strike bowler; there, a rhythmically predictable but utterly unpenetrative medium-pacer. There were a couple who were neither fast nor accurate, but *were* left-handed, which England's selectors hoped would confuse the opposition. There were also a number of Australian leftovers, unable to break into their own state side. The selectors would try them in endless new permutations, looking to fit the misshapen pieces together. They – and I – genuinely believed that if only the correct combination could be found, England would be a powerful and vicious machine that would thresh through the opposition.

There was nothing remotely vicious about the men who made up England's pace attack. I adored them, especially the few who managed to hold down a semi-regular place in the side. Take Darren Gough: you would have needed a heart of solid cyanide not to love him. From the moment he had bundled on to the pitch against New Zealand, in the spring of '94, his broad-shouldered, big-bottomed presence had energised the England side. He bustled, he buzzed, he brimmed with enthusiasm; his bowling was full of life, his batting full of dare. He reminded me of a kid from my old *Whizzer and Chips* comics: the cheeky rascal who gets one over on his teacher, then sneaks a sticky bun and hares off down the street, leaving the baker shaking his head with a rueful grin. He felt like the team's lucky mascot, even when they lost.

I was also especially fond of Phil DeFreitas, a rare veteran of the days of Gooch and Gower, a man who ran up to bowl with his head leaning over as if making a bid for freedom from the rest of his body. Stood alongside his teammates, 'Daffy' looked small and sinewy, although his stats showed him to be six foot tall. He also seemed far too pleasant a man to be a frightening fast bowler. But you could see the earnestness of his efforts in his face and that strange, contorted delivery stride. He was reliable, and while that may not sound a thrilling quality in a sportsman, England's unstable exploits were already teaching me to prize it more highly than rubies.

No bowler was more dear to me, however, than Angus Fraser. Fraser was the most reluctant of sporting heroes. He took to the field with a hangdog air only emphasised by his giant proportions, and there was little of the natural athlete about his running or his bowling. Every jogged step elicited a pang of sympathy – it all just looked such hard work. And yet he was the precision weapon in England's arsenal. In each of the giantkilling victories I had witnessed – against West Indies in Barbados, and Australia at The Oval and in Adelaide – Fraser had been the destroyer. He had done it all with an air of modesty and exhaustion, and a funny little flannel flapping at his crotch as he ran down the wicket, his finger wagging at the sky.

The pace attack is supposed to be the most aggressive of cricket's fraternities, but the men I admired didn't snarl or strut or swear. OK, I'm sure they did swear, but they didn't do it in such a way that I could hear, or lip-read, so my innocent ears remained protected. I imagined DeFreitas as a super-helpful uncle, and I could sense a gruff kindness behind Fraser's Eeyorish expression. Even Gough, who had earned the tag of housewives' favourite, was a safe choice: cuddly, not sexy. It says something, I think, that my cricketing favourites were the same as my mother's. They were all the types of solid, dependable men of whom she approved.

And then, in June 1995, Dominic Cork erupted into my life.

As I became more savvy about my adopted sport, I had quickly begun to consider myself an expert. To begin with, I had merely repeated whatever my mother told me; now I was cribbing the opinions of newspaper columnists and TV commentators. I was increasingly confident in sharing 'my' views, and these included which players should and shouldn't be in the England team. I would loudly tout the merits of up-and-coming players who I had never seen play, and I would campaign tirelessly for their selection, mainly to my mother.

Mostly we would agree, but the more I learned about the sport, the more I was prepared to challenge her orthodoxy. And I knew more than Mum about the 23-year-old newcomer who lined up against West Indies at Lord's. It was the second Test of the summer (true to form, they had lost the first) and Cork was filling our screen. His blond hair was brushed forward and to one side, in a style that hinted at a quiff – as James Dean as he could manage, without stooping to anything as cissy as gel. He was tall and lithe and seemed to be made up entirely of acute angles, from his chin to the pointy tips of his ears. His gangly limbs reminded me of a badge I'd worn in the Brownies. I'd been an 'Imp', and the anarchic yellow figure that had been embroidered on my sleeve perfectly captured Cork's angular energy.

He bowled England to victory with seven wickets in the second innings – the best bowling figures of an England player on debut, a performance that would have been eye-catching enough on its own. But it was Cork's manner that really startled me. He delivered the ball trailing the other arm in the air to create a dramatic silhouette. And when he celebrated a wicket, he leapt up to punch the air with his fist, sometimes both fists, the holler of an Indian chief on his lips.

Nothing, though, matched the testosterone thump of his lbw appeals. As soon as the ball hit a batsman's pad, Cork would jump round to the umpire in a massive burst of masculinity, his arms aloft, his legs spread, his mouth fixed open in a leonine roar. He held that star-shaped pose – back arched, knees buckling – as long as it took to get the answer he wanted. The bravado was astonishing. It was meant to intimidate the opposition and the umpires, but it horrified my mother.

This scowling, howling, chest-beater of a man fitted nowhere in the categories of England bowlers I had grown to know and love. There wasn't anything fatherly, or brotherly, or avuncular about him. I couldn't imagine Fraser executing a swift half-turn and bellowing his destiny at the heavens – well, I'm not sure his back would have taken it anyway. Mum thought Cork was crass and vulgar. I thought he was great.

When I was 11 my school friend Philippa, the one who loved Bros, had lots of other posters on her bedroom walls too: INXS, New Kids on the Block, groupings of young men lounging in ripped jeans, toplessly. My intuition told me that I was supposed to like them, but I didn't. They were so confrontational, all those naked torsos. I'd always loved Craig McLachlan from *Neighbours*, but when I saw him up there, an undersized waistcoat flapping nonchalantly open, it felt like the start of a dangerous quarrel.

By my mid-teens, it was obligatory to have a picture of David Hasselhoff or Jason Priestley on your wall, six-pack rippling, a slight sheen suggestive of— what? I had no idea. The sight of all that flesh was confusing. I could feel deeply in love with Kevin Costner in *The Bodyguard*, but the moment he revealed so much as a chest hair a strange chill would affect my insides and I had to fight the urge to hide my face and giggle. I didn't really want to see men as sexual creatures – definitely not naked ones, anyway.

The men of my most romantic fantasies were impossibly remote and tightly buttoned into frock coats: Mr Rochester in *Jane Eyre*, Monsieur Paul in *Villette*.

With no experience of boyfriends, I couldn't really fathom what having one would entail, or why it might be nice. Most of the teenage males who trespassed on my daily life were pretty offputting, especially the pupils of the boys' school that adjoined our own. At the age of 11, I had begun encountering these creatures on the coaches which ferried us to and from school. It was here they felt free to unload their minds of all the putrescence that had been fermenting there overnight, and the sexual frustration they'd been tamping down in class. I vividly remember in my first week, sitting alone and virginal on the scratchy seats, being told how ugly I was, then asked for a handjob.

Afraid of these new creatures, I decided early on simply to despise them. During school hours, they were penned in the next enclosure to us, behind a pair of black gates that were emphatically out of bounds. Naturally, therefore, that was the cool place to hang out. Ominous warnings were issued by the headmistress to stay away from The Black Gates, and for swots like me they became a place of legend where only the most dangerous girls would venture. I occasionally wondered if my life would be different if I were brave enough to tag along – then I reminded myself that the prize wasn't worth it. Who were these people? Had they faced down Courtney Walsh or castled Mark Waugh?

Caring as much as I did about cricket did not make my interactions with boys any easier whatsoever. Sure, you might think that my teenage love of the game would provide some common ground. You might imagine it would gain me some respect, or even a special place in their affections. But you would be wrong, because you would be fundamentally mistaking the motives of the boys I knew.

Discounting the dickwads on the school bus, I did have some male friends. At least I realise now that they were friends; at the time, I was never sure. We went to the same church, and the same youth group, and they – Jez, Ben and Chris – enjoyed only one thing more than their games of no-rules football, and that was ceaselessly tormenting me and the rest of the girls. Our Friday night hangouts were a constant bombardment of teasing and bickering. Unfortunately, they were no Spencer Tracys, and we were no Katharine Hepburns. It wasn't a battle of wits so much as a debilitating and drawn-out siege.

The other girls, who went to mixed schools or had brothers, were more *au fait* with the infuriating manners of the teenage male, and handled it far better. My friend Verity had a glance so icy you could see the stab wound it left. But I had no such weapon, and was the easiest bait. All the boys had to do was tell me that the England cricket team were crap and I'd turn puce and begin to splutter. Unfortunately, my team was constantly providing them with fresh ammunition: individual failures, collective collapses, bowling figures that read like darts scores. If all other taunts failed, a reminder of England's 46 all out in Trinidad was a sure thing. It would instantly prompt me to wail that they'd won '*the very next Test!!*' and the boys knew they had me on the hook for the rest of the evening.

We hung out more as we grew older, the boys, Verity and me. The boys didn't get noticeably more mature – when we went camping, they'd pee on our tent one night, and let it down the next – but, then, neither did I. I let them provoke me all the time. I guess I liked the rush of feelings, and the sense that I was defending my team's honour. My naive enthusiasm may have driven Verity to despair – 'You're such a weirdo,' she would tell me, lovingly, to my face – but it was an ideal characteristic for supporting England, a team that demanded a particularly imperishable sense of loyalty.

Discovering my voice, and my identity as a contrarian, made me feel surprisingly powerful and alive. The only thing I really hated – what made me squirm and die inside – was when the boys teased me about the players. 'How can you fancy Michael Atherton?' they'd ask, and I'd recoil as if someone had accused me of incest, or listening to Rick Astley. Ugh! The idea I might want to kiss one of my cricketing heroes was disgusting.

I had been off sick the day they taught sex education in biology, and my parents never gave me 'the talk', assuming the job had been done elsewhere. This all suited me, as I didn't like to think about the physical act of sex at all. It made me squeamish and uncomfortable and the mere mention of it – even by a girlfriend like Verity – would make me blush. So I didn't consider all those pictures of cricketers on my walls to be pin-ups. They were more like imaginary friends than objects of lust. My feelings about the England team were on a rarefied plane.

'But you do! You fancy *the pants* off him!'

And then would come the blush, the unquenchable blush, which only confirmed to Jez and Chris and Ben everything they had said, and made them say it again, louder.

It takes me a little while to reach Dominic Cork. It's not that I don't know where he is. He's regularly on the radio, and he pops up on my TV screen too, as a pundit paid to give his opinions on whatever games are going on around the world. But he's not responding to my emails or my phonecalls. Each message I leave attempts to sound more winning than the last. I know that, in reality, I'm coming off as increasingly desperate.

Perhaps it's fitting that he should be a difficult quarry. After all, Cork is more than a former fast-medium bowler with a decent inswinger and the ability to crack a ball through the covers. He was once cricket's unicorn.

In the aftermath of the 1980s, when a titanic figure known as Ian Botham had clobbered batsmen and bowlers with equal glee, there was a widely held belief that England would never succeed until they found someone to replace his all-round role in the team. People talked and wrote as if Botham were King Arthur, and the end of his reign had caused Camelot to crumble. Only the miraculous emergence of one who could both open the bowling and bat at number six would return Albion to its former glory.

The legend took hold, and selectors scoured the country for the next Botham. Over the following decade, many were invited to prove their worth. There were challengers who had the heart, but not the fitness, like Craig White; others had the fitness, but not the brain, like Chris Lewis. There were 'bowling all-rounders' who proved more use as batsmen, and 'batting all-rounders' who kept losing their wicket, and a couple of bustling figures whose greatest claim to Botham's mantle was shopping from the same XL rack. No one could do the job. Four contenders – Mark Ealham, Ronnie Irani, Adam Hollioake and Ben Hollioake – racked up the paltry sum of 17 Tests, 369 runs and 26 wickets between them.

For a short while, however, Cork had seemed the real deal. After the thrill of his debut at Lord's, England were 1–1 in their six-Test series against West Indies, only to be disgraced in the next game at Edgbaston. I was furious: not with them, but with the Birmingham groundsman, whose pitch had sent balls rocketing about the batsmen's heads, making it the perfect early Christmas present for the opposition bowlers. The result was defeat in two days and a little over an hour, and Cork was one of the few to emerge from the debacle with any credit, taking four cheap wickets and batting longer than any but the veteran Robin Smith in England's all too brief second innings.

Before the two sides met again, I had got myself a job. Well, not a job so much, in that it paid nothing. But my mum had been nagging me to get some work experience. In one of the cricket magazines I read, I'd seen an advert for a company called Cover Point that sold video highlights of each month's major cricketing events. Presuming that the workers' only task was to watch cricket all day, I had offered my limited office skills (tea-making, photocopying, etc.) for free, and they had accepted.

The business was based in the house of its owner, Paul, and consisted of a handful of men doing technical things with VHS and Betamax machines. I was installed in an attic room and asked to type up the player interviews they had recorded. Paul was a nice man with a short fuse, and I was happy to stay in my attic where I didn't have to listen to his shouty phone conversations. I spent my days transcribing the thoughts of John Emburey and Paul Downton, and eating the same ham sandwich I requested for lunch every day because I was too nervous to think what else to ask for.

The week of the Old Trafford Test, Paul called me downstairs to his office. He was going to interview Michael Atherton in Manchester the next day, he told me. Would I like to go with him?

I said yes. Of course I said yes. I said yes and I said thank you, and then I immediately regretted my decision. The waves of nausea I felt as soon as I had committed to the trip stayed with me all the way up the M6 the next morning. Paul was a terrifying driver – he actually reversed down the hard shoulder when we missed our turning – but even that couldn't distract me from the horror of meeting my favourite sportsman in the world. I was desperately prone to blushing, an uncontrollable reaction that embarrassed me more than the thing that prompted it. I knew that today, something was going to embarrass me. I was sure of it. And the only thing that could prevent my own mortification was death which, in spite of that sliproad manoeuvre, wasn't imminent enough.

At the ground we met up with Paul's cameraman and the three of us sat in the empty stands waiting for Atherton, who had headed for the showers after training. I was mute, still battling the urge to vomit. Throwing up on the England cricket captain now seemed a very real prospect, and when he finally joined us, a pink towel slung casually round his neck, I nodded my head and bit the insides of my cheeks.

My role was to hold a large, heavy and utterly phallic microphone, and since I had to stay out of shot while Atherton sat in the stands, I had to kneel at his feet. There wasn't much room, my legs were twisted painfully beneath me, and my arms were soon burning from the effort of holding the microphone still. I was far too self-conscious to look up, so I stared fiercely at the mic instead, willing myself not to drop it.

I have no idea what Atherton must have thought of this strange, mute girl with a look of desperate concentration on her face. But my policy worked: I got through the interview without turning candy-floss pink, and without speaking at all. As Atherton left, I was letting out a sigh of relief, when the cameraman remarked as loudly as he could: 'You can put your tongue away now, Emma.'

I glanced despairingly at Atherton's back as it retreated amid the stands, and I swear I saw a hitch in his step.

In spite of what was, and possibly still remains, the most embarrassing moment of my life, my trip to Old Trafford meant I felt a strong personal claim on the events that followed there. Ironically, I didn't get to see much of the first two days, because it turned out that those who worked at a cricket highlights video company did not, as I had imagined, down tools on the Thursday and Friday of a Test match. Instead of watching England bowl out West Indies for 216 then build a solid reply, I spent most of those two days watching an old man called David Steele tell a story about getting lost in the pavilion on his way to bat at Lord's in 1975. (The anecdote probably took half an hour, but my tortoiseian typing speed required I listen to it over and over, until Steele's white hair and black eyebrows were burned on the back of my retina.)

By Saturday morning, I knew I had thoroughly earned my right to the remote control. I may even have claimed to my sister Kate that I needed to watch every ball of the cricket 'for work'. Cork batted like a scamp; his shots were kosher enough, but there was something in his stance, the way his head ducked to meet the oncoming ball, that made the whole thing look improvised. He scored swiftly, and each of his runs seemed to be stolen from someone else, be it the bowler, the fielder or the cricketing gods themselves. As it turned out, they were: at lunchtime, we saw slow-motion footage of Cork's foot sliding backwards into his stumps and a bail gently sliding to the ground. Technically, Cork had been out, but since no one had noticed or appealed, he had slyly replaced the bail and carried on. It was metaphysics in motion: the tree had fallen and made no sound.

Laws of proportion and probability just didn't seem to apply to Cork. His half-century was celebrated with a standing ovation round the ground and the England players were all on the balcony to recognise him. (I remember being horrified that Mike Watkinson, a 33-year-old playing his first Test, was sporting a low-slung vest. I didn't know why it upset me so at the time, but life has since taught me that those items should only ever be attempted by Channing Tatum chest-alikes.) By Saturday evening, West Indies had lost three wickets but the ever-dangerous Brian Lara was still in, and I'd gone to bed oscillating between an irrepressible hope and a learned pessimism.

The first over of a day's play is imbued with a kind of holiness. True fans hate to miss it. Some think it sets the tone for the day's play, others that it's when batsmen are at their most vulnerable. I don't share either of these beliefs, but I do love the thrill of the build-up, as the bowler marks out his run-up with exaggerated strides and hops, and the fielders scatter enthusiastically to their positions, the most energetic you see them all day. Since my teenage days, I have kept to my own start-of-play routine. I make ready my viewing sanctum: there are the tea and biscuits to fetch from the kitchen, the sofa to pull into position. I'm all settled by the time the bowler starts his run-up and the crowd (a third empty, because the dilettantes are still missing) makes its weird lowing sound to accompany it. It's not that I believe something will happen in that first, precious over, it's just that, if England are bowling, I so desperately want it to.

I was in my pyjamas and still groggy with sleep when Dominic Cork bowled his first four balls on Sunday morning. When his fifth ricocheted off Richie Richardson's bat and into the West Indies captain's stumps, I let out a breathy noise, a zombie groan of barely sentient excitement. The next ball thumped into Junior Murray's pads, and now I was upright, my fists clenching the air in an unconscious parody of Cork's own. I couldn't have been more suddenly awake if someone had applied a defibrillator to my chest.

I knew not to expect a hat-trick. No Englishman had taken a hat-trick since 1957. The term is misleadingly familiar, perhaps because of its footballing equivalent – you're far more likely to score three goals in a 90-minute match than you are to take three wickets in consecutive deliveries. But the statistical rarity can't prevent you hoping, or tensing every muscle in your body, or shouting confusingly unladylike things at the screen – things you've never said before, phrases like 'go on, my son' and 'this one's *yours*, Corky' and 'c'mon, c'mon, *c'mon, c'mon*, C'MON!'

Mum was with me, of course. Moments of high drama like this were a testing ground, a time when I discovered just how far I could push the boundaries of our maturing relationship. Normally, a mere 'oh my God' got a quick rebuke. But who knew what was allowable under this sort of duress? I might even *swear*.

Cork stood at the end of his run-up, his hair swept horizontal, his cheeks and nose under a stripe of sunblock – a wannabe rock star on his evolution to Adam Ant. He squinted into the sun, then leaned forward and ran, his elbows pumping behind him, prancing upright as he reached the crease to fling the ball at the new batsman's middle stump. It hit neither stump nor bat – only the resounding middle of Carl Hooper's front pad.

Every man on the screen screamed their appeals, and so did I. In the heartbeat that followed, my stomach pitched and rolled. And then the umpire raised his finger, and Cork sank to his knees, his teammates leaping on top of him until he was completely obscured. Me? I cried. I wish I'd had a different reaction – that I'd leapt into a hug with my mum, or at least ventured a 'bloody *hell*' – but I didn't. I just stood there, my limbs shaking from the shock or the lack of a more substantial breakfast than custard creams.

As the unnecessary tears squeezed out of my eyes, I suspected that I didn't know myself at all. Why did such an arbitrary occurrence – three wickets in three balls – feel so miraculous? Where did these sensations even come from? Was this how Cork felt, too? Or was this strange thunderclap of feelings a mere echo of his achievement, a wish-fulfilment facsimile of emotion transmitted across the airwaves into my living room?

I still don't know. Maybe I can find out from Cork. He's finally responded. He's covering a major international tournament for Sky, and he's promised to hang around in their studios at the end of one of the matches to talk to me. The studio lot, perched on the very edge of west London, is a sequence of hangar-like buildings connected by enclosed walkways, their industrial grey brightened here and there with aggressive flashes of colour carrying upbeat corporate messages. At ground level are small plots of earth in the very first stages of cultivation. When I arrive, I'm required to have my picture taken. I feel like I'm checking in on an interplanetary colony.

The Sky Sports building is a futuristic glass cube, its entrance guarded, inexplicably, by two giant models of Mike and Sulley from *Monsters, Inc.* I climb the stairs and spot Dominic Cork before he sees me. He's at the other end of the first floor, backlit by the bright sunshine that floods through the floor-to-ceiling windows. But there's no mistaking that silhouette, its upward thrust, its pointy joints. 'I don't wear make-up normally,' he smiles, when I get near enough to see his face.

We head to the café, where the colony workers are refuelling in between shifts: Cork nods to one and it takes a second for me to realise that it's the former England captain Michael Vaughan. There's a lanyard with his studio pass draped around Cork's open-collared shirt, beneath his grey, TV-ready suit. He will have to head back into the studio eventually – there's a breaking story that the *Sky Sports News* viewers require his expert opinion on – but he's in no hurry, and he's more than happy to relive old times. After all, he says, they were the best days of his life.

He still remembers the frustration of waiting for his first Test cap – he was considered more of a one-day player – and how, when he did get selected against West Indies, he'd hurt his back playing for Derbyshire. 'I went to a specialist and said, "I don't care what you do, you've just got to get rid of this pain,"' he remembers. Three days later he hit his first ball in Test cricket for four runs. 'People say, "Why did it go so well?" and I think it's because I was that *desperate*. I so wanted to prove myself and make sure I grabbed on to my chance.'

Cork's speech is fast and fluid. I'd worried, from his reputation for confrontation, that he might be a little prickly, but you can tell that these days he's a professional talker. As for the hat-trick, I had been nervous he might not remember anything at all: sportsmen who have enjoyed the out-of-body experience they call 'being in the zone' seem to lose all conscious thought during their finest passages of play. Some later claim that they can remember nothing of their performance, like those murderers who come to with bloody hands and no knowledge of the crime they've just committed.

I'm lucky. Cork can remember *everything* about his victims. He tells me that before the start of play Atherton had made 'a little speech' to his troops. 'We were still up against it, and he said, "Look, we've got to do something, something's got to happen." And I just stuck my hand up and said, "Give it me. I'll bowl. I want to bowl."' The first three balls he bowled were 'average' and the fourth was a no-ball. 'I thought, "This hasn't been a great over."' So he refocused. He thought hard about the next ball hitting the top of off stump, and it did, albeit via the inside of Richardson's bat. 'He was so unlucky,' says Cork, 'but I thought, "I'll take that." How many times as a bowler have you had a batsman play and miss, and you get nothing?'

Carl Hooper was due in next, so when Junior Murray walked out to the crease '. . . we thought, "That's a bit strange. What's up with Hooper? Is he ill?" And that gives you a bit more spark.' Cork knew how to bowl at Murray, who tended to stay back in his crease and work the ball leg-side. 'Get it full and straight, make him play.

Soon as it hit him I knew – I didn't really have to turn around to the umpire.' But being Cork, he threw his legs wide and appealed himself hoarse anyway.

He can still recall his internal monologue as he walked back to his mark for the final ball of the over. 'I remember thinking, how many times have I seen it on TV – how many times have I seen it on the field – when the bowler hasn't got the hat-trick ball straight? So all I kept saying to myself was, "Bowl straight." I even visualised the actual ball. I knew how Hooper played. I knew if I got it slightly outside off stump with a little bit of reverse swing he'd go across his stumps. It was either going to go through bat and pad and bowl him or get him lbw.'

Cork can remember thinking how loud the crowd sounded as he ran in – like a stadium of 90,000 people, not the mere 8,000 that were there. He knew Hooper was out the moment the ball hit his pads. 'But I thought, "Will the umpire think that he can't give two lbws on the trot?" So I turned round and my appeal stance went even wider, I was nearly doing the splits.' He laughs. 'I think my whites did rip, actually. And I remember seeing he'd got a shudder in his finger, and thinking, "He's given that out, what do I do now?" I didn't know what to do. So I just fell to my knees.'

Few of us know what it's like to experience a moment, however brief, as a sporting god. Cork's pose looked, from the outside, like a moment of unadulterated ego: his arms aloft, rooted to the ground like a statue of himself, while his teammates ran up from every corner of the field. But now I hear him describe the moment I wonder if his stance was more shock than awe. 'I just didn't know what to do,' Cork repeats, his eyes wide at the memory. 'It takes a while for it to sink in.'

Fans rarely had a neutral view of Cork. His showmanship just didn't allow for it. There were those who thought that it was a fillip to see someone demonstrate such out-and-out passion while playing for their country. And then there were those who found his aggressive posturing unnecessary, who considered his histrionics thoroughly *infra dig*. These people tended to remark, sniffily, that such behaviour wasn't appropriate for a gentlemanly sport.

Of the two camps, I should have fallen in the latter. I loved the gentility of cricket, the way it claimed to belong to a different era. It offered a sheltered fantasy world for someone who craved the safety and delicacy of chivalry – a teenager who wanted the opposite sex to be courtly, not manly, and who would prefer it if everyone pretended that people didn't have sex until they were married. Cork suggested a world of men who didn't play by those rules. A world I wasn't ready for.

But if his methods got results, I wasn't going to complain. Australia was full of bowlers far shoutier, swearier and stroppier than Cork, and I'd have given them British citizenship in a heartbeat. I didn't hold with the snobbery that said Cork was an apocalyptic sign that cricketers were becoming evermore like footballers. The footballers I'd seen doing goal celebrations on the TV looked far less aggressive than Cork; they rocked babies, or did silly dance moves, or ran around with their shirts stuck halfway over their heads like toddlers.

I assumed that Cork was just a bit big-headed and decided that, in this case, it was absolutely fine to indulge his antics. It didn't occur to me that the entire thing might be a performance – that Cork was not an ever-gushing fountain of machismo, but a young man doing a war dance for the benefit of the opposition, the supporters, and himself. Beholding the grey-suited man in front of me who is courteously answering my questions, that scenario does make a lot more sense. 'Cricketers, sportsmen, we're actors on a stage,' he says. 'That's what we *do*. We can't deliver lines, but we act with our skill.'

I ask where he learned to play the part, and he doesn't hesitate: 'My dad,' he says. Cork remembers playing with his older brothers in the backyard – football, most often – '. . . and my father really drilling it into us: "You go out there and you push your chest out, and you show them. Whatever you do, you actually believe you're better than the opposition."'

And he did, such as in the summer of 1998, when he decided to wind up his South African opposite number Brian McMillan, a physically huge man, by calling him 'the bus driver' whenever he came in to bat. 'I went a little bit too far. We clapped him in at Headingley, and when he was out, I said, "There you go, off to start your engine!" And he came looking for me at the end of the game. He's a big lad, someone said he's a Hell's Angel as well . . . I *ran*. "Oh God, I'm off, see you, lads . . ."'

What did he think of being called a showboater? 'Show*pony*,' he corrects me. 'That was what Geoffrey Boycott called me. But I *loved* playing for England! I loved cricket!' I can see it even now, the zeal of a man who wants to entertain. 'I was just a guy who wanted to do well for England, and sometimes my enthusiasm took over. I didn't see it as showboating. I saw it as living the dream.'

'After all,' he says, 'would you call Ian Botham a showboater?' He, too, wore his heart on his sleeve, and it was Botham's passion that had inspired Cork to play cricket in the first place. A nine-year-old Cork watched Botham's 1981 Ashes heroics on a portable TV in a caravan on a family holiday and decided he wanted to play for England – up until then he'd only wanted to drive a Yorkie lorry. The little boy grew up to make his England debut in Botham's last ever one-day match. 'He came straight up and put his arm round me and said, "I'll look after you." And that was good enough for me. Everywhere he went I went. I was like his lapdog.'

Cork says he's never stopped being in awe of the man. 'Still am! And I work with him now. I play golf with him, and I'm still starstruck. I give him ten-foot putts – "Oh, don't worry about them, you're Ian Botham!"' Did it feel like hubris, then, to be named his heir apparent? Cork shakes his head. 'It didn't bother me in any way,' he says. 'A lot of people found it pressure, but I didn't find it pressure. I just thought it was quite nice, a compliment.'

He didn't ascend to Botham's throne, in the end. 'I was never going to be as good as him. I thought in my mind I could be, but realistically it was never going to happen.' His bowling progressed in fits and starts, and his batting never lived up to its promise, or the standard of a Test-class all-rounder. Cork thinks he just didn't practise enough: 'Generally because I was so tired from bowling, but that's no excuse.' He still played a role in some of England's memorable rearguard actions and, for fans like me, his presence down the batting order offered a reassurance more totemic than it was real. Perhaps some of his best work was done sitting in the dressing-room as the next man in, bolstering the fiction that England had plenty more batting to come.

Things went a little sour, for a time. Two years after his brilliant debut summer, he pulled out of England's tour to Zimbabwe because his marriage was falling apart; when he joined up with the team in New Zealand, he was, according to the press reports, both unfit to play and a difficult man to get on with. I heard he had an on-field spat with Atherton, I say. Cork nods – he can't even remember what triggered it. 'It was something about how he wanted me to bowl, and I just threw him the ball and said, "Well, if you can do any better, you bowl." It was very disrespectful. I apologised straight after to him, and I regret it.'

It was, he says, 'just emotions, again', and he points out that he batted in the partnership that won the New Zealand Test series on the final day. 'There were a lot of things that were said about me – David Lloyd said they considered sending me home. I never understood why. I still don't now.' Well, some of his teammates said that he didn't seem to want to be there. The problem with wearing your heart on your sleeve is that you can end up being a downer for others. 'Maybe I was a little quieter at night,' he says, 'but I was still giving it my all on the pitch. I was justified to be there.'

The quest for England's next great all-rounder moved on; other candidates received the false anointing. Cork's story had progressed from medieval fantasy to soap opera to something far more mundane – the common narrative of the nineties paceman. He fell in and out of form, and got injured from bowling too much. Sometimes he found himself left out of the team for no discernible reason. 'I think the worst time for me was 1999 when I couldn't make a World Cup squad of 30 players,' he snorts. 'I remember saying to David Graveney, the chairman of selectors, "You're having a laugh, mate. There's something wrong."'

Still, Cork did have some magic remaining – his ability to give his best when there was something to prove, and the pressure was at its greatest. 'It was like somebody giving me a can of energy drink. Like somebody had injected adrenalin into me. Lights on, here we go. *Now* it's time, *now* I'll show people.' When West Indies returned to England in 2000, Cork was recalled to the team at Lord's. Like a member of an ageing boyband reforming for a comeback tour, Cork brought out all his greatest hits. Having taken seven wickets for 52 to help set up a surefire win, he found himself sent in to bat with England teetering on the brink of defeat.

'Walking through the Long Room,' says Cork, 'I heard, "Here we go, we've lost this game . . ." It inspires you when the members are giving up. I remember going out there and losing wickets at the other end, then Goughy walking to the crease. I'm all serious. And his first words to me are: "Ay up, lad, just think how famous we'll be if we win this Test match."' England were 28 runs short of their final innings target, with only the nervous Matthew Hoggard left to bat. 'I said to Gough, "Look up there at Hoggard. He can't even watch – how's he going to bat?"' Cork scored 33 as England squeaked home, and took another man of the match award at Lord's.

That series contained the last great international performances of his career – while he played on another ten years on the county scene, his Test career was over by 2002. I wonder if the vintage Cork sitting in front of me now has any regrets about his career. He isn't apologetic about how he played the game – 'If I can't show a bit of aggression, if I can't show people I'm a winner and that I would die for the country, then for me there's no point in playing'– but he does sound just a little rueful. 'Sometimes that over-exuberance, or perhaps the over-aggression, went a bit too far. If you look back now that would be one thing I would perhaps change.'

Cork suspects his behaviour coloured people's judgement, and might even have meant he played fewer Tests than he wanted. 'I just thought, "It doesn't matter what they think, I'm playing for England." Unfortunately, you have to think, now, it does matter . . . If I knew everything I know now I'd have maybe done things a little differently.' He was, he says, 'more innocent' back then, and a little naive.

I want to share tales of my own naivety, to show him that I too know what it was like to be over-eager in the England cause. But I'm not sure that *nearly* swearing in front of my mum counts as common ground. It's one thing for a fan to want to see inside a sportsman's head, but it's unlikely the fascination runs the opposite way.

Just before Cork leaves to go back on air, I ask whether he ever imagined he might be a pin-up on someone's wall. The proposition confounds him. 'You're having a laugh, aren't you? No. Ridiculous!

I put a bit of zinc on, I'm going to war. I'm not thinking, "I'd better get me Lypsyl on and all that."' He's still scoffing when he stumbles unexpectedly on a childhood memory. Perhaps the image has whisked him back to thoughts of his own embarrassing teenage crushes and skincare regime. 'People laugh at this, but growing up, I was a very shy inward boy,' he says. 'And I would have to really force this . . . my type of . . .' he hesitates, his quick-pour conversation running dry. 'What am I trying to say? The way I am . . . I had to force it out. The person I wanted to be.'

I picture the teenage Cork in his bedroom, looking up at a picture of Ian Botham on his wall, and choosing who he is going to be. We had something in common all along.

Chapter 6

My sister and I love films. When we were growing up we both wanted to be famous actresses, and if that failed the back-up plan was to open a video store together. We wanted to carry a huge catalogue of classic films that you could rent for a pound apiece, and only a single copy of each week's latest release. That way customers who came in for Vin Diesel would end up going home with Frank Capra. It was a terrible business model, but proof we considered ourselves as sophisticated cineastes.

And yet, if you told me I could only watch one film genre for the rest of my life, I would pick the buddy movie. You could empty the shelves of romcoms, you could take away my dystopian sci-fi, I'd even give up my prized Ethan Hawke collection. Touch Jon Favreau and Vince Vaughan, however, and I'd have to fight you. I've always adored an odd couple pairing, especially the kind that involves a diffident, solitary type forced into an unlikely friendship: the perfect example would be Dan Aykroyd and Tom Hanks in *Dragnet*. I just can't resist all that hard-won affection and deeply repressed emotion glimpsed in chinks between putdowns, and which results in a loyalty so fierce its protagonists are willing to take a bullet for each other.

Having never participated in one of these relationships in real life, I have hoovered them up in fiction: Poirot and Hastings, Jeeves and Wooster, Wimsey and Bunter. I read Sherlock Holmes not for the puzzle-solving, which I was hopeless at, but for the rare flashes of warmth that prove how much Dr Watson means to him. And I have no idea what this says about my psyche, but I was the only one of my girlfriends who, watching Kevin Costner's *Robin Hood*, wanted not to be the Maid Marian who kissed him, but the Will Scarlett/ Christian Slater who nearly got hanged for him.

In the corner of my DVD shelves, next to the buddy movies, sit a few old cricket videos that I can't part with either, even though they're coated in dust and haven't been touched in ten years. They have survived numerous clearouts, just in case I ever get the urge to re-watch the 2001 NatWest Series final (it hasn't happened so far) or a 98-run victory over New Zealand at Christchurch (no, that neither). Among them is a case with a red spine which bears the title *Atherton's Innings*. I haven't actually watched this video – I've never even opened the case. I bought it as a memento of a performance that I'd already heard, seen, read and talked about to satiation. I keep it for the same reason that others might have a Smashing Pumpkins T-shirt in the back of their wardrobe. The only difference is that at no stage has owning a highlights package of Michael Atherton's 185* against South Africa in Johannesburg in 1995 been remotely fashionable.

Today, I'm breaking the seal. I fetch down an old VCR from the loft, and feed in the cassette. The video whirs to life; there's a bit of snow until the tape rights itself, and the opening credits play, a twee concoction of African dancers, sunset colours, and white men hitting things. They're immediately followed by a montage of big cats, rhinos, wildebeest and any other animals the camera has managed to pick up. I presume the producers, concerned that what's to follow is too dull for even committed viewers, just decided to go full *Lion King*.

Eventually the action moves from Kruger National Park to the Wanderers Stadium in Johannesburg, a sun-baked arena where many of the stands are half-empty. A voice begins to recap the match, and the bleached-out pictures provide a stab of nostalgia: England's overseas matches always looked like they were being played on a distant moonscape. I have the same slightly painful sensation I used to experience when I watched the overnight report on the morning news, like a cord attached somewhere between my heart and my stomach is being tugged.

Interspersed with the footage, Michael Atherton is interviewed about his memories of the game. He's sitting in a park, or a garden, presumably at the end of the tour – he certainly doesn't look any older than his on-field incarnation. His face is impassive, his voice is flat. You couldn't get a better demonstration of the word 'deadpan' from Jack Dee. Considering that the event he's talking about is one of the most famous sporting stonewalls of all time, it's fairly appropriate.

But it's not how I remember that game. He's talking about the greatest act of cricketing heroism I've encountered, one I followed with my heart in my mouth. It's my favourite innings of all time, more precious to me than the flashiest match-winning century – and I'm not having its very author ruin it for me. So I decide to get the story from someone else. The superhero had a sidekick that day; I'm going to take a train to Bristol and meet him.

It's a grey day when I make my way to Chipping Sodbury. The taxi driver doesn't know exactly where the Jack Russell art gallery is so he puts out a call. A colleague crackles some directions through the radio – 'my wife's bought a couple of his pieces' – but we still have to make a couple of passes of the high street before we spot it. Nestled amid an attractive jumble of Tudor, Georgian and Victorian buildings, the gallery's sign blends rather too modestly with its brickwork. At least I'm not visiting Russell at home. I've read that he's so paranoid about his guests knowing where he lives that he makes them wear blindfolds.

Inside the gallery, bucolic scenes fill the walls. There are English landscapes, Cotswold buildings, a street brimming with the village life of a previous century. A dark and stormy depiction of a navy destroyer looks down from a spot near the ceiling. In the shopfront, nearest the passing trade, are the cricket paintings: long canvases that capture entire grounds, while tiny white figures squat at their centre. Jack Russell has heard the door, and emerges from a back room – would I like a cup of tea? My mind flits to a piece of information stored there two decades ago. Russell was a prolific tea drinker in the dressing-room, but would barely dunk the teabag in the water, then hang it up to use again later. 'Yes please,' I say. 'That would be lovely.'

He fetches out two cups, and we sit at an old leather-covered table which, like the rest of the décor, effects an air of well-worn country living. Russell too shows signs of age: his face has plumped a little below his cheekbones, and his moustache – which seems to be made of the same durable stuff as his paintbrushes – shows a hint of grey. He is still endowed with silky brown hair that reaches past his collar and would shame a choirboy. The man is, no question, follicularly blessed.

The tea tastes good: perhaps not all of Russell's habits have stuck. His passion for painting was actually considered the least strange thing about him by his teammates, who witnessed his compulsive and fastidious behaviour towards his food, his clothes, his gear and much else. He once ate steak and chips every night for a month, and he wore the same batting shirt for eight years. 'I'm not so bad now,' Russell says. 'It was just how I dealt with the pressure – I like repetition. I used to have underpants with dots on – one dot for the first session, two dots for the second session. I'd have them washed and dry to wear the next day.'

It must have been exhausting doing all that laundry on top of your regular job, I say. 'That's why rooming with me was a nightmare. In between games I was washing stuff in the bathroom sink, then I'd be hanging it over lightshades to dry it off.' Although that was only the half of it – Russell would tape up his wet paintings, too. 'I think Angus Fraser still gets headaches from the paint fumes. In Cape Town Neil Fairbrother was actually sick out of the window.'

A couple of customers come in and browse the paintings but Russell shows no interest in talking to them. 'It's very rare for me to sit out here,' he admits. I tell him I've heard that he's such an introvert that on tour he would stay in his room for days at time. 'That was probably to recharge my batteries,' he says. 'That's when I get some energy back. Certainly if I was having a bad trip, I would hide away a lot. If I was on a good trip I'd be out painting everywhere.' He used to ask spectators to take his paintings home for him, rolled up in tubes. I try to imagine how that conversation would have gone in customs. 'Have you been asked to carry any items for someone else, madam?' 'Yes, just this large hollow receptacle that an international sportsman asked me to bring.' 'And what was his name, madam?' 'Jack Russell.' 'Right. Step over here, please . . .'

When Russell goes to top up our tea, I browse the gallery. There's a small but vivid depiction of a landscape whose hills seem to rush vertiginously beneath you, as if you were flying over them at speed. There's a bust of Jack which makes him look far more eccentric than he is in the flesh. At the back of the room there are three glass cabinets filled with memorabilia, some for sale, some for show. Signed bats and shirts, an Aussie sweater, stumps, bails, and the wicketkeeping gloves of A. E. Wilson, his Gloucestershire predecessor – it's a treasure hoard, a mini-museum. In one corner of a cabinet I find a watch with the inscription: 'Don't let the buggers get you down, Michael.' I ask Russell if it was a present from Atherton, but he can't remember.

Among the trophies there's a cricket ball set on a plinth. I read the plaque, then stare at it a long while. It is a genuine artefact from England's second Test against South Africa in Johannesburg in '95. It's the ball with which Russell broke the world record for the number of catches in a Test match.

Sometimes scorecards struggle to describe a cricket match. They can give you all the facts and figures – who scored what and when, which bowlers took the wickets – and still fail to tell you the story of the game. The Johannesburg scorecard does a decent enough job with the first innings. South Africa 332 all out – a maiden century from Gary Kirsten – and England 200 in reply. It tells you that Atherton had won the toss, even if it can't add a withering aside on what a mistake he made putting South Africa in to bat. And what it does record, rather elegantly, is the apex of Jack Russell's wicketkeeping career:

c Russell b Malcolm
c Russell b Cork
c Russell b Hick
c Russell b Cork ...

and so on. The 'how outs' begin to read like a mantra. In the second innings, Russell had already caught South Africa's top three when Jonty Rhodes edged a ball from Angus Fraser and it flew right, far and low, to the spot where first slip should have been. 'My best ever catch,' Russell tells me. 'I'd been working on that with Alan Knott for two years and then suddenly it happened.' It was Russell's tenth catch in the Test, equalling Bob Taylor's 15-year record. That night, Russell couldn't sleep. 'It's not every day you're going to wake up and the world record's, like, one catch away. I remember sitting up all night drinking tea and watching the lightning storms. I probably had about two hours' kip.'

His big moment came after an hour of play the next morning. I've seen it on the video. Considering some of the leaps he's made earlier in the game – snaffling the ball while horizontal in the air, like Superman – his world-record catch is fairly simple. You can see Cork, the bowler, give a little nod of recognition, and Russell runs to him, jumping up to wrap his arms around the tall man's neck. 'He always says, "I got it for you,"' laughs Russell. '"You didn't have to do nothing, you just had to catch it!"'

It's after this that the Johannesburg scorecard reveals its limits. The numbers are all there: the 100 not out from Brian McMillan which hammered home South Africa's advantage; their captain Hansie Cronje's declaration, at 346 for 9. England were given an impossible, fantasy total of 479 runs to win the match (the most any Test team had chased down back then was 406, and that figure has only risen to 418 since). But none of those numbers, large though they are, capture the hopelessness of England's case. Because South Africa declared 27 minutes before lunch on the fourth day, with more than five sessions of the match still remaining. No one had ever batted so long in the fourth innings to save a Test match.

Surely, I ask Russell, even the England team believed that they were on the road to defeat?

'You don't say it,' he says. 'But you think, "Christ, this is going to be hard. How do we get out of this? Well, Athers, you're going to have to bat most of it." That's what I remember thinking: "If Athers can stay in for a long time, we've got a chance."'

When it came to long innings and feats of defiance, Atherton had previous. He had, in fact, demonstrated his extraordinary durability in his very first century for England, back in 1990 against New Zealand. It was before my time, and I only know it through our friend the scorecard, who tells me that Atherton hit 151, with 16 boundaries. I imagine that one of the chief reasons I've never come across this innings on, say, a highlights package, is that it was eight and a quarter hours long. That's the kind of effort you appreciate in retrospect, but no one necessarily wants to watch.

It was, nevertheless, a sign of the young man's character. Atherton was 22, he had played in just two Test matches – and it was the first time he had been asked to open the batting for England. He immediately lost his venerable partner (and captain) Graham Gooch, but while his more experienced colleagues wobbled and fell, Atherton stayed standing. It's a rare enough feat of stamina to bat through an entire day; the new boy came back and made it past lunch on the next. By the time he got out, he had shepherded his team past scores of 0 for 1, and 45 for 3, to 302 for 7. He was named man of the match.

It became Atherton's greatest trick in the years to come – sticking it out when others couldn't. Commentators occasionally talked of his 'grim determination' at the crease, but he never seemed especially grim to me. Sure, his resting face was no Chuckle Brother, and he made it a point of principle to stare down a bowler who was trying to intimidate him, but sometimes, when a fast bowler fizzed a quick one past his ear, you'd see him unleash a grin you didn't even know he was capable of. One of my favourite pictures of Atherton comes from his first tour as captain, just after Courtney Walsh has landed him on his backside with a bouncer. He's sitting looking up at the giant bowler looming over him, and he's laughing.

It was obvious he enjoyed himself most when the bowling was at its fiercest, and that series in the West Indies was the perfect showcase of Atherton's bravery and staying power. He averaged over 50 against Curtly and Courtney's fire and brimstone; he scored 144 in a defeat in Guyana where more than half of England's scores were in single figures. He led his team in the field for ten hours straight while Brian Lara scored a world record in Antigua – then went out and batted another nine. It would have been only natural to crumble under the weight of Lara's achievement; Atherton's lengthy century ensured England did not.

His qualities of grit and patience seemed out of place with his youthful looks. Atherton was fresh-faced until he was at least 30, while his innings suggested a far greater maturity, the indomitable spirit of someone who knew themselves – their strengths, their weaknesses – and could not be tempted into actions rash or dubious. After inheriting the captaincy, Atherton's batting only improved. His extra duties magnified the sense of responsibility he already possessed; he was a leader made of the old-school mould, a man who would ask his men to do nothing that he hadn't done himself and who would, if they fell behind, carry them on his back. I had notions of him as Captain Scott or Ernest Shackleton, compassionate enough to risk his life for his men, unflinching enough to shoot the dogs.

He became the rod of steel that ran through England's batting order, the only thing protecting them from total collapse when the earthquakes hit. He didn't even have to make a big score to prove his fighting credentials: in Brisbane in '94, he watched six partners come and go at the other end of the pitch while he put on a masterclass of defence, and hung on for a four-hour 50. His style of play was the perfect reflection of his personality, and his stubbornness was the greatest gift he had to offer his team. Russell says he had a name for him: 'Mr Obsidian, I used to call him in my head. He's just like the hardest rock on the planet to me. He was without question the toughest guy I've played with. You couldn't knock him over.' He shakes his head, then grins. 'I used to beat him at chess, mind.'

I laugh – that must have annoyed him. 'Oh, he hated it. Hated it! We played a bit in South Africa and I think I beat him every time. I had no brains so I used to just attack' – he mimes thrusting the pieces forward indiscriminately – 'and I had him on the back foot all the time. We had a little chess set on the aeroplane, and I was thinking, "I'm beating a bloke from university here, and there's me from a council house, secondary modern school."'

Russell was one of the few surviving players who had made his Test debut before the England captain, and could remember him as a raw recruit. He ought, on paper, to have been one of Atherton's most difficult managerial prospects: a reclusive loner, a possible OCD sufferer, a self-confessed oddball whose instincts were always to do the opposite to the crowd. And yet Russell clearly adores him. He remembers his captain's kindness and concern – the times he let him off practice, or intuited that something was wrong and knelt down beside him in the nets for a chat.

'Some people couldn't get close to him,' says Russell, 'but I always got on well with him. I never felt at any time that I couldn't talk to him . . . which is weird, because some people say he wasn't a great communicator . . .' Well, I say, some players have told me he could be distant. 'Yeah, that's the word I was after. But I never found him that. Maybe because I'm slightly distant as well!'

When Russell joined Atherton at the crease in Johannesburg, an hour into the final day, Atherton had already been batting for six hours. He had gone in to bat just before lunch the previous day, and lost four of his colleagues before the close of play. I remember listening for his century on the radio, and the fright on 99 when he fended a ball into the hands of Kirsten, stationed at short leg. Happily, it popped straight out again. Atherton hooked the very next ball for four and raised both arms aloft, a huge smile breaking out on his face. He even hugged his batting partner, Robin Smith – Atherton was a man who usually celebrated with nods and handshakes – and, quietly, privately, as he walked back to his crease, he kissed the England badge on the front of his helmet. It was all over in a few seconds, but it was a demonstration of emotion that I had never seen before.

Smith was out four overs later. Russell remembers the noise as he walked down the players' tunnel, a small slope with a tin roof. The home fans would clatter the roof as a new batsman took the crease – in Russell's case, they barked as well. 'They were trying to put me off. And actually it made me more determined.' He met Atherton in the middle of the pitch. 'He said something like, "Good luck, Jack," and I looked into his eyes and I knew he was going to do it. I could see it in his face, honestly. I thought, "Christ, someone had better pull their finger out here and stay with him. Because he's going to do this, this guy's going to do this today."'

If you were choosing a man to bat for your life, you probably wouldn't pick Russell. I don't think even Russell would pick Russell. In my Johannesburg video, he stands at the crease like a hobbit who has accidentally wandered out of the Shire and arrived, dwarfed, in the realm of men. He shuffles to the ball, crabways, his bat thrust out ahead of him in the same earnest yet fearful pose of a priest using a cross to ward off a vampire. But, really, his style reminds you of nothing more forcefully than this: that a batsman is merely a man holding a medium-sized plank of wood.

He had recently adopted the curious habit of wearing dark glasses when he went out to bat. Most people, faced with a posse of men routinely hurling hard, heavy objects in their direction, wish to give themselves the best chance to see them. (In fact, at the other end of the crease, Atherton was doing eye exercises to sharpen his focus.) But a few weeks previously, facing Devon Malcolm in the nets, Russell had been bothered by the glare of the African sun and decided to put on sunglasses. He wore them for the rest of his career, and if they made him look like a small, blind Tom Selleck impersonator, at least they kept the dust out.

Russell will not, I hope, mind me writing this; he has already confided that he 'wasn't a batter's rear end, really' and that was certainly the impression he conveyed at the crease. And yet, the looks weren't the whole story. In his previous two innings, he had scored 91 and 50 not out, innings that were as inventive as they were dogged. In the first Test at Pretoria, washed out by rain before England could even complete their first innings, Russell had found a novel way to frustrate South Africa's bowlers without touching the ball. It involved making to hit the ball outside his off stump, then elaborately withdrawing his bat and playing, essentially, an airshot against an invisible ball.

'Two or three times I had edged to slip and it didn't quite carry,' he explains. 'I thought I've got to do something here or I'm going to get out.' That's when he remembered a trick he'd seen a Kent player, Mark Benson, use at Canterbury, playing down the wrong line of the ball. 'He'd never nick them. So I started playing like that. People think I invented that shot – I didn't.' But it infuriated the South Africans, so he exaggerated it even further. Here in Johannesburg, it was making a starring appearance.

At the other end of the pitch, Atherton was doing the thing he did so well. Since the turn of the millennium, cricket has changed beyond recognition, beyond belief. It has entered an era of muscle-bound big hitters, and of shortened attention spans, when quick scoring is enticed with powerplays and super-overs, and a fast game is a good game. But even as Atherton hunkered down, his slow, steady compilations seemed to belong to bygone days. There was something old-fashioned about his virtues of patience and reliability. He drew comparisons with Geoffrey Boycott, the slowest scorer of them all, a man who guarded his wicket with the same jealous sloth that Smaug sat atop his pile of gold on Lonely Mountain. I was too young to have had to sit through a Boycott innings, but even I could tell you that the associations were not kind.

Plenty of people found Atherton boring to watch, and plenty of my friends told me so. It is certainly true he played more than his cosmic share of dot balls. But that never bothered me. I liked Atherton's crisp defensive shots, the way the bat dropped so perfectly down behind the ball like the needle on a set of kitchen scales. There was something pleasing about their geometry, their studied correctness. It's possible, when you watch him play forward to the ball, to see him as a young boy, practising his positions.

Unfortunately, my video is only an hour long, meaning it skips a large number of the deliveries that Atherton defended – 400 or so. It focuses instead on the balls he scored from, and a few that threatened his wicket or his skull. There's one spell where Donald bowls so straight at his head that it's not obvious which way Atherton should go to avoid getting hit: sway back or duck forward? Just once, I think I can spot the nanosecond when he makes his decision. But even at 24 frames per second the camera struggles to capture it.

As for boundaries, there are plenty. Most are his trademark shots, like the ball clipped off his legs, Atherton's most elegant and economical stroke. He's also regularly seen hooking the ball as it flies up around his head, a deed that marries bravery and concentration in equal measure. Great batsmen can make the bat look weightless, a feathery extension of their own limbs; and it's true that Atherton didn't do that. When he cuts a ball square, he does so with a flourish, but you can see the effort in his arms and his posture. If his bat is a weapon, it is a broadsword, not an épée.

When he passes 150, he barely celebrates. In the background, you can hear the banging of corrugated tin. Atherton has batted eight and a half hours but there are still two and a quarter more to go. He knows the courage and the effort will be worth nothing if he doesn't see it through.

Russell knows too. He has been here before. In 1990, England needed to bat out the final day at Bridgetown, Barbados, to save the fourth Test against West Indies, and go into the final Test 1–0 up in the series. Russell had batted five hours and the finish line was in sight when he lost his wicket with a little over half an hour to go. The last few wickets were blown away by Ambrose; there were ten minutes of play remaining when West Indies won the game. It had been a heartbreaking experience, says Russell: 'I couldn't go through that again. I thought, "I'm not having that again." I kept saying to Athers, "Remember Barbados, remember Barbados."' Russell had picked up another superstition around that time – he needed to tap his partner's pad with his bat in between overs. 'I don't know if you can see the marks on Athers' pad but by the end of the day I was bashing it. I was so pumped. After tea I'm shouting,' – he pulls his lips back into a snarl, and growls – '"Remember Barbados!"'

I have a favourite picture of the two of them, taking a break at the end of an over. Atherton is crouched low, his helmet in one hand, propping himself up with his bat. Russell leans in close to talk to him, and Atherton, looking up at his much shorter companion, is grinning. There's something cartoonish about it – there ought to be a speech-bubble coming out of Russell's mouth. Perhaps it's part of a storyboard: a frame from the animated adventures of Captain Atherton and his faithful sidekick Jack Russell. It always makes me smile, this image of the little terrier yapping excitedly at his big-pawed friend. Because whatever their differences, they had one big thing in common – they would never say die. Russell's quirks, while barmy, weren't without purpose; they were a form of dedication, a way of asserting control, of giving himself the best chance he could. Russell tells me that as a young apprentice cricketer he had been a 'bolshy, mouthy teenager', someone who had rebelled so much he'd been threatened with the sack. So he had created his own disciplines, and let nothing stand in their way. He'd even gone to Monday night practice on his own wedding night.

South Africa's captain, Hansie Cronje, had experienced just how obstinate Russell could be. He'd been in charge of the South Africa team when they played Gloucestershire on their tour of England two years previously. It was a warm-up game, and Cronje expected Russell's side to declare on the last day to give them another chance to bat. Russell refused. 'I'm not going to give South Africans batting practice just before a Test match,' he says. 'I put England in front of my own fans' entertainment.'

Cronje was furious, but the Gloucestershire faithful even more so. 'I nearly got lynched by my own fans. There was a mob of them, hundreds. It's the only time in my life I had to go out the back door to my car. The chief exec had to help me out with my kit.' Russell reckons that incident helped him out on the field in Johannesburg. 'I knew I had the psychological edge over them. Hansie Cronje knew I wasn't going to . . . I've got to watch my language here . . . mess about.'

As the time ticked by, the England dressing-room had come to a standstill. Even players far less superstitious than Russell were refusing to move places. Dominic Cork, padded up as the next man in, kept the same seat all day; he got so nervous that he had to get a football out in the dressing-room. 'I was doing headers with Mark Ramprakash because I couldn't watch any more,' Cork had told me when we met. 'My legs had gone, I was shaking, I had pad rash.' (I'm still not sure what pad rash is, but it sounds disgusting.) Russell says that when he saw Cork at the close of play, he was exhausted. Atherton, by contrast, didn't seem tired at all. In the lunch and tea intervals, while Russell ran round frenetically preparing his gear for the next session, Atherton calmly read a newspaper.

The longer the pair batted, the more wound up Russell became. 'I hit a four late on and I was angry with myself: "What are you doing? You're supposed to be blocking it! What are you *doing*?"' Then he saw umpire Darrell Hair taking the bails off the stumps. 'I was going to have a go at him. I actually wanted to say, "What are you doing? I've got to bat here for a week yet!" Then I thought, "What? Is it the end?" I was so focused I could have been there all night.'

The scene that followed is the one I remember best; the one that was played at the start of the 10 o'clock news, after the headline that Yitzhak Rabin had been shot in Tel Aviv. The video shows a round of handshakes in the middle, and the batting pair turning to walk back to the pavilion; but the crowd is already invading the pitch, and the pair have to jog, then sprint, to avoid being absorbed by the well-wishers. To any neutral observer, it must look like England have just won a famous victory.

Back in the changing-room, Russell can still picture Atherton sitting opposite him as the beer flowed, and giving each other a short nod of recognition at a job well done. 'He said, "Jack, you kept saying 'Barbados'?" "Yeah," I said, "Remember Barbados." He said, "Jack, I wasn't even at Barbados." We joke about that. All along, I'd forgotten he wasn't at Barbados.'

It's hard to remember that I'm talking to English cricket's most infamous introvert. There's nothing shy about him here; he bubbles with enthusiasm. I've met the only other person who can get as excited about a legendary ten-hour stonewall as I do. And I'm loving it. Because it occurs to me that my ludicrous emotional attachment to this game, and this innings, is a little less crazy if he still feels the same way too. I even feel envious of the part he got to play. 'It was like life and death to me,' he says. ''Cos I knew Athers was going to do it, and I didn't want to let him down. If I'm honest, I just couldn't face letting him down.'

Military history is one of Russell's obsessions, and some days after the game he fulfilled a lifetime ambition to visit Rorke's Drift. A pilgrimage to the small garrison where 150 soldiers of the British Empire held out against 4,000 Zulu warriors was the perfect coda to his and Atherton's achievement. It was so good, he went twice.

They weren't to know it at the time, but Atherton and Russell's careers had both reached their zenith. As captain, Atherton's stock tended to fluctuate wildly depending on the state of whichever series England were playing. He had stared down calls for his resignation in the West Indies, Australia and at home with the same unflinching gaze he gave Donald and Ambrose. Of his 26 Tests in charge, Atherton had now won or drawn 16; in the past two summers, his side had emerged from series against the hardboiled teams of South Africa and West Indies unvanquished. His batting, however dull you found it, was unarguably the most important feature of the England team – he was even, ironically enough, the lynchpin of England's one-day efforts – and he had a personal average, as captain, of nearly 50. The asterisk next to his Johannesburg score was his crowning achievement.

Russell's 29 not out was far from his highest Test score: in fact, he reached the second of his two Test centuries the next summer, against India. But the selectors – and Atherton – began to prefer Alec Stewart in the wicketkeeping position, and by the time Russell next toured with England, in the early months of 1998, England had a new cricket board, a new chairman, and a new attitude to non-conformism. It was the latter, he says, which broke him.

Russell had always worn the same hat. It was one of the facts that every fan knew about him. That hat had been with him throughout his career; it had survived 49 Tests, 16 county seasons and a small microwave fire (caused during an ill-conceived attempt to dry it out). His wife lovingly cleaned, starched and repaired it every year. But on arrival in the West Indies, Russell was told by the manager Bob Bennett that if he refused to wear the new, team issue hat, he would be sent home. There was more – he wouldn't be the only one to go. 'It came down from up high: if Jack wears his hat, Bumble and Athers are going to be sacked.'

I must look surprised, because Russell is nodding his head in verification. 'You didn't know that, did you?' asks Russell. I didn't. But I wouldn't have believed it either, even if I don't like to say that to the earnest man whose loyalty was being tested. Even the most obtuse and rule-bound cricket official would not recall their captain and their coach, David Lloyd, for the sake of a piece of headwear. But Russell is adamant – 'it cost me a fortune in phonecalls to solicitors' – and after a tense flight to Montego Bay, where the first Test was to take place, Russell agreed to wear the new hat. He did, however, elicit written assurances that he could cut the brim down, and when they finally took to the field, the new hat looked so scruffy Atherton thought he was wearing the old one.

The damage done inside Russell's head, however, was worse. 'I had the worst tour of my life,' he says. 'It was like they'd chopped me in half. My soul had gone inside.' It didn't help that he got the wrong kind of runs the day before the first Test, when he was expecting to win his fiftieth cap. 'I remember being on the floor like this –' Russell drops on to all fours, his most complete dog impersonation so far '– and Athers coming over to me and saying, "How are you doing?"

And I was saying, "I'll be all right, I'll be all right." But I couldn't even get up.

'Athers made the decision for me, which was good, because I was going to crawl out if I had to. I wouldn't have had white gear though, it was all . . . well, I won't go into detail. But it was terrible. By the time I got to the changing-room I burst into tears.'

Russell did eventually make it past 50 Tests, but that winter was the last time he played for England. As the cricketing authorities sought a more professional structure to the game, the environment became tougher for individuals like Russell and Tufnell, who didn't fit a mould. Tufnell had said as much to me in the pub: 'They didn't know anything about different strokes for different folks. It was all just "have a shave".' This was another of the edicts from Lord MacLaurin, the new chairman, says Russell. 'He wanted us to all look tidy, which was fair enough, because I was one of the scruffy ones, to a certain degree. He wanted us all shaved. But you don't shave on a morning when you're going to be sweaty all day. He couldn't understand that.'

Russell speaks of Tufnell with great affection: he clearly empathises with the teammate who preferred to do things his own way. 'Tuffers just wanted to bowl. He didn't want to do any running, he didn't want to warm up, he didn't want to bowl in the nets. If I asked him to give me some practice deliveries, he'd bowl three balls and go off for his breakfast, which was coffee and a cigarette. But just give him the ball and he'll win you the game – he doesn't need to be a marathon runner. That's where it got too much, towards the end.'

Still, it's notable which of the pair Atherton sympathised with. Not the extrovert whose streak of genius ran along a fault line of unreliability, but the recluse who turned up at practice on the very day he got married. In return, Russell appreciated a captain who always told him to his face when he was dropped from the team. 'I never felt uncomfortable in one of Athers' teams, I never felt like I didn't belong here. There were insecure people in the dressing-room, but that's not Athers' fault. They were people still struggling with their own careers.'

Russell says he had one, brief insight into the pressures of captaincy, when Atherton was suffering back pain the day before a Test. The chairman of selectors asked Russell to step in if necessary, and Russell was instantly flooded with the myriad concerns the captain had to handle on a daily basis. By the next morning, after an evening of sleeplessness, he was exhausted – and luckily his captain was fit to play. 'I don't know how he did it. Such a massive burden, let alone trying to score runs – and he would carry it. He was the toughest, hardest, stubbornest bloke I ever played with. He's just magic, Athers.'

It's coming up to lunchtime, and Russell needs to pop into the bank and the butcher's. It's fun to think of him doing his errands around this little market town like a character in *Postman Pat* – it suits him. He shows me out through the back of the shop, via a corridor stacked with boxes and files. 'Recluse's corner,' he calls it. He prefers it to the front door: this way he can slip in and out without ever being seen.

Back at home, I try to re-watch my Johannesburg video, but the recorder's not having any of it. Something's gone wrong with the tracking – no matter what buttons I push on the aged remote control the screen spasms every five seconds, and Atherton and Russell disappear under a blizzard of static. I'm not too bothered. For me, the individual details of that match have never been as significant as the concept – the perfect marriage of style and situation that kept Atherton at the crease so long, and kept Russell with him. It has never been about the shots that were played, or the chances that were missed, but the symbolism of a captain who stood at the helm and steered his foundering vessel to safe harbour, against all the odds.

Maybe it's my old-fashioned fondness for an increasingly archaic notion of duty and commitment that make it so important to me. Perhaps I've a yen for the days when leaders inspired not through their ability to turn computer algorithms into billions of dollars of stock options, but because of their physical and mental courage in the face of danger and adversity. That's why I love a sport that can make a virtue of mulishness, and find glory in a five-day draw.

My encounter with Russell had shown me that the brand of loyalty I've always idolised doesn't live on only in the pages of fiction, or Hollywood bromances. It's not just something that a fan projects, hopefully, on to her sporting heroes – it can be as real as her imaginings.

It endures, too. Russell told me how, even now, 'If Athers asked for help to do something, you do it, because you've got a bond. Because even though we didn't win a lot, we had some special moments, and we've been through something together.' And then he paused. 'Now I come to think about it . . . I ain't got any friends, really. Not *friend* friends. I'm quite singular. Remote. But when you talk of Athers and Angus and Stewie and those guys . . . I'd trust them.'

And I knew that was the highest compliment Russell could give.

Chapter 7

People used to instinctively wrinkle their nose when you told them you lived in Luton. They probably still do; it may be ten years since the place secured the Crap Town of the Year title, but it recently came runner-up for Ugliest Town in the UK. I always found plenty to love about it in spite of its concrete seventies eyesores: the pink flamingo statues that stood for no good reason in the Arndale Centre, but served the same function for the Luton youth as 'beneath the clock at Waterloo'; the spiral exit ramp from the car park that my sister and I treated like a fairground ride and dubbed 'the curly wurly'.

There was, too, a football club that even fans of Premiership teams knew about. This wasn't because it was a thriving sporting concern but because it was the answer to various trivia questions: the giantkillers of Arsenal in the Littlewoods Cup final, the hosts of a horrifying night of hooliganism in 1985, one of the only teams in the league with an Astroturf pitch. You supported Luton Town by dint of having an LU2 postcode; whether you cared for football or not was fairly irrelevant. I went to the ground a few times with my friend Jonathan; it was cold, and the games were tedious, but I liked the feeling of belonging, of subscribing to a common heritage.

My cricketing allegiances were not as automatic. I had England, and that was non-negotiable, but a true fan was also supposed to have a club or county side. This was what grounded you, the earthy, rootsy diet that nourished you in between internationals. Supporting just the national side was, in those days when the English game as a whole was paid for and marshalled by the counties, the mark of a dilettante. So many kids are, of course, baptised into their sporting faiths before they're old enough to make the decision for themselves; Dad, or sometimes Mum, has them in football replica kit as a toddler and before they know it, boom, they're consigned to a life of lower-division misery with Notts County. But since I'd come to cricket relatively late, I had the freedom to choose.

Strictly, a Lutonian's 'home' team was Bedfordshire, but it was only a minor county and did not play first-class cricket. I dismissed it as too small fry for my grand passions. Geographically, the next nearest teams were Northamptonshire and Middlesex; both offered a range of supportably high-profile players. I hated Northants' colours, a vile combination of brownish maroon and yellow, so they were out. Middlesex were a tempting proposition. They played at Lord's, the only ground I'd actually been to; they could boast a couple of my favourite England players (Angus Fraser and Phil Tufnell); and the three swords on their badge were pretty hardcore.

Also up for consideration was Atherton's county side, Lancashire. It seemed, even to me, a bit of a stretch to support a team 170 miles away from where I lived, a place with which I had no history and whose principal city I could not have pointed to on a map. The only Lancastrians I could name with any certainty were the fictional occupants of the Rovers Return, and that purely because my nan had been a massive *Corrie* fan. There were no precious holiday memories to the Lake District. I harboured no profound love of the Manchester music scene – I hadn't a clue who the Charlatans or the Stone Roses were, and genuinely thought Morrissey was a shorthand for the actor in *Men Behaving Badly*.

I remember, when cricket was still a novelty, sneaking upstairs to watch the TV in my parents' bedroom one Saturday afternoon, having discovered that Lancashire were playing a Cup final at Lord's. Downstairs there were chores to be done, and I stayed guiltily quiet when I heard Mum call for me, hoping she'd assume I wasn't in the house. On the screen, the Lancashire captain Neil Fairbrother was standing in the field, biting his nails as Dominic Cork knocked his bowlers disrespectfully around. I found myself clenching my fists every time a fielder threw the ball, willing them to run Cork out, but they never did. Lancashire lost the game, and I felt a pleasurable ache of disappointment. The whole experience was enhanced by the knowledge that I had avoided doing the hoovering and secretly skirted my mother's wrath.

Those sensations were enough to seal my commitment. I started looking for Lancashire's results on Ceefax, reading up on their matches, and familiarising myself with their faces. I doubt I understood the word 'yeoman' back then, but I recognised something wholesomely ordinary in the features of players like Graham Lloyd and Gary Yates. Mike Watkinson looked as if he could be one of my dad's commuting buddies. And it made me happy to discover that Ian Austin, a man who bowled with such parsimony, was actually shaped like a snowman.

Apart from a family trip to Scotland, I had never knowingly gone north of the Watford Gap. The fact that my new team contained straight-talking men who had grown up in the blunt, uncompromising environment of league cricket, and I was a preppy Home Counties girl of no little privilege, didn't really occur to me. Sure, it was love across the divide, but I had no idea just how wide that gulf might be. And so, thanks to my utter lack of self-awareness, I felt no embarrassment about it at all, and identified myself with them freely.

My mother, who preferred Middlesex herself, was supportive of my choice. She had always admired Fairbrother's England performances, and could scarcely blame her daughter for following an entirely unrelated northern team when she had been a Liverpool football fan since her teens (something to do with Tommy Smith). I had chosen well – over the next four years, my team reached five Lord's finals, which gave me plenty to get excited about.

I wanted to wear my allegiance, literally, on my sleeve, and would pore over the Lancashire CCC mail order catalogue, coveting its replica shirts, embroidered caps and engraved pewter mugs. (I even wished I had a baby so I could snuggle it into one of their red rose-embossed baby-grows.) The clothes in the catalogue were modelled by the players themselves. They managed to prove that there is indeed a skill to leaning naturally against a fence, and that not all sportsmen possess it. On one page, a youngster with an upward profusion of blond hair appeared in various poses and casual wear. He smiled gamely at the camera in a hideous white tracksuit, while a woman wearing a matching jacket perched her hand affectedly on his shoulder. Still, he looked, of all the players, the most suited to the role of catalogue model. He might not have been Boden-handsome, but he could have held down a spot in Argos.

John Crawley was the great new hope, not just of the Lancashire side, but of England too. He was also, to those in the know, an Atherton mark II. His path had followed the England captain's almost exactly: he had been a pupil at Manchester Grammar School, a few years below Atherton, and had, in time, broken the older boy's school batting records. He had gone to Cambridge to read history, just as Atherton did, captained the Blues, just as Atherton did, and earned a Lancashire contract . . . well, you get the idea.

By the time I was filling out my own UCAS form, Crawley was making his England debut. He had only graduated the year previously, but he'd already scored vast amounts of runs for his county and made big centuries for the 'junior' national side known as England A. People said of Crawley that while he might look like Atherton's shadow, he had the talent to surpass him. He was, the experts agreed, a far more gifted batsman, and his very existence seemed to justify everything I had admired about the England captain himself. It made me feel rather smug.

I had never felt so ambitious for another person. (If I'm honest, I'd never really felt ambitious for another person at all – other people's achievements tended to grate.) It must have had something to do with the timing – he was just out of Cambridge, I was just applying – but when I looked at Crawley, I saw someone with a destiny, and I wanted him to achieve it. I cared deeply that he should win a regular place in the national side, and I was perfectly confident he would. He was, I felt sure, to be a key component of England's glorious, world-beating future.

In my thoughts, he has always remained the corn-haired, gawky youth of the catalogue, a symbol of potential and aspiration. It's why, when he got older, and fell out with Lancashire, and had Cherie Blair argue his employment case against them in the high court – incidentally one of the most glamorous things to happen to county cricket in the past 50 years – I kept only a half-ear on the outcome. I was losing my interest in Crawley even as he was losing his hair.

It is no spoiler to say that he did not become one of the country's greatest Test batsmen, or an integral part of an Ashes-winning side. But he had a very successful county career, and by the time he retired, from Hampshire, he had amassed tens of thousands of first-class runs. I have no idea what happened to him after this. I'm rather warmed to discover, via a quick Google, that he's making use of the degree he took. He's teaching at a small but ancient establishment, the kind that was founded by a wealthy medieval churchman for education in Latin and Greek, and which now incubates future international rugby players. It's something of a tradition, albeit one that's fallen out of style, for retired cricketers to retreat to teach in the public schools of England. And we've already established how much I love an outdated convention.

His subject, naturally, is history. I feel that this is a sign. Partly because it was one of my own favourite subjects at school, and partly because it seems almost supernaturally apt, when I'm trying to track down England's past. If Crawley is immersed in history every day, surely he's the ideal person to give the considered, long view of the dark ages of English cricket?

He's impossibly busy during term time, so he invites me up to his home over the Christmas holidays. I drive up the M1 with a cold and *Now That's What I Call Christmas* blasting on the stereo. The satnav makes frequent and aggressive interruptions: 'Hang all the mistletoe, and IN 200 YARDS, KEEP RIGHT.' It's a clear winter day, although for much of the journey all that affords is an unencumbered view of Northamptonshire's flatlands and wind-farms.

It gets prettier once I turn off the motorway. There are fields and trees, a good-looking village with a cosy pub. A little way outside it I turn through Crawley's gate; he comes to meet me at the door, an excitable pair of chocolate Labradors following him. I've all but lost my voice, so I croak out my greetings in the only register I can manage, which is somewhere between Bryn Terfel and Barry White.

Crawley is already different from how I'd pictured him: a creased, lined face, and a comfy-looking ensemble – soft-collared shirt, blue jersey, taupe trousers – that suggests he's been the country gentleman for a while. You would never guess that the man before me is younger than Stewart, Atherton or Thorpe. He invites me through to the kitchen and puts on the kettle, and we chat about how he came to be living and working here, equidistant from the Lancashire hills where he began his playing career and the south coast where he finished it. He says that when he retired he tried out a job in the City, but the 5 a.m. commute was killing him after three weeks. So: school.

As we wander through Crawley's very pleasant house to a day room, we pass evidence of his own children. A piano and a music stand both display rather advanced pieces – they're clearly already discovering their talents. I wonder if it was always Crawley's dream to be a professional cricketer. 'It wasn't, actually,' he says. 'I enjoyed football, and I was probably just as good at that until about the age of 14, 15, probably. What I didn't ever develop was any pace, and without pace you can't progress.' But he had always played cricket with his elder brothers. 'Mike Atherton and my eldest brother were in the same year and they were always around, so I was playing with them and progressing.'

Atherton was a decent footballer too, he says. 'Everyone was well aware that he would go on to do great things.'

'Then you came along and broke his school records.'

'Yeah, but I think they've all been broken again since,' he grins.

It's not that long since Oxford and Cambridge universities, with their dispensation to play first-class cricket against the counties, were a customary career path for the brainy cricketer. Crawley's brother Mark went to Oxford, but when I ask why he chose Cambridge instead, he answers obliquely, explaining that he couldn't study modern languages as he'd wanted. 'And, yes, Mike had gone there. We went to different colleges.' It strikes me that maybe he doesn't want people to think he was following in Atherton's footsteps.

I wish I could, in all honesty, claim the same. Studying English at Cambridge had been my goal since I was ten (the only other thing I wanted as badly was a best actress Oscar that I could keep, with a mixture of irony and false modesty, in my downstairs bathroom). But when it came to choosing which college to apply to, the usual questions of prestige or teaching or suitability didn't especially interest me. One afternoon in the summer of my lower sixth, a couple of our teachers took a small group of us on a day trip to Pembroke College, Cambridge, whose pen of English tutors was considered particularly fine. I wandered through the cloistered courts and passed through the ancient oak doors with a sense of awe. And then, at the first opportunity, I slipped away from the group to check out Atherton's college, Downing.

It was the exact opposite to Pembroke – a large, geometric congregation of Georgian buildings facing each other grandly across an open quad. There were small purple flowers crowding in large Grecian urns outside the library, and students milling on the stone flank of steps that led to the chapel. The place seemed to radiate calm and a stately beneficence. I fell for it instantly. I had been primed to since the day I'd read its name next to Atherton's entry in the first *Playfair Cricket Annual* I owned. This was where my hero had studied, even if, in reality, his cricketing obligations meant he had barely been here in the spring and summer months. By the time I had regained my group, my insides were buzzing with my secret expedition and Cambridge's hidden medieval treasures had nothing to offer me in the face of Downing's majestic austerity.

The sensation stuck. I found enough supporting circumstances to convince myself and my parents that Downing was a good choice, even if my teachers remained bemused. In the course of time I was invited for an interview and reiterated these reasons to the Downing admissions tutor, a large man with an extremely large beard and a thick plait of ginger hair that ended halfway down his back. He looked like a hippy version of W. G. Grace, which is perhaps why

I came clean about my admiration of Michael Atherton. He turned very earnest and told me how good a student Atherton had been: 'He almost got a first, you know!'

Back at school, I had never felt under so much pressure. I loved my subjects and my teachers, but I was studying alongside 120 highly strung young women, and we all felt our lives were about to be decided for good. The atmosphere was febrile; there were occasional outbreaks of hysterics, and not the funny kind. Having spent most of my life considering the classroom a competitive arena, sixth form was my Cup run, the build-up to the ultimate decider.

Luckily, I had Alex. I hadn't come across Alex before sixth form, but it had turned out she was taking all the same classes as me. We were the only two girls in the entire school taking Latin, which made lessons a rather intense experience, and we were soon akin to sisters. She was kind, funny, smart, and the first school friend I'd had who made me feel completely at ease. She often knew what I was thinking before I said it and, despite being cleverer than me, she always made me feel *more* confident, not less. She patiently showed me how to translate our Latin homework, and when that didn't work she let me copy hers.

We had plenty in common: we were the first girls in our school to play truant so we could see back-to-back Shakespeare plays in London. And though Alex had no love of cricket herself, she took mine seriously. In the few periods of the school week when we weren't sitting next to each other in class, we would write each other letters. She filled hers with wild and witty imaginings of my secret life as a spy on life-or-death missions for the sake of the England team. If anyone in my life encouraged and fed my cricketing lunacy, it was Alex.

Instinctively, my new friend seemed to understand that cricket was my safety valve. I had other hobbies and interests, like music and drama, but they were contaminated by my own involvement, polluted with self-interest. Someone would play violin better than me, or get a better part in the school play, and suddenly my hobby was another blaring reminder of my own failures. But I wasn't a cricketer, and I had no influence over the results – I couldn't stop England losing if I tried.

When England were playing I cultivated my anxiety, a scratchy little ball of 'what if?' that I fed and cosseted like a pet. When they lost, it hurt, but it was a good, clean hurt, something invigorating, refreshing. It made me feel alive, and took my mind off the fact that I was turning 18 and had still never had a boyfriend, or that the goal I'd built my little life around was looming, or that everything I'd known was about to end, and something utterly unknown was about to begin.

So I poured myself into my alternative world, the way some of our classmates poured themselves into their earphones, communing with Cypress Hill and The Prodigy like shamans. My parents had given me a pocket longwave radio one Christmas, and it went with me from class to class (where it was occasionally confiscated), and to the common room, where I sat on a tattered foam chair in the corner inhaling microwave odours and watching the ritual stirring of Pot Noodles. I'd remain there in free periods, writing Alex letters, cocooned in the world of *Test Match Special*, where the brutal things happening on the pitch were described in gentle tones and the harsh reality of England's fate was softened by Vic Marks's chuckle.

My hopes and dreams were fused with those of the England team. Their performances, their failures, were somewhere my own tightly wound emotions could cut loose. John Crawley became my proxy, his achievements a modest covering for my own zealous ambition. After all, it wasn't selfish to want to see Crawley do well, or arrogant to express pride in his scores – I could crow when his name was picked for the England team, and no one would think less of me.

I do not tell Crawley this as we sit in his living room drinking tea. But I do want to know if he was feeling the same desperate pangs to prove himself as I felt on his behalf. I remember the hype, the big county scores, the comparisons with Atherton. Atherton was, in fact, one of Crawley's biggest fans. I have got a match programme in which Atherton talks him up as a possible England captain of the future. Was stuff like that a help or a hindrance? Bit of both, says Crawley. 'I never had any issues with any kind of nepotistic tendencies because of the similar background or because we'd known each other a long time. That never really came up. And he was very fair.'

The summer of 1996 was a good one for both Crawley and me. I'd had an offer of a place at Downing; Crawley had got back into the England side. I got good A-level results; Crawley one-upped me by scoring his first Test century, against Pakistan. Up until that point, he had been a predominantly leg-side player – an observation that is usually an implicit criticism, since it makes a batsman look limited, as if they can only score the easy runs that come when a bowler is off-target. But against Pakistan Crawley revealed a selection of wristy cover-drives in an almost baroque style. He played three of them in one over against Pakistan's feared spinner Mushtaq Ahmed; they came with a final flourish of the bat that wouldn't have looked out of place in a cotillion.

Crawley remembers having to wait overnight to get his 100 because of the rain; he also remembers facing his Lancashire teammate Wasim Akram. 'I think he was very nice to me in that first series,' he says. 'He and Waqar Younis were great because they tried to push the game on, which gave you opportunities to score, which is when I was at my most comfortable. I didn't enjoy the likes of

Glenn McGrath or Curtly Ambrose because they're just metronomic and they're so good at what they do the cricket becomes almost boring. They just wait for a mistake and never really bowl you something which actually gets you out.

'But with Akram and Younis it was just a different game: they're trying to get you out every single ball. And I enjoyed it. I had a few play and misses and was fortunate the ball didn't reverse swing hugely in that particular game. I remember in the second innings, having got a hundred in the first, Wasim said enough's enough, and bowled short ball after short ball. He had this ability to get the ball up to throat height from a decent length . . . I ended up fending off to silly point or someone.'

That series marked the beginning of Crawley's longest run in the England side. The fickle finger of the selectors is a recurrent theme in my conversations with nineties players and Crawley's Test career was as pebbledashed as any – picked for a Test series, deselected for the next, brought back for a couple of games, dropped for a few more. The England dressing-room had a speed-dating feel about it; players never knew who they might find themselves sitting next to, or whether this was their own last chance to make a good impression. Phil Tufnell, in his excitable way, had even acted out a little scene for me when we met in the pub. 'You just put your kit down,' he said, 'and there's another bloke in the dressing-room: "Hello, mate, all right, mate; good luck today!" "Got any advice?" "I dunno, just do what you did for your county and hope for the best!"'

It could make for a selfish environment. 'You're playing every game to stay in the next one,' Graham Thorpe told me. 'When blokes who have done well in their first couple of Test matches say, "It's all for the team," it's not, really. That beginning is all about you.' No one could feel settled in their place, and there was even an undercurrent of *schadenfreude*, because if someone else had a bad day, that was all the better for your prospects.

I knew that England selection was quixotic, but at the time I never really considered the impact on the players (they didn't tend to mention it back then, presumably because they didn't want to antagonise the selectors). My romanticised image of the England team was of a tight-knit crew, the kind of gang I hankered to be a member of. In reality it was a collection of names assembled at something approaching random, with one eye on each other's failures. It doesn't sound like a warm, nurturing place. 'No, well, it wasn't,' says Crawley. 'But we knew what the set-up was like. No one can whinge or cry that that was unfair.'

Personally, he thinks he was given 'more than enough chances . . . I have no qualms about that. There were times when if I'd just kicked on in the odd game . . . ' He thinks, specifically, of a winter tour to Australia when he scored a couple of stylish 70s, then made two 0s in the final Test. 'Athers always says the best way to survive in those circumstances is not get 0 and 1 but get 20 and 25. Then you're just not doing badly enough to let them drop you.'

At the end of the Pakistan series I felt sure that Crawley had finally come of age in Test cricket, and he scored another century in his very next game in Zimbabwe. It was not, however, a happy tour. England were held to two draws by the hosts, a team that included part-timers like Eddo Brandes, a Harare-based chicken farmer. It was a humiliating result and one not helped by the insistence of the new coach – David Lloyd, who had replaced Ray Illingworth – that England had 'flipping murdered 'em'. Crawley laughs a choking sort of laugh. 'Well, we did play better than them but we didn't actually win, so . . . yeah. We didn't quite murder them.'

The England team were notoriously grumpy throughout the trip, thanks to Lloyd and Atherton's decision to ban wives and girlfriends on a five-month tour that continued to New Zealand. 'We did do some whinging, and we shouldn't have done. But of all the managerial mistakes that was the biggest one . . . that's where a huge amount of the problems happened. And it was a shame because Zimbabwe is such a lovely place.' That's not what a 25-year-old Crawley wrote in his tour diary for the *Sunday Telegraph* though. 'Absolutely nothing to do,' was how he described Bulawayo. 'A document of . . . melancholy and despair,' was how Ian Wooldridge, the great *Mail* sportswriter, described Crawley's diary.

England lost all three of their one-day games against Zimbabwe, and moved on to New Zealand, where they drew a sure-thing victory in their first Test. I was exasperated. I had long been in thrall to the England team, held emotional hostage by their ups and downs, but I was beginning to discover that I could be irritated by them too. In previous winters I had staunchly defended their incompetence with the argument that they were young, inexperienced, and their time would come.

But Alex had brought the fresh perspective of an outsider to my thinking, and was sharpening my mind to a more critical edge. After all, we were nearly old enough to vote: it was time to demand answers from my team, rather than trusting them blindly. In our letters we discussed the cricket team's ongoing crises with a radical, almost revolutionary bent. Our correspondence began to envisage coups in which we stormed English cricket's HQ. Some were non-violent, others gleefully bloody.

Crawley always survived our imaginary takeovers, and for a while he kept his place in the real-life team as well. He played in 12 consecutive Tests until the end of 1997, and made a few decent scores, but far more single-figure ones. He just couldn't seem to hang around. He calls it a career of 'fits and starts', and regrets the way he would 'grind to a standstill' against pace bowling. Jack Russell recalled an innings against West Indies when they were batting together and 'Creepy couldn't get a run, he was frightened to do anything.' 'I wish I'd had a bit more of a risk-taking outlook,' Crawley nods. 'But you think, "If I get caught on the boundary hooking, then it's not going to look good."' This time it's him who reaches for the comparison with Atherton: 'When he was struggling he'd always battle to get 25 or 30 and then it would get better. Perhaps my technique wasn't quite as solid as his, so when things were going wrong, they were going horribly wrong.'

He's interesting, Crawley. His sporting past doesn't seem to hang on him the way it might a player who has gone into the media or coaching. He's polite, and happy to talk and, in one sense, he's almost unbelievably ordinary. If you were introduced to him as the local history teacher, I don't think you'd guess for a second that he had once been an international sportsman. The chief characteristic that I can discern in him is reasonableness, but as to what lies beneath it, I'm at a loss. It's like the country clothes and the Labradors – is this who he is, who he's grown into, or a life he's adopted as his own? Is this the same man who, in earlier incarnations, loved to battle Shane Warne, or hired the Prime Minister's wife to pursue his case in court? I can't help but feel there's something omitted, or just absent. When I ask him his first impressions of Atherton he uses a curiously old-fashioned phrase: 'I always held him in the highest regard,' he says. 'He practised hard, he thought about the game, he was determined to do well. He was very impressive all the way through.' But when we talk about Shane Warne, he is noticeably more effusive: 'Wonderful guy, wonderful captain, magnificent bowler.' I wonder if there's something I'm missing.

Still, he's pretty honest about the stuff he didn't enjoy. That included some of the touring. He struggled with the length of some of the trips abroad and 'didn't embrace it perhaps as much as I should have'. He was the victim of an unprovoked assault one night in Cairns, when he and Dominic Cork were walking back to the hotel after dinner. Cork had recalled how sudden and violent it was: 'I remember hearing this guy go, "Watch this, guys," and then he just punched him, knocked him down. He looked out cold to me. I picked him off the floor and had to get him home in a taxi.'

Crawley admits he found Australian tours particularly tough. 'The whole country is against you – if you're going out to supper, people would say, "You guys are rubbish." In the end you set up a bunker in the hotel or have dart boards in your room and entertain yourselves that way.' But really, he reckons, the biggest problem was not being ready for the England call when it came his way. 'I just wish in hindsight I'd had one more year of county cricket before going into it. But it's not something you could control.' I laugh a little – I can't imagine that if he'd been given the option to defer an England cap for 12 months, he would have given it much consideration. He agrees. 'Everyone wants to play for England as soon as possible . . . so given the choice at the time, you would jump at it.'

I think of my place at university, the prize I'd worked towards since I was ten. However prepared I thought I was for those stone halls of learning, I was certainly not ready for their freedoms, their cheap booze and their horny young men. Living in halls and making new friends didn't faze me. My enthusiasm made me popular with the second and third years looking for recruits to college choirs, drama societies and the like. And my sporting knowledge and passion, for the first time in my life, seemed to be interesting to the opposite sex. My experience of romance had been limited to the singular and unlikely heart-throb who stared down from my ceiling wearing Henri Lloyd casual wear, and a single, ill-judged snog on a train platform. I knew that I was playing catch-up with the rest of the female race.

On my second evening at college, in a bar dank with overexcited Freshers, I realised that the boy I was talking to wanted to kiss me. I was surprised, flattered and desperate to make the most of the opportunity; it seemed only seconds later that his large lips were pressed, too hard, against mine. Beneath the foggy mixture of physical sensations – a drunken buzzing in my head, a revulsion at the wetness of the exchange – was a small stabbing thrill I'd not encountered before. I felt proud to have experienced it.

Boys and booze, the two elements that had never interested me as a teenager, quickly became a perpetual distraction. Downing outperformed other Cambridge colleges in only two activities: rowing and drinking. I never stepped in a boat, but I spent plenty of time in the bar. The result was not a dangerous and infamous sexual history but a long string of mostly disappointing snogs that made me cringe with shame. Among the pleasurable moments there were plenty of scratchy chins and clashing teeth, and once the tingle of sexual feelings wore off, I often felt horror, shame, or both. But it still took me a while to learn to say no.

After all those years of swotting at school, I became a lackadaisical student who rose at lunchtime and never bothered with lectures. I still phoned my parents like the good daughter I wanted to be, and whenever I spoke to them I felt conflicted about my secret rebellion. They sounded so pleased that I was having a good time. They didn't know how often the good times had ended with me throwing a guy out of my room so I could peacefully lie down and vomit into a wastepaper bin.

Talking to Crawley I discover that he was not a model student in the first year either. It's hard to get any work done when you're missing an entire term playing cricket in New Zealand. (Note to his current students: he turned it around through the application of hard work in the second year. Please don't take this as an excuse to slack off.) He recalls freezing his nuts off on the field at Fenner's, the university cricket ground, preparing for games with lock-ins at the Cross Keys, and gatecrashing May balls. He once attempted to climb his way into one college ball with members of the Combined Services XI: 'Unfortunately one of the Marines fell off a very high gate and we ended up in A&E because he'd fractured his hip.'

It's an enjoyable peek at Crawley's less guarded, less sensible side. But, like me, he's not keen to dwell on it. The Labradors need feeding, and I take my leave of him and his gorgeous dogs, and drive away. The Carpenters come on the radio and the car is awash with their sepia sound.

I think of Mum, and my last summer in Luton, and the Lancashire cricket jumper that I loved to wear until I put it in the washing machine and shrunk it. When Lancashire had reached the NatWest Trophy final at Lord's Mum had bought us tickets, and the Lord's ticket office, perhaps noting our Home Counties postcode, had seated us in a tranche of Essex fans, many of them wearing their team's custard yellow one-day kit. Essex bowled Lancashire out for the pitiful total of 186; with every wicket that fell, I slumped a little lower in my seat. By the time my mum was getting out the picnic, I felt too sick even to enjoy the pork pie she had bought specially for the occasion. I loved pork pie.

Crawley top-scored the Lancashire innings with 66. When I asked him about it, he told me he thought it was the best he'd ever batted. 'The ball was just going sideways,' he said. 'I remember looking as we watched the Essex lot come off – they're grinning and chuckling – and thinking, "Well, guys, you don't quite know what you're in for. You've got to bat on that pitch against Peter Martin, Ian Austin and Glen Chapple.'

What followed was one of the most extreme mood reversals I've ever undergone. 'Such a change! In one moment such a change! From perfect misery to perfect happiness . . .' I finally knew how it felt to be Harriet Smith in *Emma*, and asked to dance by Mr Knightley. Martin, the friendly giant known to us fans as 'Digger', got a catch behind off Paul Grayson, and another to see off Nasser Hussain. Over in the opposite stand, a group of Lancashire fans had cranked up their favourite chant, and I joined them in a joyous solo: 'Ooohhh, Lanky-lanky! Lanky-lanky-lanky-lanky-Lancashire!' My mum, more alert than me to the black looks I was getting, ordered me to sit down and shut up.

But I couldn't stop my legs from jiggling; I was watching a miracle unfold. With each wicket that followed – and they followed fast – my celebrations became increasingly uncontained. Graham Gooch, the granddaddy of Essex cricket, stuck it out for an hour before Jason Gallian, a man whose medium-pace bowling was scarcely a thing of terror, trapped him lbw. I leapt up in my seat, spraying sandwich crumbs over the already irate opposition fans; Mum and I knew Lancashire had broken them. Chapple – a whippy looking kid with a face covered in freckles and strawberry blond hair – finished with six wickets for 18 runs, Essex were bowled out for 57, and how I escaped a lynching I don't know. It was all over by early afternoon; as we picked our way back to the concrete stairway, we heard people grumbling about a disappointing game, a terrible wicket, a waste of money. I felt I'd just been at the game of my life.

History is many sided. Despite all these eyewitness accounts I'm compiling of the nineties, I'm finding it hard to get a handle on what being in the England team was really like. There's fondness in people's voices as they remember their playing days, but there's also talk of selfishness. I hear of cliques, but no one admits to being in one. Crawley hasn't given me much of a steer – he's spoken about few of his England teammates by name, and his memories of that time were a little colourless, like an overexposed photograph.

So I enjoyed hearing him talk about his Lancashire teammates. There, you could detect real warmth, a place he had, perhaps, found home, at least for a while. 'It was an unusual situation, because many of the team had grown up with each other,' he had told me. 'Some from the north of the county, some from the south, but we all met in the bar after a game, no cliques. Everyone got on really, really well. Not to say there weren't arguments – but they were proper friendships, basically.'

Here, finally, was the fulfilment of my most cherished teenage imagination, the cricketing life I'd pictured: a band of brothers straining their sinews for each other on the field, and sharing a frothy pint at the end of the day. I'd been right to pick Lancashire all along.

Chapter 8

A confession: my mum and I used to be pretty mean to my dad.

Dad has never had any interest in people kicking or hurling balls around. He'd rather be doing stuff than sitting on a sofa watching other people do it in high-definition. He likes motorsport, and he has a ridiculously extensive knowledge of racing cars that reveals itself during Grand Prix weekends and boring motorway journeys. But woe betide him if he dared to comment on a cricket match that Mum and I were watching.

Sometimes his observations were sweetly naive, sometimes actively dangerous ('England seem to be doing well for once,' spoken fate-temptingly before a mid-innings collapse). Occasionally, like an idiot savant, his random comments would hit an accidental truth ('They don't look like they're ever going to get that guy out,' voiced before an opposition batsman scored a double-century). But mostly they were just annoyingly ill-informed and made the assumption that, whatever was happening in the game, England were going to lose it. It didn't matter what Dad said, we would react in the same way: shush him loudly, tell him he didn't know what he was talking about, and bristle until he left us in peace. Which, unsurprisingly, he was happy to do.

I am not proud of our behaviour. I love my dad, and I respect his brilliant brain so much that he is the only person in the world I care about beating at Trivial Pursuit. But it stirred something deep and ugly when he weighed in on the cricket. Yes, Mum and I spent a large proportion of our time loudly discussing the defects of our team; yes, we would decry this batsman as 'useless' and that bowler as 'a total waste of space' – but it was not OK for other people to say the same stuff, even if it was true. You were only allowed to agree that our team was crap if you actually supported our team. And that excluded Dad.

At the core of our behaviour was this, irrational, truth: fans are capable of feeling completely opposing emotions towards their team at the same time. We can be frustrated by them, irritated by them – we can even hate them for the way they disappoint us – and in the same moment we can feel as protective of them as that mummy T-Rex attacking Jeff Goldblum in *The Lost World*. We love them like brothers and sisters, and they repay our bond by annoying the hell out of us.

This complicated dynamic extends to individual players. For me, it was no better embodied than in the person of Andrew Caddick. Caddick had first joined the England team in the same 1993 Ashes summer as me, so we had that in common. He was a bowler who had grown up in New Zealand, and modelled his bowling on that of his home country's greatest ever player, Sir Richard Hadlee. Hadlee took a world record 431 Test wickets and became an ambassador for the sport. Caddick took 234 and became an ambassador for a helicopter sales company.

I had begun with great hopes for Caddick. At first he struggled to differentiate himself from all the other mediocre England seam bowlers, but in Barbados in 1994 he had taken vital wickets to close out a historic victory. England had ignited a spark of talent, and Caddick had revealed his true potential. And so, with almost cosmic inevitability, he got injured and didn't play for the next two years.

Caddick's shin splints weren't the only issue, however. There were rumoured to be other reasons the selectors wouldn't pick him. These were transmitted to fans like me through a sort of code: newspaper writers would tell us that Caddick was 'not a team man', and my lawyer mother explained that this was a way of saying that other people didn't like him, without being sued for libel. He was 'difficult' and 'sensitive'. Sometimes he was termed a 'problem player', a term I definitely understood, because I'd been studying *Measure for Measure* and that was one of Shakespeare's problem plays. Caddick, according to the shadowy accounts I was reading, appeared to be Claudio – a man with a slightly selfish bent, unwilling to take responsibility for his own failings.

His personal attributes did not help his appeal. Caddick's mouth skewed naturally towards a grimace, and his large nose vied for attention with a pair of outsized ears. His body language in the field sometimes suggested a wish to detach himself from the events taking place around him; when a batsman drove him through the covers, he would stand with his hands on his hips, a hard-done-by air projecting all the way to the back of the stands. It didn't help that he was often bowling in tandem with Darren Gough, whose gregarious behaviour and electric smile only made Caddick look more sour-faced by comparison.

No, Caddick was not a player who gave you the warm and fuzzies. Even his name, with all those hard-edged consonants, lent itself quite easily as an expression of frustration and a pseudo-swear word. Just as there are players who we find ourselves naturally drawn to, there are those who become lightning rods for our anger and our disappointment, and little did poor Andy Caddick know how often his name was taken in vain in my house. Still, if I ever heard anyone else dissing him – calling him a flat-track bully, or questioning his mental toughness – I would swiftly remind them of his achievements. Didn't they see his 7 for 94 at Sydney? Didn't they know he took four West Indies wickets in a single over? I always cheered Caddick's good days, and celebrated his successes. He was no villain, more an odd cousin who I had little in common with, and whose bad habits I deplored. He was still, crucially, family.

These days, I realise how little I really knew of his true character. I imagined his prickly ego, on no particular evidence; I labelled him a selfish player, where I might have called the same behaviour 'single-minded' in others. Now I'm older and wiser, with a greater understanding of how the media can exaggerate and distort, I actually feel a little ashamed of how eagerly I believed everything bad I heard about Caddick, how happy I was to jump to conclusions. I'd seen a faulty, flickering hologram, and taken it for the real deal.

So there's a hint of penitence in my soul when I ask him if he'll meet up with me. He lives in Somerset, but he's in London for an awards dinner and offers to meet me for breakfast the morning after. This is why our chat takes place in the nondescript lobby of a Marriott hotel, a place whose greatest asset is its proximity to Paddington station, where Caddick will catch a train back home. He is waiting for me in the breakfast bar, at a Formica table that looks out on to the A4; the man whose uniform used to be a set of whites is now wearing a suit and looming over a forlorn looking coffee, the very image of a man on a sales trip.

We chat about the awards dinner, which was the other side of town, at a swanky five-star location; it's an event Caddick goes to every year and loves, because it brings him back together with some of his old playing buddies. 'It's always good fun to catch up,' he says, and I'm surprised on two counts. Partly to hear him use the word 'fun' (he always seemed so serious), and partly to discover that he's so fond of his former colleagues. There's clearly a sentimental side to Caddick that never got reported.

He tells me that he and Dean Headley had been discussing how proud they were to play during the nineties, when the opposition was so consistently tough. The conversation runs into other things that were better back then too: the standard of second XI cricket, the coaching set-up. And, he says, the players: 'If you put today's bowling attack up against the one from the nineties – if you line up the whole team against each other – ours was better. Because you're only as strong as the international teams you're playing against. That nineties team would beat today's team 5–0.'

If there had been a soundtrack to this conversation, we would just have heard the loud needle-scratch as the record was ripped from the turntable. I don't know how to reply to his assertion: it is so palpably untrue. When we meet, Alastair Cook's team have just beaten India 3–1 at home; they have won 11 out of their last 17 series. The England team of the nineties couldn't win a Test against a team of Zimbabwe part-timers. But Caddick does not sound like a man used to being told he's wrong, and I don't want to argue with him so early in our conversation. So I listen on as he talks, his opinions gathering momentum, threatening to squash me where I sit. Today's players are 'a bit sterile – you know, you look at it, there's not that many characters in cricket now.' And they don't appreciate what the team of the nineties did for them financially. 'We sowed the seed allowing them to have more player-power. That's the bit that sometimes gets me: I don't think the players now understand what our era went through to get them to where they are now.'

His telephone rings – it's an important work call – and as he walks away from the table I hear him straight-talking a colleague in the same strident voice. I reel towards the hot buffet plates of stringy bacon and watery eggs. I can't say I hadn't been warned. 'Some people didn't get on with Caddy because Caddy talked a load of rubbish and annoyed people,' Jack Russell had told me bluntly, back in Chipping Sodbury. 'He'd come out with the most strange comments.' And then he had recounted the story of Brian Lara nicking behind on his world-record-breaking score of 375, and Caddick's (non-ironic) announcement: 'See, lads, I told you I knew how to get him out.' 'But that's just innocent Caddy,' Russell continued. 'A lot of people didn't want to room with him, but I used to take him with a pinch of salt.'

There was a more endearing side to Caddick. Everyone agreed that he was an extraordinarily kind and helpful teammate. He was the handyman of the dressing-room, the man who cut Thorpe's bat handles down to size, or solved Hussain's problems with the TV remote. Phil Tufnell was especially grateful for the times he fixed his Walkman and showed him how to use his phone. 'He was a good lad,' said Tufnell. 'Slightly different. He might have rubbed a few people up the wrong way but never in a malicious way. He was as good as gold when I played with him.'

So I stuff my bacon in a roll, and I head back to the table. And when Caddick returns, I ask him bluntly: what did he think of his reputation as an awkward sod? Was it unfair? 'Maybe I would ask the wrong thing, give the wrong vibe, but that's because that's the person I am,' he says. 'I'm not a yes man, never have been, never will be. If there was something to say I'd say it. It might have been the wrong thing at the wrong time but I'd rather say it and get it off my chest than sit there.' What he didn't like, he said, was the press putting him in the same category as, say, Tufnell. 'They're stereotyping me as someone who's an issue. I thought, "How can you compare me and Tufnell? We're chalk and cheese.

Phil's an absolute nutter and I'm just Joe Bloggs who wants to help everybody.'

My own mental processes never bore much scrutiny where it concerned cricket. Whatever powers of rationality I had were wilfully ignored by the part of my brain that had fallen in love with the England team. Since the summer that Atherton assumed the captaincy, I had been waiting patiently for the time he would usher in a new age of victory. And I fell, like a sucker, for every flicker of fight they showed. If England drew a Test, I saw it as a win. Their consolation victories – which arrived, like messengers in a Greek tragedy, just too late to prevent a bloody annihilation – were the sign of a golden future. Call it optimism, call it naivety, but it never occurred to me that Atherton would fail to turn England into a successful side.

You can dismiss this as the delusion of a girl with a desperate crush, if you like. But I wasn't the only one holding out hope. Looking back through my old match programmes, I came across this, written in 1996, by Simon Barnes, the eminent sportswriter: 'When was there last an England captain as greatly, as universally admired as Atherton?' By the start of the 1997 season, Atherton had been given the honour of captaining England 40 times, and was fast approaching the record for most Tests as England captain, held by Peter May. He had talent, brains, and guts, and he still seemed the obvious, and only, candidate for the job. Surely, surely, the trophies would eventually follow?

As they prepared for an Ashes summer, England could, in fact, boast one prize: their first overseas series win in five years. After the embarrassment of Zimbabwe, England had triumphed in a three-Test series in New Zealand and Atherton himself, who had endured a torrid run of personal form in Africa, had topped the runs table with an average of over 100. 'England finished the winter with something to build on,' noted the wisdom of *Wisden*. 'Time would tell whether the foundations were strong enough to withstand the gale due to blow in from Australia.'

There aren't many international sports where a team measures itself entirely on the result of a single bilateral contest, but then cricket's system of individual rivalries is unique. It took 100 years for anyone to invent a world championship that rated the Test nations against each other, and it will be another 100 before anyone really cares about it. Until then, England will go on defining their success by one thing alone – whether they beat Australia in the Ashes.

I learned this central principle of England fandom early and, like any obedient recruit, I accepted it without question. Australia were the ultimate enemy. And since they had not lost an Ashes series in almost ten years, they were also bloody tyrants. To me, who had experienced absolutely nothing of real-life oppression, Australian sportsmen presented themselves as a ravaging horde of destruction. They were Genghis Khan, Attila the Hun and the boot of Rome. They were Tamburlaine, humiliating their subjugated foe with their Aussie swagger and their ruthlessly economical bowling. I knew it was never right to hate people, but I also knew that God allowed a special dispensation for Australia's cricket team.

None of this made any rational sense. Australia was a country I had visited and loved; my dad's mum had moved there and married a native. I had family in Perth and Queensland and the Northern Territory; I loved the Australian sun and the Australian sea, and the Australian capacity to cook sausages on a barbecue every single day. But I couldn't help myself. In the midst of my teenage turmoil, I had found somewhere to direct my feelings of resentment, shame and inarticulate anger. It was a pleasure to imagine Australia's plain-faced wicketkeeper Ian Healy as an evil gnome. It was a relief to mock

Shane Warne's fluctuating weight, and to laugh at Mark Waugh's stupid hair. The fact that such behaviour was completely endorsed by my mother only made me worse.

By the time the Australians arrived in May 1997, I was obsessed with the idea of beating them. I was also particularly vulnerable to the idea that, this time, we might. For this I blame D:Ream and Tony Blair. The general election that month was the first time I had been eligible to vote and my late-teenage social conscience had hit the sweet spot between innocence and earnestness. On election night, my friends and I stayed up celebrating each seat won, until the limo finally delivered Britain's new Prime Minister to Downing Street for breakfast. We went back to bed drunkenly convinced that life was soon to become immeasurably better for everyone. By the time the cricket came round I was pumped so full of Hope and Expectation that my optimism was running at unsustainably high levels.

Thus my first-year exams seemed of very little significance, certainly far less important than the outcome of the one-day series that England and Australia were playing in the build-up to the Ashes. Luckily I had a friend, Ben, who felt the same. We agreed we should revise together, swapping the relative luxury of the college's library for its fetid TV room, which was situated in an airless basement with sticky floors, broken furniture, and an unshiftable smell of dirty laundry. The TV itself was a 14-inch model that someone had clearly sourced in a Rumbelows liquidation sale. This was good news because no one else in the entire college could be bothered to fight us for its use.

Ben and I watched England win the first one-dayer. We watched them win the second. We saw them complete the series 3–0, and we wondered if we were having a joint hallucination brought on by the lack of fresh air. What we had failed to learn about Chaucer or linguistic theory was more than made up for by what we'd learned about the Australia team. We had discovered that they were beatable. We knew that their captain Mark Taylor was in a terrible run of form, and a personal crisis so deep he was prepared to drop himself from his own team.

I sat my final paper on the opening morning of the first Ashes Test. I remember returning to halls and Ben asking in a very serious manner if I had heard the score. 'One hundred and eighteen all out,' he said. I groaned, and threw myself dramatically on to a nearby sofa, muttering curses into a cushion until I spotted the mischief in his face.

'Wait,' I said. 'Is that us – or them?'

'*Them*,' Ben smirked.

D:Ream were right; things *did* only get better. Nasser Hussain scored a double-century and England declared 360 runs ahead. Even their eventual victory target – 118, one of those modestly gettable scores that England were experts at failing to make – didn't trigger their usual panicky self-destruction. Atherton and Stewart despatched the task like men who needed to get home for a dishwasher delivery. Within an hour and a half, England were 1–0 up in the Ashes.

The crowds in the stands had swiftly bastardised Skinner and Baddiel's Euro '96 anthem: 'They're coming home, they're coming home, they're coming, Ashes coming home.' It was a grammatically ugly rewrite, but I hummed the tune to myself as I walked round college with an air of invincibility. A sensible person would have tempered their excitement. I should have remembered that this victory went entirely against the form guide, and that Australia were bound to retaliate hard. Instead I dared fate by laughing at their failings (until now, I had only dared laugh at their haircuts). I even went as far as to publicly pity their captain, who was being called on to resign by the Australian press. I told Ben, in a voice rich with condescension, that it actually made me sad to see Mark Taylor, who seemed a nice enough man, looking so forlorn and batting so ineptly. 'Life's too short to feel sorry for Australians,' said Ben.

You would think that a pair of literature students might have recognised hubris. But we didn't. When England got themselves bowled out for 77 in the next Test – their lowest total against Australia in 50 years, their lowest at Lord's in more than a century – I chose to ignore the portents, since, thanks to two days of rain, my team still managed to draw the match. I even convinced myself that England were on top in the next Test, having bowled Australia out for 235 and reached 74 for 1 in reply.

And then, Nemesis awoke, and her name was Shane Warne. For a weapon of vengeance the Australian leg-spinner looked pretty unthreatening, with his blond surfer's mop and his two-step lollop to the wicket. He sent the ball careening harmlessly wide of Alec Stewart's leg stump; Stewart was still turning to meet it when it leapt from the pitch and twisted back on itself, revealing its secret pre-programmed mission and flying from his bat to the hands of slip. It was one of the greatest leg-breaks the world had seen since Warne had made his Ashes debut four years previously; unfortunately for England, it was also just the beginning.

His deliveries hung in the air with the slow-motion menace of grenades in a war movie, and spat off the pitch like shrapnel. Each time Warne took a wicket the umpire paused lugubriously before raising his finger, as if allowing time for the batsman and fans alike to take in what they'd just seen. Other bowlers could knock you over, and challenge you to get up from the mat. Warne was able to implode a match from its centre. He was a black hole, to which everything eventually succumbed: your hopes, your mind, your futile resistance. England eventually lost by 287 runs; Australia had levelled the series, but nothing about the contest looked even any more.

It was here, at the halfway point of the summer, that Caddick found himself dumped from the team. He had taken 11 of the 45 Australia wickets to fall in the series so far, a joint-highest tally that matched that of his bowling partner Darren Gough. 'I can remember turning up for the next game at Headingley,' says Caddick, 'and Mike Smith the left-arm bowler got picked ahead of me.' He screws his face into an expression that marries disgust and derision. 'And I'm sitting there going, "*What*?"'

Mike Smith was about to turn 30. He had never played for England before. But he was topping the county averages that season with his swing bowling. He was also a left-armer. The selectors believed he could prosper at Headingley, where conditions were often favourable to swing. And so Caddick was sent back on the long drive from Yorkshire to Somerset, and Smith took his place in the team.

The lucky-dip style of selection that England favoured at this time may have been frustrating for the players, but I kind of liked it. Every time you reached your hand into the bran tub for a new name you could still hope that, despite all previous disappointments, you were going to come away with a decent prize. There's always been something in me that suspects the grass is greener on the other side, that's tormented by the path not chosen. I would rather have all and sundry given a chance to play for England than be tortured by the idea that there was hidden talent treading the greensward somewhere in Glamorgan or Leicestershire, never to see the light of Test cricket. Plus, it was fun. There was a constant stream of new men to become acquainted with, and if England couldn't win, they did at least provide a variety of ways to lose.

So Smith got his chance, and nearly took his first Test wicket when a ball took the shoulder of Matthew Elliott's bat and looped gently to first slip. Instead of succumbing graciously to Graham

Thorpe's upturned hands, it bounced off them, vaulting over his head in an elegant arc, teasing him to follow. Thorpe turned and threw himself despairingly after it, but the ball dropped a finger-length out of reach and hit the ground just before he did. Elliott went on to make 199; Australia marched from 50 for 4 to 501 for 9 declared. England lost by an innings, went 2-1 down in the series, and Mike Smith never took a Test wicket. It was his only match.

He was not the only player of that period to be robbed of a chance of redemption. Joey Benjamin and Simon Brown at least got to celebrate wickets in their single-Test careers; batsman Alan Wells made a duck and 3 not out in his only two England innings in 1995 and, four years later, the Scottish all-rounder Gavin Hamilton took no wickets and made no runs in his sole appearance. The England team was a high-turnover employer in the nineties – 28 of their picks played fewer than five Test matches. But there was always, to me, something especially melancholic about the one-Test wonders. Selected purely out of expediency – a mature presence (Wells), a home pick (Benjamin), left-handedness (Brown) – they were the cannon fodder of the nineties, whose debuts were their epitaphs.

Smith's luckless career is not, however, what Caddick remembers of that episode. Caddick's own eviction from the England dressing-room was proof to him that the England management did not take him seriously: 'Playing a bowler who got 80 wickets in a season at the expense of a player who was trying to establish himself was always the easy option. That happened a couple of times to me. You just think to yourself, "What do you have to do to get your foot in the door and feel part of the team?"'

It's a theme that comes up repeatedly in my conversation with Caddick – belonging, feeling valued. He's the first player to tell me, candidly, that he didn't enjoy playing for Atherton. 'I don't think Athers was a very good man-manager,' he says, and I think of what Crawley said about the disastrous decision to ban wives and girlfriends from Zimbabwe. 'He was a lot more distant than most captains,' says Caddick. 'He always had his favourites, and that was hard work.'

I've heard other players talk about cliques within the team – 'too many people with different agendas,' as one player put it – although everyone I've spoken to has denied being in one, with the exception of Graham Thorpe, whose friendship with Nasser Hussain and Mark Ramprakash earned them the title 'the brat pack'. Even Caddick admits that 'Ath would hang out with anyone', so it wasn't that Caddick felt socially excluded. 'I just felt as a captain he would always take the more comfortable option,' he says. 'Back in that period you had to be not only a very good player but you had to be well liked. Whereas now they don't care what you do off the field.'

'I'm not sure that's true,' I say. I think they do care. Look at the case of Kevin Pietersen, exiled from England because his presence was considered toxic to team unity. 'No, but he's a complete arsehole,' Caddick replies.

I snort a laugh. There can be something rather endearing about Caddick's honesty. It might not be entirely self-aware, but I think his ability to believe what he's saying, even against all the evidence, might just be his superpower. It was certainly the key to his longevity: he was one of the last of England's nineties players to retire, playing county cricket for Somerset until the age of 40. 'I still believed I was the best fast bowler in the country,' he admits. 'No matter what age I was. And that's just me. If I didn't believe that I wouldn't have played, 'cos it's just too hard, too painful.'

He has always had that attitude, he says: '"Stop wasting my time, give me the ball." I didn't believe anybody else could do the job better than me. "Just give me the ball, we'll get off the park quicker."' And that didn't used to wind people up? 'It would always wind people up. And that didn't bother me in the slightest. If they don't like it, tough, because that's how I grew up. Find someone better than me and they can do my job. But my whole career all I wanted to do was keep proving people wrong.'

It is fatal for a sportsman to start doubting himself, or his ability to win. By contrast, sports fans have to come to terms with the fact that we are, by and large, losers. Unless we win the lottery of life – born to Australian parents, or blessed to grow up in Manchester in the late 20th century – we know that at any time the spectre of defeat is likely to cross our paths and ruin our day, our week, our year. We hazard ourselves, again and again, and we aren't even doing it for the exercise. We're not gaining physical benefits, or a social life, or status in the eyes of our peers. We're doing it solely for the hope of a hit of victory, and a vicarious one at that. It's a strange choice we make, to stake our emotions so wholeheartedly upon such meaningless outcomes. Sport is, by its nature, utterly trivial; a team's success or failure doesn't matter anywhere outside of its own universe. I suspect that this is why, paradoxically, we overinvest ourselves. We go all in, like a goldrush victim spying a fleck of something glittery in the ground. When our team win, we're an instant millionaire; when they lose, we're bankrupts. That's the only way I can explain why fans like me keep supporting teams that keep letting us down. We've given so much of ourselves to this fictitious universe that we can't withdraw from it until it has paid us back in good feelings. We become trapped in that gambler's mentality. No matter what trophies our team win, or how far down the league we fall, we can never get out. As long as there's another fixture, as long as there's a revenge match, our sporting narrative goes on.

There may be those who take the long view of sport; those who, with the advantage of age, can support a team with equanimity knowing that the wheel will turn and, one day, an England football team will win the World Cup again. That's not how it was for me. It doesn't matter how poor my team's form is, I don't watch a game without believing that this time, somehow, they can win. That's why sport is magical – because anything can happen. And until it does, defeat cannot wither us, nor custom stale its infinite variety.

For four challenging years my innate optimism had held out against all the evidence. England were going to get better, be it in the next Test match, or the next series. When they finally lost the Ashes at Trent Bridge, it wasn't their submissive performance that hurt – by now, they were even phoning in their failures – but the fact that the excitement of Edgbaston seemed like another lifetime. I'd had a glimpse of a parallel dimension where England were winners; and now here I was, abandoned back on regular Earth, in a never-changing reality where England got thumped by Australia, their bowlers bowled short and wide and their batsmen displayed the grace and calm of C-3PO. With the Ashes gone, the team were once again the whipping boys of the British press. The journalists who called for Atherton's resignation sounded certain of their quarry. For the first time, I started to doubt: what if he wasn't going to do it? Maybe Atherton would never lead his team into the promised land. The thought was like cold steel sliding between my ribs.

Towards the end of the summer I went backpacking in India – I had never even owned a backpack before, but it was a chance to hang out with friends and take my mind off a difficult summer. So I didn't see the last Test at The Oval. Instead of watching England steal a dramatic, consolation victory, I was suffering from vomiting and diarrhoea in £1-a-night hotel rooms near historic Indian locations. These were not the kind of amenities that ran to TV or radio, and the newspapers were all in Hindi, but I did get incredibly accurate bulletins from receptionists, waiters, and random people in the street. It was apparent from the scores they gave me that I was once again missing a classic – a desperately low-scoring match, the advantage shifting rapidly from side to side. I tried to create the game in my head, concocting a narrative from the few names I could pick up: Thorpe and Ramprakash scoring some runs, Tufnell and Caddick taking the wickets. I pictured the two bowlers – the problem children of the side – coming together to prove their doubters wrong. Tufnell would be bounding around with wide eyes; Caddick would be accepting the plaudits – as good as he'd said, all along.

By the time I got home, England's failure to win an urn full of pretend ashes was a footnote to the summer. My friends and I had been alerted to Princess Diana's death only when a couple of young Indian men ran up to us on a train platform, shouting her name at the first white people they'd seen that day. We had only half believed their claims, and had entirely missed the grief-a-thon that followed – by the time we flew home, the funeral had been and gone, and we felt like astronauts returning after a five-year mission, unable to appreciate or understand the collective change in our countrymen.

I felt far more emotional about how the cricket had turned out than about any royal's passing. The mood swings the Ashes had taken me through had been violent and intense, and I had never felt so grateful for a season's end. A final scoreline of 3–2 didn't sound so bad, but somehow it was less honest, more mocking, than a 4–1 drubbing. It suggested that England had come close, when in truth they had never had as much as a fingertip on the urn. I knew that, at some stage, I was going to have to stop lying to myself and face the facts. England weren't getting any better.

In January 1997 when England were at the nadir of their winter tour Derek Pringle, former player turned *Independent* columnist, had wondered what their problem was. 'England appear to have more wastrels with talent, like Chris Lewis and Andy Caddick, than any other country,' he wrote. 'One of the challenges of captaincy must be to tame and harness such mavericks . . . Atherton's major fault is perhaps that he expects unconditional support, rather than a battle of wits with his players. It is a preference that tends to promote sheep rather than wolves.'

Maybe it's no surprise, then, that Caddick's greatest performances came under another captain. But 1997 was at least a turning point – the first time he played with Darren Gough. The two would eventually become England's best opening bowling pair of the decade. They were never so much a partnership as two ultra-competitive and sometimes hostile individuals, desperate to outdo each other. Caddick remembers first meeting him when he was still living in New Zealand and Gough spent a winter playing club cricket in Christchurch. 'Good lad,' he says. 'Bubbly, very down to earth. It was quite funny because he's not always the brightest, he doesn't make the brightest comments.'

Caddick says it's not true that they were never friends. 'There's a lot written about the fact that we never got on. But we got on like a house on fire. You always take a little bit of time to get to know people, but as the relationship grew we gelled very well. The beauty of it was that the competitive edge was not only on the field but off the field as well. That's what made it such fun.' He tells me they regularly went to the cinema together on the eve of a Test match, just the two of them. It sounds positively romantic.

They certainly had chemistry: Caddick's rhythmic bowling, delivered with plenty of height and bounce, seemed to trouble batsmen more when it was combined with Gough's high-energy skidders at the other end. Caddick's greatest achievements came later in his career – 7 for 46 in South Africa, an Ashes ten-fer – and he tells me that he recently re-watched his famous four wickets in an over against West Indies in 2000. 'Years ago I asked Sky to do me a DVD of all my Test wickets, which I sometimes click on,' he says. 'And this time I watched Nasser when I got the fourth one: I ran over to him and he just stood there, he was just blown away. The buzz . . . it wasn't the actual doing the job that gave you that, it was the buzz you got from the crowd, because they were just ecstatic.

'We partied that night, but Goughy and myself had to come back in the next day to do a photoshoot and press conference, which pissed us right off.' That was all in the future, a future where Nasser Hussain was the England captain, and the imperturbable Duncan Fletcher was his coach. 'Nasser instilled what was needed for us as players to believe in ourselves,' he says. 'The Atherton–Lloyd era wasn't the right era for me.'

Lloyd was, he thinks, 'too passionate' to be effective as a manager. He remembers watching him pace around a ground in New Zealand during a particularly tense match, smoking a pipe filled with blueberry-flavoured tobacco and talking to himself 'because he couldn't take the pressure. Things got to him. He wanted the team to really knit together. He wanted players to be in with his team effort. It didn't matter what you were like as a cricketer, you had to be the right bloke to be in the team. And that was the wrong attitude to have . . . It wasn't a period of being able to relax and do what you do naturally. That's what I felt.'

Caddick, like Jack Russell, doesn't have especially fond memories of the West Indies tour that followed the 1997 Ashes, an ill-fated and turbulent venture in which the first Test had to be abandoned due to a dangerous pitch, and England managed in the remaining Tests to convert winning positions into draws and losses. Lloyd's characteristic intensity was very much in evidence. 'One hundred and eighty days, we were training every day. That's one of the things people watching Test cricket don't understand:

when you're on tour, it's not about the 11 till 6. You don't take into account the amount of travelling we do, booking in and out of hotels non-stop . . .'

Caddick's own performances were a microcosm of the team's: every good day followed, inevitably, by a horrible one. I didn't know much about the technical aspects of bowling back then, and that probably made me even less tolerant of the bad days. I always wanted to know why, when it was so obvious that landing the ball too short and too wide was the problem, the bowlers would continue to do so. 'We don't intentionally bowl like that,' says Caddick, when I finally get the chance to ask. 'But sometimes it just comes out wrong, there's no reason.' That's the problem with bowling – when it's going badly, there's just no stopping it. A struggling batsman will soon be back in the pavilion and out of his misery. Bowlers are subject to a lengthier torment, trapped in the field by their own ineptitude, the engineers of their own destruction.

Caddick took seven wickets as England levelled the series 1–1 in Trinidad (his part in the victory there was, wrote Matthew Engel in that year's *Wisden*, 'especially inexplicable, since his new-ball bowling had been dreadful'). Unfortunately, that was as good as it got for either the bowler or his team. Caddick was dropped from the fourth Test, which England lost by a thumping margin, and a monsoon ruined any chance of a result in the next. The hope of saving face with a series draw in the sixth Test disappeared in a single session on the second evening, when the West Indies openers, Philo Wallace and Clayton Lambert, smashed Caddick and Headley's bowling all over the Antigua Recreation Ground.

'Myself and Dean got a bit of a dressing down from David Lloyd,' remembers Caddick. 'And we said, "Well, what do you want us to do? We bowl where you say to bowl, they smack it out of the park. We bowl bumpers, they smack it out of the park."

'That was just a one-off. Never happened again. You get thrown to the wolves and you've got to turn up the next day and dismiss it and carry on. The press came hard at me and blamed me for losing a Test match, and you go, "Well, there's another ten guys in the team. OK, I didn't bowl that well, but there's another ten guys."'

Whose fault is it when a team sucks? Is it the individuals, for not doing their job? The leadership, for not inspiring the individuals? The selectors, for not picking the right leader and players in the first place? Failure seems to be circular. The batsmen I've talked to have spoken of the extra pressure you feel under when you take guard with a 600-run deficit. The bowlers have pointed out how hard it is to win a Test when the batsmen never give you a decent score to bowl at. I ask Caddick why he thinks England failed so repeatedly. Why was the opposition always better than his own team? 'A lot of it was that they had more self-belief,' he says. 'I've talked about this with a lot of players and I think we were just as good – it was just the belief.'

'You're saying that England's players were as talented as anyone else's?'

'The talents were just as good, yeah. On a par.'

I look him in the eye, and wonder. It's a ballsy claim. After all, one of England's best excuses for losing as often as they did is that they simply didn't have the same near-miraculous giftings as the men they were up against. If Caddick is right – if the players had plenty of talent, and still couldn't win – then they've only themselves to blame.

In cricket, however, one man alone takes responsibility for the team's results. The captain is a breed apart: the person who directs play on the field, and plans strategy off it; the man supposed to inspire his troops, lead by example and set the tone at all times. Only two men, Allan Border and Clive Lloyd, had captained their national team more often than Michael Atherton, and they were both legends. But the Caribbean was Atherton's eighth series defeat. Of his 52 Tests in charge, he had won 13, drawn 20, and lost 19.

I tended not to dwell on these statistics; as the coaching handbook insists, I always focused on the next game, not the last. But they were starting to hang around his neck like an albatross with an abacus. Plus, Atherton was having a terrible time with the bat. He averaged 20.72 for the previous 12 months, and he hadn't scored a century all year.

Things reached a head on the last day of the West Indies series. Just when England looked like they might salvage some pride and bat out the final Test for a draw, Graham Thorpe ran out his partner Nasser Hussain. With the series already won, Ambrose and Walsh had been merely going through the motions; now, at the first sniff of victory, they ran off the field and changed from their trainers into their spikes. They came back out, ended the game in a single session, and the England players were soon back in their dressing-room licking their wounds.

The changing facilities at the Antigua Recreation Ground were pretty basic: a toilet with no door, and a mattress in the corner where Tufnell took his naps and smoked clandestine fags. There was nowhere to store gear, so it spilled haphazard across the floor. Into this jumble – a not entirely cheerless mess that might have served as a metaphor for England's past five years – Atherton stepped. His message was brief and unsentimental: 'Boys, that's it. I'm done.'

If Atherton didn't seem emotional about his resignation, others were. Thorpe said he felt 'almost slightly responsible' because of the run-out: 'Athers never showed heaps of emotion anyway. But it was pretty sombre. I remember Nasser's emotions more than Athers' – Nasser was in tears.' He wasn't the only one: Angus Fraser hid his head under a towel, and the moment was made all the more poignant by the fact that, outside, the crowds were cheering Atherton's opposite number Brian Lara as he received his first Test series trophy.

It was the Easter holidays, and I heard the news that Atherton had quit from Mum. She tried to put a positive spin on it: 'Well, we knew it was coming, didn't we? And he'll be a lot happier now . . .' There was no shock, just a heavy sadness settling behind my ribcage, making itself comfortable there. It was like late-stage grief, the kind you might feel for a loved one who dies after a long and debilitating illness: no bargaining, no anger, no denial, just a painful longing, an aching absence.

When Take That had split up, the Samaritans had set up a helpline for distraught fans. There was no such recourse for me. But I did have a mum who understood, and who was prepared to indulge my misery for the next few days. I sat around mournfully, listlessly, a hospital patient happy to be coddled and consoled with puddings and ice creams and cups of tea. No defeat had hurt in quite this way, because there was always another game, or another series ahead, a chance at redemption. Atherton's departure was final. I thought of Edgar's speech in *King Lear*: '. . . the worst is not, so long as we can say, "this is the worst."' This certainly felt like the worst. Atherton's defining characteristic as captain had been his tenacity, his refusal to give up on his team. His departure didn't just feel intensely personal; it signified the death of a dream.

Chapter 9

Caring too much isn't the sole province of the sports fan. Perhaps the players I have most in common with are those who couldn't quite put their own game into perspective.

At the start of the 1990s the two finest young talents in England were – almost incontestably – Mark Ramprakash and Graeme Hick. They were both brilliant batsmen. Throughout their long careers they were the scourge of every county side; no batsman in the country came close to matching their dominance. Unfortunately, that is rarely the first thing posterity remembers about them. Instead we talk, wistfully or whiningly, of their abject inability to do the same job for England.

Ramprakash and Hick arrived on the international scene garlanded with praise and expectation; by the end of the nineties both wore the lead mantle of unfulfilled potential. They became accidental symbols of England's fragility. Whenever they failed to impose themselves on their opponents, whenever they wilted in the white heat of Test cricket's spotlight, they reflected the team's wider weaknesses. Their problems, which seemed so entirely in their own heads, became emblematic of the national side's own psychological frailty.

My mum and I were divided on their advantages. I had a soft spot for Hick, the soft-faced giant who would loom benignly at the back of the balcony or the wicket celebrations. He had a generous smile and a gap in his front teeth, and he looked like a man of simple tastes and humble character, the kind who would get led into trouble by a wily village girl in a George Eliot novel. He looked like the kind of man you could rely on, no matter how often his scores proved the opposite. Whatever the numbers said – and they often translated as 'failed', 'failed miserably' and 'blew it' – I would still get a completely contrary reassurance from seeing his name on the teamsheet.

My mum always favoured the flash kid, Ramprakash, who had a cover drive to die for, and a pair of sparkly eyes set above a pair of perfect cheekbones. I suspect my mother had very conflicted feelings towards Ramprakash, who looked like a Prince Charming off the pitch but, at the crease, seemed to need some serious mothering. Caught in some bowler's crosshairs, his fear and stress apparent in every false move and tentative stroke, Ramprakash roused her most maternal instincts.

Mum loved to see him do well. As a result, she used a rather different yardstick for his achievements than for anyone else's. 'It's nice to see Ramps make some runs,' she'd say, as he battled to 35. Or, 'He'll feel a bit better about himself now,' as he took a simple catch at short leg. I, who had far less patience, would try to call her out on this blatant lowering of standards. 'You've got to give him a proper chance,' Mum would say. 'It takes some people a while to come out of their shell.'

She was proved right eventually, although not necessarily by Ramprakash's England career. My family have been avid *Strictly Come Dancing* viewers since its very first series; my sister has learned more about cricket from watching Darren Gough, Phil Tufnell and Michael Vaughan fleckle their way around the floor than she ever did in the years that Mum and I tortured her by trying to teach her the game's ineffable intricacies. Ramprakash seemed an odd choice for the show: an introvert who was clearly uncomfortable with the emotion and physicality of it all. But, over the course of 12 weeks of Saturday nights and Sunday results shows, Mum and Kate and I saw him transform from someone with a horror of flashing his chest in the Latin numbers to a spotlight darling.

Ramprakash's successful campaign owed no little part to the many, many votes phoned in from my parents' house (Mum justified the phone bill to my dad by reminding him that all the money was going to Children in Need). When he triumphed in the final, Mum cried. And while this isn't necessarily a unique occurrence – Mum also cries at black-and-white war films, *Morecambe and Wise* sketches and Facebook videos of elephants – I know it was because it represented the metamorphosis he could never manage for England.

So she's jealous when I tell her that I'm going to meet him. 'Ooooh, you're going to see Ramps?' she says, in the strangely high, girlish voice she slips into when she's too excited to be her serious-woman-of-substance self. 'Can I come?' I pretend to consider her request for a second. 'No.'

Wandering out of St John's Wood tube station to meet him, I feel a stab of guilt. Mum and I have walked this pavement together every year since she first introduced me to the game. Over the course of the Tests and one-dayers we've attended together, Lord's has taken on a special significance for us. It has been a proving ground for me, and every year has marked my progress towards becoming a grown-up woman, someone who could be her equal. With every match we sat side by side in the plastic tip-up seats – indulging in adult occupations like doing the crossword and drinking sparkling wine – I became a little less her daughter and more her friend.

It's also our home ground, and our many visits have given me a sense of ownership of it; by the time my tread reaches the Wellington

Hospital it's pretty much a swagger. I should really walk all the way round to the Grace Gates to state my business, but I've always preferred the more convenient North Gate, and with my gilding of confidence I nod at the security guard and stride past him without breaking step. I can't quite believe it when that works.

Skirting the Nursery Ground, I arrive at the shiny cube of the indoor school. Ramprakash isn't here yet, and there's no one practising in the nets this morning, so I can stick my head between the tall green curtains and catch a glimpse without fear of a broken nose. I've never liked indoor cricket nets particularly – noisy places with the acoustics of a swimming pool and something of its humid air; the constant gunshot of bat hitting ball, chased around an echoing space by a garble of instructions, usually makes me feel queasy. But this is empty, still, immaculate. It feels like a cathedral.

At the reception a noticeboard advertises clinics and coaching courses, and also the upstairs café, where you can order a burger and fries half an hour before the end of your session. (It's nice to know that even in this uber-professional environment, the amateur ethos still lives strong.) I head up there to see if I can get a coffee, but the shutters are down, and there's a small but serious-looking meeting taking place at one of the tables. I wander back outside to the Nursery Ground. Ramprakash arrives, and greets me with a flash of a smile. 'Sorry to keep you waiting,' he says.

'No worries. I'm afraid the café's closed.'

'Shall we walk to the high street? There'll be plenty of places there.'

We head up the road, and I glance at the shops in recognition. The newsagent where I pick up a paper on the way to the game. The charity shop that can provide emergency sunhats or scarves, depending on the weather. The Jewish deli where I once blundered in with a hangover and asked for a bacon sandwich. I feel another twinge of guilt that Mum's not here, especially since Ramprakash is turning out to be exactly as charming in person as she has always imagined him.

He's wearing a crisp, dark overcoat, a navy scarf running elegantly along its lapels. He looks just as debonair as he did in white-tie-and-tails on *Strictly* and asks polite questions with a quiet, gentlemanly air. All the other cricketers I have met have looked like someone you might chat to in a pub; Ramprakash looks like someone you'd talk to in his limo as he's driven to a meeting. We cross the road to a smart-looking café; inside there are only one other set of diners, a trio of women in their fifties. One of them looks up as we enter and does a double-take, as if spotting an old friend. 'It's . . . Mark!' she says, before she can stop herself, or work out how she knows him. 'Hi,' he says, smiling and offering his hand, rescuing her from embarrassment. It's one of the most gentlemanly things I've seen.

We take a table in the corner and order some coffee and pastries. He sits stilly and waits for my questions. I feel a bit tongue-tied. I want to ask about his difficult years – the nervous innings, the single-figure scores – but I don't want to seem rude. You can't just turn up and remind a man that, between 1991 and 1997, he averaged 17.20. You can't say to a man who's played for England 52 times, 'Why weren't you better?'

So I ask him about the year he met Steve Bull. For most of the nineties, England's tours had been run along the old, amateur lines; players travelled abroad with just a tour manager and a physiotherapist. But as the decade went on, and their woes continued, the idea of taking a more professional route was, gradually, taking hold. Bull was the first sports psychologist assigned to accompany an England team on tour, and Ramprakash has said in the past that meeting Bull was a significant moment for him. 'Very much so,' he says. 'We had two or three chats and all of a sudden where Test cricket had been an ordeal for me, suddenly I had someone to speak to about it.'

It's strange to hear that he had no one to talk to before. He frowns a little, then nods. 'There's no doubt that I could have tried to seek out advice from people better before. I should have tried to do that.' It sounds, I say, like he thought he was supposed to handle everything by himself. 'That was me. I'm introverted and at that time I was very tunnel-visioned. It was all about the cricket. I wasn't very self-aware . . . and back then, there was an onus on the player taking responsibility for their own career. For want of a better expression, getting his shit together.'

He flashes a smile, and I giggle, possibly too much. I'm feeling pretty out of my depth. I had already torn a flaky chunk off my croissant and begun the messy process of dismemberment when I realised that Ramprakash was eating his raisin Danish with a knife and fork. And sitting opposite him as I am, there is one fact I can't avoid or, apparently, handle. Ramprakash is handsome. Properly handsome. He is, as Derek Zoolander would say, 'Really, really, ridiculously good-looking.' He has the eyes of the mysterious stranger in a daytime soap, the one with a hypnotic stare and a dangerous past. They can pierce you with a penetrating look, then crease into something impossibly winning. As for that smile, he keeps it in reserve, like a matinée idol. There's a wry, half-smile here, and a quick twinkle of teeth there. Then, when he unleashes the full thing, you feel like you've won the lottery.

I drag myself back to reality, and realise he's talking about the mid-nineties, the very period I have been scared to bring up. 'It had become an ordeal in terms of the nerves and the anxiety and the pressure I placed on myself,' he's saying. 'What I didn't do well enough was control my emotions.'

Before the days he learned to channel his simmering fury into an Argentine tango, his temper was rather less refined. Ramprakash, the man who could look so timid and out of his depth at the crease, was a champion bat-thrower. Dave Roberts, England's physio in the early nineties, remembers a time Ramprakash got out for a duck, marched straight into the dressing-room showers, bat in hand, and smashed every shower-head off the wall. And yet he sits here, so well-mannered, so suave. I can't imagine it, I tell him. I can't picture this raging, swearing alter ego, this desecrator of bathroom fittings.

'I didn't handle the bad days very well at all,' he says, thoughtfully. 'So on a good day I would be hardworking, professional, ambitious. And on a bad day I was intense, not able to express my true feelings, not able to see the big picture. And there's lots of bad days in cricket, that's inevitable.' Especially as a batsman, when a single good ball can scupper you? 'Exactly. So I think far too often I let things get on top of me and I didn't have a way of being philosophical about how to handle the ups and downs of a cricket career.'

As a fan, you're constantly agonising: what if the umpire had given that lbw against Steve Waugh? What if Atherton hadn't played at that McGrath delivery? How much happier would my life be, right now? We fans love to think that no one else understands what we're going through. And that's true because – quite rightly – no one cares. We create anxieties out of nothing, then inflate and indulge them. It's the kind of pathological behaviour that, if it concerned anything but sport, would see many of us assigned to a psychiatrist's care. But society accommodates it, so our friends and family are expected to tolerate our babyish reactions.

When England were on the slide, I was either snappish and petulant or self-pitying and morose. When they won, I was unbearably loud and filthily smug. I'm surprised I didn't lose friends during the height of my cricket mania, but I was probably worse to strangers. If some poor sap was introduced to me and told that I liked cricket, and then responded with a self-deprecating: 'I don't know much about cricket, I've always found it a bit boring,' they would be trapped in a blast of righteous anger and lectured about the joys of the game until they succumbed either to my argument or a protective coma.

Of course, for Ramprakash, cricket wasn't just a game, it was a career. It was his livelihood, his public identity, and the root of his ambition and pride. It was, in his words, 'all-consuming'. No wonder he was described as intense. 'If the team was losing, or I wasn't performing, I found it very difficult to relax away from the ground and make friends and have great times and stuff like that. I wasn't able to deal with the whole environment, really. I can recognise that now.'

Ramprakash had played cricket with Nasser Hussain and Michael Atherton since he was 14, but even their support wasn't enough. 'I remember in 1994, Mike Atherton put me at number three against West Indies. He placed a lot of belief in me by doing that, which was great, but I never really believed I should have been batting there because I hadn't established myself in the side.' He would fail, and fall into a rage, and push people away 'But if I was feeling down that I'd got out, the worst thing that you could do to me was ignore me and give me space. When I'd calmed down I really valued someone coming and talking to me.'

We pause to consider this vicious circle, and to eat our pastries. In the background, Elvis is singing a song about loneliness. Anyway, says Ramprakash, 1997, that's when he finally started to tackle the problem: 'I was drafted in to the last Test match at The Oval and I had dinner with Alec Stewart one evening before the game. I was talking about the difficulties of the pitch, but he was very certain: "You've got to go out and play your own way. If it's there to hit, hit it, and what will be will be." One of the things I've always admired about Alec Stewart and Graham Thorpe is they did exactly that.'

The pep talk worked – Ramps made 48, his first double-figure score in seven attempts. 'And we beat Australia, and then I got picked for the tour of West Indies.' Also on the tour was Steve Bull. 'I remember talking to him in the hotel in Guyana, and for me it opened up a new world.'

Bull listened to him without judgement. And then he did something that no one had done before – he offered him practical tips on how to control his thought processes. Ramprakash started listening to music that helped him relax. He began visualising the next day's play, 'so that when I'm going into bat now I've almost rehearsed it the night before, the fall of the wicket, the noise of the crowd, taking guard, facing the first ball.' He stopped thinking of batting as purely survival. He started picturing his idol, the West Indies legend Viv Richards, to help him remember the joy of batting, the freedom of scoring runs.

In the Guyana Test, Ramprakash top-scored in both England's innings. And in the next match in Barbados, seven years into his international career, he scored his first Test century. Ramprakash looked assured and in control from the moment he walked to the middle, the horrors of the past entirely erased. His 154 was a showcase of all the exquisite shots we England fans had so rarely seen him play, and his feet skipped under him like Fred Astaire's. He looked like a man who had fallen in love with his sport all over again.

At the time, I was having my own personal epiphany. I was going out with a boy. Tom was a medical student who lived upstairs from me, and I'd been smitten with him since my first summer at college. He was tall and attractive and brainy. We had middle-of-the-night conversations about things that felt profound and important. We played Frisbee. We went to parties where we drank 'cocktails' that were just vodka with orange juice and food colouring. I introduced Tom to my favourite poets, and he snuck me into a dissection class so I could stick my hand inside a human leg.

He wasn't perfect. My most romantic dream was of cosying up with my new boyfriend on a grass bank, a wicker hamper overflowing with Frazzles and champagne while a game of cricket proceeded in gentle fashion before us. Unfortunately, Tom didn't like cricket, and when I suggested an afternoon spent watching the university team take on Middlesex at Fenner's, he gave the idea short shrift. I went alone, and sat in the icy cross-blast that blew straight from the Arctic, while a student called Ed Smith scored 40. If anyone had told me then that Ed Smith would later play for England, I might have ditched Tom altogether.

Actually, Tom and I seemed to spend most of our time breaking up or getting back together. He was a reluctant boyfriend and I was an over-eager girlfriend; it was, in that respect, a disastrous match. But we had plenty else in common, including a mutual taste for the dramatic, and while our friends got tired of the tears and the stormings out and the passionate, unexplained reunions, we didn't. Nothing in my life had prepared me for the heaving, multi-coloured wash of feelings I was now experiencing. Love was, on the whole, a far more exhausting venture than I had pictured. I'm sure that a third of the tears I cried were just from fatigue.

By the summer of 1998, my relationship statistics were something along these lines:

College discos, dinners, parties: 50+
Actual dates where we went out, just the two of us, like grown-ups: 1
Postcards carrying what I thought were meaningful pictures (sent): 15
Letters containing what I thought was beautiful prose (sent): 6

Surprise bunches of flowers (received): 3

Conversations about our relationship: too many to count

Times he held my hair out of my face while I was sick: 2

Times I kissed one of his friends: 1

It was the last one that broke us up for good. I naively confessed to the crime, which had gone unseen by anyone else; I begged forgiveness and blamed the viciously magenta cocktails I'd been drinking. But Tom was growing tired of all the histrionics and, besides, this way he could spend his final year of university as a free man.

I had thought I knew what heartbreak was. All those times I had seen England's batting splinter like matchsticks, or their bowlers squander match-winning positions, I had assumed that nothing could hurt more. Now I knew: following England had merely been a training ground. Each time I'd seen Atherton dismissed in single figures had just been practice for this barrage of misery, of waking up each morning to discover new bits of my heart that hurt.

Cricket was, apparently, the only language in which I could process my pain. 'Tom rang,' I wrote in my diary. 'Managed to steer conversation to break-up and its stupidity. Tom executed superb backward defensive and blocked crease with stubborn refusal to talk about it.' Later I wrote him a long letter using various sporting metaphors to explain how I was feeling, forgetting that none of them would mean anything to him. His reply included a note of tender concern: 'I am a little worried at how your daily intake of sport seems to have affected you.'

In fact, it was the other way around. The break-up was seriously affecting my sporting consumption. England were playing South Africa in a home series, and were, for the first time in five years, being led by a new captain, Alec Stewart. But my heightened, headache-inducing emotions now eclipsed anything caused by their results.

The question of whether Tom would ever go out with me again was far more important than what would happen in the next session of play. When Atherton scored his first century in over a year during the first Test, I barely noticed; when they collapsed in a heap in the second, it didn't even leave a bruise.

The university year was over and I headed back home, where I spent a good week under a duvet and a cloud of self-pity. This was how I watched the third Test, a game that even the crowds had abandoned by the final day; the TV wide-shots struggled to hide a backdrop of empty stands. That was no one's fault but England's. It had been another rotten performance and, forced to follow on, they began the final session of the match six wickets down then lost Mark Ramprakash in the first over after tea. Defeat was inevitable. I kept watching anyway. Misery loves company.

Time passed. Two more wickets fell; the end was as nigh as Bill Nighy saying Night Night in his nightie. But Robert Croft stuck in his crease, clam-like, and Darren Gough, painfully curbing his usual flamboyant instincts, stayed with him for over an hour. It was the most boring innings Gough had ever played. It was also, perversely, the most gripping.

There were still seven overs of play remaining when Gough nicked to slip. Seven overs for the last man, Angus Fraser, to withstand: it was an eternity, especially with Allan Donald running in, his hair parted so he looked like the villain in a silent movie, missing only the pencil moustache. Every ball travelled smartly and purposefully towards Fraser's feet and the stumps behind them – it would only take one to get through, or catch him on the pad, and Croft's three-hour resistance would be in vain. After each delivery, Fraser turned and walked away from his crease, as if he didn't trust himself to spend one more second in front of his wicket than he had to. I leaned in to the screen, feeling suffocated.

In Donald's last over of the day, I held my hands out in front of me, silently counting off the deliveries on my fingers. Six. Five. Four. Three. Two. A thump – the ball hit Fraser's pad – the entire South African team were screaming. I was screaming too: 'No, no, NO!' The umpire's finger stayed down, the match was a draw, and I had entirely forgotten about Tom. England had dragged themselves out of the pit, and they had taken me with them.

My relationship with the team was changing. Take the captaincy, for instance. I had expected it to feel like an injustice and a betrayal, seeing Stewart lead the team out on to the pitch at the start of the summer, Atherton falling in behind, just one of the infantry. But it had turned out to be, at worst, a phantom ache. If I was honest with myself I actually felt a little relieved. When Atherton shed the burden of captaincy, a weight had fallen from my shoulders too. The outcome of each game suddenly felt far less personal. If England lost with Stewart as captain, I could always say, 'I told you so.'

Paul at Cover Point had given me a summer job, and while I was still eating a ham sandwich every day, I had at least grown enough in confidence to eat it in my colleagues' company. I sat listening to the conversations around me: serious, grown-up men with serious, grown-up opinions. I considered my own wide-eyed enthusiasm. It suddenly felt very unsophisticated. When Paul, for instance, asked, 'What's the score?', he said it coolly, not with the breathy urgency of someone arriving at the hospital to which a loved one has just been admitted. The men around me experienced cricket, it seemed, in a very different way. It wasn't that they cared any less than I did – if anything, they seemed more obsessed with the game. The guys at Cover Point talked about literally nothing else; they had fresh thoughts on the subject every moment, statistics easily at their recall, and could reminisce endlessly about past matches. But it was clear they didn't love the England team the way I loved it. Their love wasn't tender, or callow. Following England, to them, didn't mean blind, devoted loyalty to a cause; it meant demanding a team that could compete. You didn't prove your allegiance by defending your team's weaknesses, but by showing you knew better than anyone else how to fix them.

More than anything, though, they loved the game itself. They wanted to see close contests, and intriguing battles, and brilliant players showcasing their skills. It didn't matter who these skills belonged to, be they English or Indian, Sri Lankan or South African. I would come into the office to find them talking excitedly about yesterday's 'incredible game' and the 'brilliant result' and feel completely confused, because England hadn't been playing; it would turn out that they were talking about a World Cup qualifier between the Netherlands and the United Arab Emirates, in which a welder from Utrecht had scored a whirlwind hundred.

Personally, I was always so caught up in my team's results that the nature of the match – what Paul called 'the beauty of the game' – had never really occurred to me. To me, an exciting match was any that England looked like they were going to lose but managed to draw. The idea that I might be able to detach myself and appreciate a game for its sheer entertainment value was anathema.

The limits of this approach became apparent when I convinced *The Cricketer* magazine to let me report on a game for them. They sent me to cover the Princess of Wales Memorial Match between MCC and a Rest of the World XI at Lord's, in which a constellation of stars, from Sachin Tendulkar to Brian Lara, were playing. I remember sitting in the press box feeling confused, because I didn't know which side I was supposed to be supporting. My scribbled notes indicate that Tendulkar and Shivnarine Chanderpaul both hit sparkling hundreds but my piece for *The Cricketer* gave no detail on these, and concentrated, curiously, on the fact that the coin used for the toss was an 1848 florin. The magazine's editor generously published it anyway, and paid me £40. I asked Paul to read it and give me some feedback. 'Well,' he said, in his typically blunt manner, 'you didn't actually write about the cricket.'

But I was getting an education, because England's series against South Africa was turning out to be the sporting event of the summer. It's traditional to compare a topsy-turvy match to a rollercoaster ride, but this resembled the entire amusement park. The big drop of the second Test was followed by a nerve-shredding cling to the wall-of-death at Old Trafford. The fourth Test turned out to be more like a pirate ship, the advantage lurching back and forth between the teams, until England were set a target of 247 runs in the final innings.

They were making it, too. They were 82 for 1 when Allan Donald came back on for the final spell of the day. Fired up, he speared a ball into the ground that leapt across Atherton, just grazing the batsman's glove as he turned sharply out of its path. Atherton was still hopping gently on his back leg like a ballerina as the ball was caught by the wicketkeeper. Donald celebrated the catch, Atherton stood his ground, and South Africa appealed to umpire Steve Dunne. Dunne looked back at them like a chinless country parson from a Wodehouse novel asked to decide between two terrifying dowagers in the village cake contest. He glanced sheepishly down at his thumb. Atherton had got away with it.

Standing your ground when you know you are out is a contentious area. It is not technically cheating, but it does run contrary to some people's strongly held belief in the Spirit of Cricket. I had a vague, Sunday school notion of this Spirit. It was, I understood, like the Holy Ghost, a benign, bodiless godhead that looked over our shoulders, encouraging us to be better people; its high altar was Lord's, its priests were the MCC, and its commandments were written down by human hands in The Laws of Cricket. I tended to invoke its name when England's batsmen were getting bullied by West Indies fast bowlers, or when Shane Warne was over-appealing. But when it was a case of my favourite player doing the decent thing by admitting he was out, or keeping his head down and finishing the job, the Spirit of Cricket could kiss my ass.

Donald smiled at Atherton. It was not the smile of a man who has just encountered the appealing ambiguities of his sport and found them delightfully whimsical. It was the smile of a man who has just unmasked his wife's lover and is already plotting his murder.

The half-hour of play that followed was a battle for all time. Donald bowled the angriest spell of his life. You could measure his rising levels of rage in the increasing speed and viciousness of the deliveries, and on his face you could read each thought as it appeared: 'You cheating son of a bitch . . . I'm coming for you . . . I'm going to kill you.' Atherton, by contrast, was fiercely impassive, his mouth set in a straight, uncompromising line. After every ball he stayed where he was and stared his enemy down. He was the silent, fearless hero of a Western, and Donald was his arch-villain, raining curses and threats, and howling in rage when one of his henchmen, Mark Boucher, dropped a catch.

I re-watched the spell recently; it was not, as I remembered it, merely a procession of projectiles whizzing past Atherton's head. There was the one that Atherton hooked high in the air, chased by a sprinting Makhaya Ntini, his long legs straining, unsuccessfully, to reach the ball. There was a ball to Nasser Hussain that seemed at first sight to pass straight through the batsman's body like a Victorian parlour trick. It was an epic spell, and one on which an entire summer hung. If Atherton or Hussain succumbed, there seemed no doubt that England would be scuttled, and the series would be lost there and then.

They survived. England won the Test; they went to the final game scores level. This was entirely new to me: an evenly matched series against a major opponent where my team had a chance – at least 50 per cent! – of winning. There was something different about that England side, too. They had never looked so organised, so in-sync, so like a . . . *team*. They took nerveless catches. They bowled with purpose. They celebrated wickets with great swoops of synchronised joy.

The last game was a microcosm of the summer: subtle and shifting, its result a secret until the very end. For the first time, I found myself appreciating, not dreading, its unexpected reversals – the ebbs and swells, advances and retreats were adding an entirely new dimension to a game I already loved. I was like a music lover who had been entirely satisfied with the facile burps of an off-kilter brass band, now hearing for the first time the grand strains of a symphony. It was what Paul had been talking about – the beauty of the game, regardless of the result.

The result wasn't entirely irrelevant, of course. England won. They had beaten one of the world's top-three teams in a full, five-Test series: in the five years that I had followed them, it was their greatest achievement. I remember Ramprakash taking a catch in that final victory – an incredible one-handed effort, at full stretch – that seemed to sum up England's renewed confidence. In previous series you suspect he wouldn't have got near that ball, but here he was, a salmon snatching a fly in mid-air.

Ramprakash didn't score many runs that summer – his greatest contribution with the bat was a not-out half-century – but it's clear, as we chat, that the series still means a great deal to him. 'That win was massive,' he says. 'Because all summer we were told by our own media that we weren't even worthy of taking the same field as them. All we heard about was how good Jonty Rhodes was, Hansie Cronje, how quick Allan Donald was. This is from our own media! And to bounce back and win was really fantastic.'

I tell him how strange it had felt, the day that England won, that I had no ceremony of my own to perform, no friends to go out and mark the occasion with. It turns out, however, that even England's own celebrations were fairly limited. The domestic season wasn't over, Ramprakash reminds me. There were still county games to prepare for, so even this, their biggest win in five years, only merited a half-hour of drinking beer in the dressing-room.

'I think that group in '98 were probably the best England side I played in,' he says, thoughtfully. The team toured Australia that winter; they didn't win the Ashes back, but they did at least put up a fight, holding out for a draw in the first Test, and pulling off a surprise win in the fourth, entirely against the run of play. 'There was a lot of frustration building up in me that we were playing against this very, very good side and we couldn't quite get over the line against them,' Ramprakash recalls. 'You're always under the cosh. We were 2–0 down, got hammered at Perth and Adelaide. Every day you're up against it.'

So the win in the fourth Test in Melbourne has always held a particular place in his heart. 'I got a catch at square leg, and got very excited about it,' Ramprakash smiles. And his new, less anxious approach to batting was paying dividends: he scored 379 runs, more than anyone but his friend Hussain, and finally felt he was contributing to the team. 'I'd had some good games in the Caribbean, had a very tough series against South Africa, I then went away and topped the averages in Australia, so I had a great 18 months. I think I got over 1,000 runs in a calendar year at over 44, something like that, right?'

Of course he's right. Cricketers, for all that they pretend they can't remember their statistics, rarely get the good stuff wrong. Did he think he'd finally cracked it, I ask? That he'd conquered his demons to become a true England player, a deserving member of the team? 'I'm not sure I *ever* felt that I'd cracked it,' he says, shaking his head. 'I'll never forget, the next summer I got 0 in the first Test against New Zealand, which we won, and the second game we lost. After that I was going to be left out. I'd had 18 months in the side, topped the averages in the West Indies and Australia, and after two games, three innings, I was going to be left out. The only reason I wasn't was that Nasser broke his fingernail or something' – Ramprakash lets out a schoolboy snigger – 'so he wasn't in the side. I just look back at that and think, "You know what? I was never quite able to feel part of the England team."'

The words are charged but his face is calm. I realise that the thing that makes Ramprakash so compelling is that he still feels completely unknowable. He's honest about his England failings, open about his mental struggles, and yet I sense I'm only meeting the half of him. Somewhere beneath the surface charm is another person, someone you feel you'd be lucky to get to know.

I think of Hick, the man to whom the word 'enigma' was bonded like Araldite. He certainly didn't look particularly enigmatic: tall, square-set, a cartoon version of himself. My life's-worth of preconceptions are of a shy, silent man, someone who would rather smile a response than verbalise one. He made his debut in 1991 and played his last game for England in 2001, after a career that spanned 65 Tests and finished with both a better average and more first-class runs than Ramprakash. Still, I get the impression he's not quite as beloved. Maybe it's because he never did *Strictly*.

Hick moved to the Gold Coast four years ago, where he's using his experiences to help coach the next generation of Australian players. He has talked openly about his past, and put his own batting struggles down to the fact that, in his head, he was always playing catch-up.

As a Zimbabwean, it had taken him seven years to qualify to play for England, and during that time the great expectations surrounding him had mushroomed to Alice-in-Wonderland proportions. His first outings for England did not live up to them.

I ask Ramprakash about Hick – whether he ever compared himself with his similarly struggling teammate. Did they talk together about their common problems? Ramprakash shakes his head: 'I think it would have been a good thing if we had. We never had dinner, we never really worked together outside of the cricket ground. Graeme was very introverted, a lovely, lovely man. I wish I'd got to know him a lot better – that's a regret.'

We get up to leave. Ramprakash refuses to let me pay for our pastries, and disappears quietly to settle the bill. On his way back, the trio of ladies at the next table ask for their pictures with him. He smiles for the selfies and offers each woman demure but sincere thanks. They quiver lightly. He checks on the England score – they are closing in on a victory against Sri Lanka – and gives a small nod of satisfaction. Then he dons his elegant overcoat and shakes hands goodbye, leaving a small flutter of hearts behind him, mine among them.

It has become standard to measure both Ramprakash and Hick by what they failed to achieve, rather than what they did, and it's tempting to imagine that these older, wiser versions, who have learned the key lesson of perspective, might have spared their younger selves a lot of pain. But how do you tell a young sportsman playing for his country not to care so much? It's like telling a 19-year-old who's just been dumped by her first love that she needn't take it so hard.

Neither of them ever disavowed the game that caused them so much torment. Instead, they use their experiences as cautionary tales, advising and empathising with younger players in a way that no one helped them. It's a reminder that sportsmen don't have to be symbols, they can just be human beings. Ramprakash and Hick don't need or deserve pity, and sportsmen who don't have the careers we imagine for them don't necessarily spend the rest of their lives feeling unfulfilled. Sport must have its losers as well as its winners. All a player can hope to do is to enjoy the ride they have.

Chapter 10

The England cricket team are about to play in a World Cup. The game they played against Sri Lanka, the day I met Mark Ramprakash, was part of their warm-up campaign. They have been preparing meticulously for the tournament. A year ago, England played back-to-back Ashes series just in order to clear their schedule, and for the past six months they've played nothing but one-day cricket. It is hoped this will help them finally break their World Cup hoodoo – England have never lifted the trophy, and it is 23 years since they last made the final.

It is generally believed that England are rubbish at one-day cricket, but that isn't fair. Since the 'one-day international' was invented in the 1970s England have won half their games, which makes them, quite literally, average. They actually won the majority of their matches in the seventies and eighties; things didn't start to go downhill until 1992, the year they lost to Pakistan in their last World Cup final.

I've always found it hard to know how I'm supposed to feel about one-day cricket. Having two different kinds of game played on the same stage by the same players is unusual, especially for a team sport. Rugby has sevens, but the Six Nations squad doesn't turn out for it. Golf has fourballs and foursomes, but we only have to get our head round those every couple of years when the Ryder Cup comes along. Perhaps the closest comparison is men's tennis, where the majority of professional games played are three-set affairs that few people outside the tennis world even notice happening. This is why Andy Murray could win all the ATP tour titles he liked in Shanghai or Cincinnati and people still thought he was a failure until he won a grand slam. If Test matches are grand slams, and the Ashes is Wimbledon, then one-dayers would be the Rotterdam Open of cricket.

So should I care if England are no good at them? From the head-holding and hand-wringing that accompanies their continued failure at the format, I must assume that the answer is yes. It is not acceptable for a true fan to keep up only with the Test score, not when short-form cricket is such a prize commodity – especially in places like India, where cricket is loved and valued more highly than anywhere else. The one-day international informs and influences the longer game, and for that reason alone a fan should accord it respect.

On the other hand, even the most dedicated cricket correspondent doesn't expect us to care about every single encounter – there are so many one-day games in the calendar that we would soon wear ourselves out. That goes double now that Twenty20 games are also competing for our attention. The most miniature form of international competition is still, in cricket history terms, an infant. But it already has all-star leagues, top prize money and its own World Cup, so try as you may you can't get away from its toddler's screams.

When I started watching cricket in 1993, Twenty20 wasn't even a twinkle in a marketing man's eye. Home one-day series were played in traditional whites. England would start or finish the summer season with a few one-day bouts against whichever side was touring, and the winner would be handed something called the Texaco Trophy, which was clear and glass and looked like a piece of Soviet art. No one really remembered the results, although they were seen as a useful indicator of a Test side's form. For me, the one-dayers were bookends that held the Test matches in place. If England won, I was happy. If they lost, I worried what that meant for the Test side, while trying to convince myself it meant nothing at all.

My philosophical crisis began as one-dayers started to proliferate and self-seed throughout the sporting calendar. Tournaments popped up in the middle of summer, or in between winter tours. Some took place in entirely unexpected locations: England would suddenly be playing Zimbabwe in Australia, or India in the Middle East, or South Africa in Bangladesh. There were triangular tournaments, and quadrangular tournaments, and tournaments that geometry had never even considered. The one that really lost me was the 1998 KnockOut Trophy, which involved all the major cricketing nations in a World Cup-style format but was *not* the World Cup. It later became known as the Champions Trophy, even though teams did not need to be a champion of anything to compete in it.

You would have thought that all the extra cricket would have made me deliriously happy – I was the kind of young convert this fast-paced fun was supposed to attract. Instead I found it baffling. One of the things I loved most about cricket was the sense of adoption it brought, the way it wrapped me up into its long, intriguing and often bonkers history. But most one-day tournaments of the nineties had no heritage at all (*Wisden Cricketers' Almanack* called them 'a bewildering variety of competitions with no legitimacy beyond the profit motive'). You never heard people reminiscing warmly about a famous seven-match series of the past, or extolling the romance of the Akai–Singer Champions Trophy (unless you found a frisson in the shotgun wedding of an electronics company and a maker of sewing machines). Mostly, the games and their results seemed to be instantly forgotten, victims of an Orwellian march of progress.

Another problem that no one wanted to acknowledge was that one-day cricket could actually be more boring than a five-day Test. Limited-over matches were designed to cater for those with shorter attention spans. Their self-contained nature was meant to satisfy the sports lover's craving for an exciting finish. But the reality was frequently less thrilling than its inventors had imagined. When the opposition posted a good score, there was nothing more dull than watching England tramp stodgily after it, their defeat a foregone conclusion. And the spectacle was rarely any better when England batted first.

Nor did anyone but me seem to notice, or mind, that this supposedly simpler, more enticing version of the game could be off-puttingly complicated. There were ever-changing fielding restrictions that I never fully grasped (still haven't, if I'm honest), and an impenetrable mathematical formula for parsing rain-affected matches. The Duckworth/Lewis method has always, to me, sounded like an oxidisation process for metal ore, and about as fascinating.

But the one-day game continued to expand, and as the decade went on, various players considered specialists in limited-overs cricket were brought into England's side to try to improve results. There were batsmen with reputations for scoring quickly (not something you could accuse many England players of in those days). There were bowlers who practised the dark arts of 'death bowling', which stopped batsmen hitting out in the final overs of a game and included the ability to land the ball on a batsman's toes. 'Death bowlers' made them sound like an elite division of the SS, but they were often about as fatal as a Bourbon biscuit.

I always felt slightly sorry for the specialists who were invited to the England camp to perform their sole trick and were then ignored for the rest of the year, and sometimes the rest of their lives. The practice increased towards the end of the decade – from 1996 to

2001, 36 different players received their first one-day call-ups, and 12 of those never got a Test cap. I understood the reasoning for the division of duties but I still thought it a shame – the way they were drafted in to fix a problem, like a plumber on an emergency call-out, and never got to feel part of the bigger picture. I'm sure I was projecting my own fears upon them, but I spent an unhealthy amount of time worrying whether men like Neil Smith, Paul Franks and Vince Wells felt like second-class citizens.

Alan Mullally had no such aura of tragedy and, of all England's one-day players, he is the one I would most love to meet. He was not, strictly speaking, a specialist, since he played 19 Test matches for England and was intermittently called upon whenever they were short of a third seamer. (He was a left-armer, and we know how the selectors loved a leftie.) His Test career, however, was not his crowning glory. In fact, it was for some a symbol of all that was ineffective and underwhelming about English cricket in the 1990s. Which is why, if you Google Alan Mullally, the search results have titles like: 'crap cricketers' and 'nearly men' and 'WORST FIELDING EVER' – or 'did you mean: Alan *Mulally*?' (the latter turns out to be a very successful chief executive of Ford Motor Company).

On the other hand, he achieved something no other England player of his era got anywhere near. He was once ranked as the number-two bowler in the world at one-day cricket. The rating system that gave him the honour had been in place only two years and his tenure at the number-two spot was far briefer. But during those blissful few days he was poised between Glenn McGrath, an Australian machine with more World Cup wickets than anyone in history, and Muttiah Muralitharan, the Sri Lankan who boasts, among his many world records, an unbeaten 534 one-day wickets. Mullally, by comparison, finished with 63.

How he ended his career, a year later, still one of the world's official top-five one-day bowlers remains one of the great mysteries of English cricket, especially since he rarely played in a series-winning side. There was nothing particularly threatening about his bowling: he was an elastic surfer dude, long arms and legs stretched into rubbery motion as he approached the crease. His bowling was designated fast-medium, and even that flattered him a little, but I liked his enthusiastic energy and I always wanted to see him do well. I persuaded myself that Mullally could become a wicket-taking strike bowler, even when his figures contradicted me then laughed in my face (match figures of 2 for 142 should never give anyone heart). I suspect this was because he always seemed a nice guy and someone who thoroughly enjoyed playing for England.

Mullally was never much profiled in the papers while he was playing – that tells you all you need to know about how his international career was valued – but the couple of interviews that I've read with him since his retirement reveal a very funny man. (He was once told at an eye test he had 20/20 vision. 'I said, "Doc, have you seen me bat?"') He comes across as someone who, perhaps, was able to take the trials of his job a little less personally than his colleagues, someone whose genial personality helped him skim over the adversity and injustices that others found so paralysing. Perhaps that was his secret. Perhaps that's why he played for England such a surprising number of times.

For that reason alone it would be fascinating to hear his take on the England years, and I don't anticipate any trouble getting hold of him. He doesn't have an agent or a publicist and he sounds a pretty helpful sort – according to the *Southern Daily Echo*, two years ago he was helping out a tiny village team in Hampshire who couldn't get the numbers together. I've soon found a phone number and an email for him. I get a generic voicemail message when I call, so I send an email, and wait for a response.

Mullally began his international career at the age of 26; the ODI itself was only one year younger, and going through an identity crisis. Arriving on the scene in the seventies, it had been a rebel, wearing different clothes, refusing to play by the usual rules, and was, depending on who you asked, the bright future of cricket or a threat to its very existence. By the mid-nineties, however, it was part of the establishment itself, which made its efforts at counterculture rather forced. The game was at an awkward stage of its evolution, caught between two eras like synth music in the eighties: it was trying very hard to be cool and edgy, and achieving exactly the opposite.

For me, the most obvious manifestations of this were the outfits. Cricket has no special relationship with fashion; there is nothing stylish about cricket whites, and anyone who thinks they are sexy probably needs their head examined (though those people have, in the past, included me). But you get used to them. The costumes commissioned for a team's one-day outings, on the other hand, were each a fresh horror. One stripy monstrosity worn on an Australian tour was a high-concept and messy attempt to deconstruct the Union Jack (a curious idea since England play under the flag of the St George's Cross). There were other, more childish affairs that boomed ENGLAND in cartoonish writing across their chests – and also, on one occasion, vertically up the trouser leg.

Commentators loved to call the limited-overs game 'pyjama cricket', but even the nightwear rails in BHS looked better than this. It said something about how desperate the costumes were that even Adam and Ben Hollioake, the two brothers who had the most bona fide sex appeal of anyone to play one-day cricket for England in the 1990s, never found a mainstream following. If they had been dressed in anything other than those hideous outfits, I'm sure that more of my girlfriends would have taken notice.

But in 1996 I was still excited at the prospect of my first World Cup. It was particularly delicious because I could now boast that England's cricketers were better than their footballers – Graham Taylor's players hadn't even made it to the USA for the 1994 World Cup finals. (Two hundred teams competed for the chance to lift football's greatest prize, compared to the Cricket World Cup's 12, but that wasn't going to ruin my claim.) I was annoyed when I discovered that instead of getting to spend my half-term holiday immersed in *Test Match Special* and setting up camp in front of Ceefax, I was going skiing with my family. The vague assurances I had won from my parents that there would be some way to get longwave radio in an Austrian Alpine chalet were never redeemed.

My faithful friend Alex had promised to save me cuttings from the newspapers while I was away, and when I got home there was a brown envelope containing all the news of the tournament so far. And the news was this: my team were in terrible shape. Picking through the reports, I felt like a minister perusing a brief on an overseas territory that was slipping towards military chaos. 'Atherton challenged to restore order,' said one headline; 'England prove nothing,' added another. The team had lost to New Zealand, and were run close by the Netherlands. Atherton had dropped himself down the batting order, where he was still scoring no runs. When England lost to South Africa, they could only scrape through to the quarter-finals as the lowest qualifying team.

I didn't get to see any of the games until a month or two after the competition had finished. I was back at my holiday job at Cover Point, where Paul was making a highlights video of the tournament. There were hundreds of hours of unedited footage to be logged, so he sent me to a rented editing suite in St Albans, where I was required to watch some of the games, noting each boundary and wicket, and any exciting or controversial moments. I sat in a tiny grey booth surrounded by dusty Betamax tapes, clipboard in hand, scratching out timecodes and annotations longhand. 'Brilliant boundary!' I would write. 'Damien Martyn smashes it through the covers for four. One of the best shots of the match – definitely worth watching!' After a while, Paul wondered what was taking me so long and demanded to see my work. 'You're just supposed to write "4" or "wicket"!' he exploded.

It was here, in my drab little cupboard, that I encountered the most exciting one-day cricket of my life. The 1996 tournament was held in India and Sri Lanka, and was the first time I had seen any subcontinental cricket at all. When the Sri Lankan pinch-hitter Sanath Jayasuriya batted against England in the quarter-final, his entire innings felt like a highlights reel. He clubbed ball after ball to the boundary, their trajectories drawing giant bell-graphs in the sky. He even landed one on the roof of the pavilion.

I knew nothing of Sri Lanka before that tournament – I couldn't have even pointed it out on a map. But there was something positively magical about their cricket team. They were led by Arjuna Ranatunga, who looked more like a pizza chef than a professional athlete. They had players who were, quite literally, head and shoulders shorter than their opponents (causing an Australian commentator to remark at one stage: 'That's a big wicket for the little Sri Lankans.'). But they were deft and bold, adaptable and resourceful, and however far they fell behind in a match they just kept coming back.

I had a particular fondness for Aravinda de Silva, having been at Lord's to see his brilliant Cup-final century against Lancashire the year before (his team, Kent, had lost, which was why I was able to be magnanimous about it). First against India, and then in the final against Australia, he rescued his team from unpromising situations with his attractive fast scoring. By the time that Ranatunga hit the World Cup-winning runs on my TV monitor and waddled down the pitch to celebrate with De Silva and their teammates, my eyes were misty with tears. This, I realised, was a kind of cricket I had never seen played before.

My parents were both good at sports – they met playing hockey – but managed to produce two daughters with no sporting aptitude whatsoever. Lacrosse, tennis, sprinting, swimming, cross-country . . . my sister and I were mediocre at them all. One holiday we took a boat up to the Scottish lochs and my dad was confident enough that one of us would be a natural at waterskiing to invest in child-size skis and wetsuits. He sat me down on the edge of a jetty and put a towrope in my hand. I loved my dad, I trusted him entirely, and his confidence in me was infectious. I had watched him gliding magically and thrillingly along behind the boat on his skis, and if he told me that I could do the same, I believed him. The unusual rubbery costume seemed in itself to give me a special anointing.

'You won't go too fast, will you, Dad?'

'It's actually easier if I go faster,' he replied. 'That way you're less likely to fall over. Now just hold on to this, and when the rope runs out of slack, you'll feel a little pull.'

I didn't know what slack was, but I took hold of the towrope and watched him return to the boat and take the wheel. A minute or so later, I was jerked violently off the jetty and deposited face down in a freezing cold loch. Luckily the shock was kind of numbing. When Dad came back to pick me out of the water, he told my mum loudly and convincingly that I hadn't hurt myself, and I believed that too. But I didn't try waterskiing a second time, and, after what she'd just witnessed, my sister wouldn't try it once.

So no, I was no sportswoman. Once I started spending most of my waking moments thinking about cricket, I guess it wasn't so strange that I wanted to have a go at it myself. What *was* strange was that I was convinced I was going to be good at it. Before I had ever so much as held a cricket ball – and against all the evidence accrued in my PE classes – I pictured myself as a natural fast bowler. I don't know why I didn't hanker to be a batter; maybe batting just seemed too technical. I suspect, however, it was my love of theatre that drew me to bowling. Nothing else is quite as dramatic as the moment you hear the clunk of the stumps. I wanted to experience that moment of wicket-taking ecstasy, to punch the air and roar like a lion, not to inch my way methodically towards a decorous hundred.

At 15 I told a teacher that I would like to learn to play cricket, and asked if the boys' school next door might give us some lessons. My request, assumed to be a thin attempt to intermingle with boys, was refused – but later, in the sixth form, I was told that if I could find a group of girls who were interested we would be allowed through the infamous black gates for an emphatically single-sex nets session. No one else I knew actually wanted to play cricket but a few friends agreed to come along and make up the numbers for me.

We were met by a tall man who had obviously drawn the short straw in the teachers' lounge. He led us in some desultory stretches, then pointed at a heap of kit. My friends and I spent a good amount of time knee-deep in pads and helmets, working out how to strap ourselves in. By the time we were ready a couple of boys who had stopped to gawp at the unprecedented sight of females in their nets had been co-opted to help. Today, of course, there's a positive evangelism about teaching girls to play cricket; urgent response teams swoop into schools at the first sniff of interest and unroll a missionary programme for potential converts. But this was not that. The laconic teacher and his sniggering aides found the scene in front of them openly amusing, and what instruction they did give was centred, notably, on the prettiest of our bunch.

Worse, I discovered that there was something I didn't know about cricket, after all. And that was pretty much everything. Standing at a bowling crease for the first time, I couldn't understand why the other end was so far away. I knew the length of a cricket pitch by heart, but 22 yards never looked this long on the telly. The corridor of green telescoped away from me, and far in the distance, the stumps winked back, impossibly small.

It was like being trapped in a nightmare designed by M. C. Escher. I ran up full of vim, but every time I let go of the ball, it thudded down just a few yards from my own toes. It would bounce a couple of times, then roll gently towards the feet of whoever was batting. Sometimes it came to a stop halfway there, so they had to walk over and tee it back to me. The teacher eventually came over and told me to let go of the ball earlier. After that I was lobbing it all over the place – sometimes in the vague direction of the batsman, but more often into neighbouring nets. I felt cheated. Where was the thrill? Where was the sense of power? The teacher explained that you had to start slow, but I didn't want to. What was the fun in slow?

That was our first and last net at the boys' school. I was the only girl who might have pushed for more, but the experience had left me low. My beloved Alex, who believed in me more than anyone of her intellect had a right to, thought I should give playing another go, so she took me along to a friendly church match her brother and her dad were playing in. It was, she promised, an entry-level game where novices were welcome. Everyone had a turn to bat; when it was mine, I put on a pair of pads that reached halfway up my thighs and were heavy as sandbags. I wondered how I was supposed to run in them. It turned out not to be a problem – I couldn't manoeuvre the giant piece of tree in my hands, either, and I was out lbw to my first ball. The church folk generously let me try again. The next delivery hit my stumps.

So that was it, for a while. I was neither bowler nor batsman. Instead, I poured my frustrated energies on to the rounders pitch. I had enjoyed the game since the days when we lived in the countryside, and Dad used to mow the traditional diamond into the long grass on the common land outside our door. It never really counted as sport, because you were supposed to be nice to everyone, give endless second chances, and bowl the ball slowly to make it easier to hit. But, inspired by my cricketing idols, I started to hone my underarm bowling. Fast-arm-over-the-wicket might have been beyond me, but I learned to be quite skiddy when facing a kid holding a piece of rolled-up newspaper. At youth group, and later at university, I would stick my hand up and ask whatever alpha male was skippering my team if I could maybe 'have a go at bowling?' I would then take a hustler's pleasure in skipping to the mark and shooting the ball at the batter's knuckles.

I loved fielding even more. I was used to hearing the adage 'girls can't throw' from Jez, Chris and Ben (to be fair, several of my girlfriends seemed intent on proving it true). But I *could* throw, and I could catch too. Not just the odd running catch out in the deep – the boys always loved to banish the females to the far reaches of the field where they couldn't be a handicap – but close, reflex catches. I found it exhilarating, the jumping without thinking, the way your body seemed to know where to go before your brain did.

Knowing I had no skill as a batsman or a bowler, I decreed myself a specialist fielder. From now on, this was the role I filled in the imaginary cricket team I belonged to. Taking catches was the only thing I could do that replicated the experience of my cricketing heroes, and I luxuriated in each memory, replaying them in my head, transplanting them from the rounders field to the slips or short leg, painting in a backdrop of Old Trafford or the MCG. My favourite was the time a ball had disappeared over my head so fast and high I never even saw it – I just leapt and stuck out my arm, and was surprised as the rest of my teammates when I looked at my hand and saw a dirty white sphere stuck in it. I have no idea whether we won that game, but I do know that I ran around for the rest of the afternoon as if the fate of humanity rested on my efforts. It was probably the closest I've ever come to feeling like a real sportsperson.

Perhaps it's because my own athletic career was so derisory that I have always felt so in awe of my cricketing heroes, whatever their individual shortcomings and however poor their results.

Meanwhile, I still haven't heard from Alan Mullally. I've asked a former teammate for advice on where to reach him, and he's told me that Mullally now lives in Australia. 'We haven't been in touch since last year,' he says. 'I don't think he does email either. You know, since he's not been well.'

I didn't know, I say.

'Well, he's had a few problems.' He doesn't use the word, but somehow I can read it in the tone of his voice: depression. 'I think he's been quite open about it.'

It turns out he has. Later that morning, I find a radio interview that Mullally gave with a Hampshire radio station in 2013, just after the England batsman Jonathan Trott had left an England tour with 'a stress-related condition'. Mullally talked about his own experiences, which were triggered by his retirement, a divorce and the loss of his father. He said he could empathise with Trott: 'There's days when you don't want to get out of bed. There's days when you don't want to eat, you've no motivation, and it's like a big dark cloud over your head . . . For me, retiring from the game [was] a big loss, from being with the lads seven days a week for your whole life.'

Mullally had always wanted to play for England. Born in Southend to an Irish dad, he was taken to Australia by his parents when he was young, so he grew up and learned his cricket in Perth. But he replanted himself in the shires, and had spent ten years on the county circuit, just another invisible servant of the bowling fraternity, when a sports reporter called him and asked how he felt about being picked for England. It was the first Mullally had heard of his Test call-up. For the next five years, he was someone England turned to whenever they felt the need for economy over excitement.

At college, Ben and I felt extremely affectionate towards him, even as we nicknamed him 'the Dreaded Alan Mullally'. We were happy to see him firing his stuff from around the wicket and wide of off stump – sure, he was never going to take wickets from there, but at least the batsmen couldn't reach it to hit it. It was his batting, though, that we really loved to watch. Mullally was literally the worst batsman in the world. In his 27 Test innings, he made 12 ducks. But that didn't stop him trying – he walked to the crease in a spirit of adventure, determined to at least attempt to bat in the heroic way he pictured in his head. He was almost inevitably unsuccessful.

As I came to terms with supporting a losing team, I had begun to appreciate some of the innate comedy in England's performances and predicaments. The team's failings were so suffused with the surreal and the silly that, once you started to relax and take it all a bit less seriously, there was plenty to entertain you: Phil Tufnell cocking up a throw from deep in the field; Ian Salisbury trying so hard to spin the ball that he landed it on midwicket. Mullally's batting was of the same ilk; even Mum, who couldn't bear to be in the room for a mid-innings collapse, would ask me to call her back from the kitchen when Mullally was in.

This made it all the more impressive when his most memorable contribution in Test cricket arrived not with the ball but the bat. After a run of five ducks in seven innings, and with the game on a knife-edge, Mullally hit an unexpected 16 off an increasingly irate Glenn McGrath in an Ashes Test in Melbourne. England won it, in the end, by 12 runs, making Mullally a bona fide hero. His career taught me a valuable lesson: that it was possible to enjoy both your strengths *and* your weaknesses, and to discover who you are through your failures as well as your triumphs. That it was enough, sometimes, just to go and have fun.

In my university years I learned to adopt that philosophy and tried everything, regardless of how good or bad I was at it. I tried drinking Guinness (terrible). I tried dancing (better). I tried being a flirt (pretty good), being a socialite (awful) and being a domestic goddess (genuine disaster). I even tried being a footballer for a season. The only kind of football I had played before was the no-rules game at youth group, which bore the same relation to soccer as those medieval versions banned by royal proclamation in the Dark Ages for causing too many deaths. It had trained me in an aggressive, combative style, and I would no doubt have been a snappish midfielder with a nasty edge if I had ever got close enough to tackle anyone. Thankfully, my fitness levels did not allow that.

Come the summer, the women's football team reformed as the women's cricket team. It was a chance to redeem my aborted playing career, and with new confidence – the confidence to be terrible at stuff – I signed up to play for them. I practised bowling a tennis ball at a tree on the paddock at the bottom of the college quad; the tree's trunk was three times wider than a set of stumps, which made it a particularly encouraging target. We only made it through one round of the inter-collegiate tournament in the end – the opposition teams had actually played cricket before – but I somehow snagged a couple of wickets with my loopy lobs, and when we rounded off the summer with an impromptu game on the paddock, I took an unforgettable hat-trick against the tree.

Of the many identities I tried out at college, lackadaisical student was probably my favourite. After all those years of swotting at school I had finally cut loose and, by the final year of college, I found I needed to cram two years' worth of learning into a few months. It was the summer of 1999, and England were hosting the World Cup; instead of researching the teams (and ways to get tickets), I was forced to spend the last weeks of my university education in the library, catching up with the novels, plays and poetry collections that I had previously only pretended to read.

Maybe it was the stress of exam term that turned me sour, or maybe the sense that I had been cheated out of a pan-global cricket tournament taking place in my own country. Either way I decided to effect a total and utter disinterest in it. Friends who asked my opinions on the tournament got a sarcastic remark about the 'so-called Carnival of Cricket' (the official tagline for the tournament); their well-meaning inquiries about England's prospects would receive a sceptical snort.

There was nothing wise or sophisticated about my cynicism. It was true that England hadn't looked in great form before the tournament, but despite their many one-day deficiencies they had a surprisingly good record on home turf, so much so that my June copy of *Wisden Cricket Monthly* predicted that England would finish top of their group and make it to the semi-finals. As it happened, however, my grumpy outlook was almost immediately vindicated. The World Cup kicked off a week before my first exam, and its opening ceremony, which consisted of a few fireworks sputtering in the rain, was widely derided as the most embarrassing and underwhelming attempt at sporting pageantry ever seen.

When England beat Sri Lanka and Kenya in their first two games, I maintained my toffee-nosed distance. Alan Mullally was having a golden spell – he took a wicket in his very first over of the competition – and his parsimonious bowling style was serving him well. He was man of the match when England beat Zimbabwe and seemingly secured their passage into the next stage of the tournament. Only a defeat in their final first-round game, and Zimbabwe recording an unlikely, first-ever win against South Africa, could stop them.

For one of those events to occur was a misfortune, but both happening was sheer carelessness on England's part. When news of the Zimbabwean upset reached their dressing-room, the team seemed utterly undone: their batting toppled to India, and when Mullally was last man out, England were humiliatingly short of a modest target. The hosts' role in their own World Cup was over before the tournament anthem (by Dave Stewart of the Eurythmics) had even been released. There were 16 matches still to play, and England would be involved in none of them; it was, without question, England's worst World Cup performance. I felt a huge and perverse pride that I had adopted such a doomy demeanour from the start.

Four World Cups later, England are about to outdo themselves. They have already lost three of their four group games in Australia and New Zealand – even their sole win against Scotland had a wobbly moment – and those six months of intensive preparation are looking like a terrible waste of their time. I wake to increasingly dire despatches from *Test Match Special*. Sometimes, when I turn on the radio, I hear the cheerful tones and muted Aussie accent of Alan Mullally.

I've still not managed to reach Mullally for a chat. There was a brief conversation on Twitter before the tournament, but the Skype call we arranged rang out and after that he went quiet. I take the hint, eventually, and stop bothering him. I enjoy his commentary stints, though. It turns out he's a natural: a fresh, thoughtful voice among the old-timers, dispensing wisdom in a wry, relaxed style. He doesn't grumble his disapproval or lay into players. He seems to appreciate the positive in a team's performances, and to remember that it is, after all, only a game.

Maybe that perspective is what's needed. England lose to Bangladesh, and crash out before the knockout stages even begin. It is an abysmal and ignominious end to their campaign. My Twitter timeline ticks over with jokes referencing 1999; several people ask if the World Cup song will be in the shops at the end of the week. The dishonour of being England's worst World Cup team has finally passed on, and the shibboleth that England are a terrible one-day side continues.

Chapter 11

It is generally agreed by historians that English cricket reached its lowest point on 22 August 1999. Humiliated in the World Cup, the national team had regrouped under a new captain, Nasser Hussain, to face New Zealand in a four-Test series. New Zealand were unofficially the worst team in the world, thanks to *Wisden Cricket Monthly*'s recent invention of a world championship table, which ranked Test nations in order for the first time. When Hussain's men lost to them 2–1, it was England who slumped to the bottom of the pile and the *Sun*, echoing the *Sporting Times*'s famous obituary of 1882, ran a front page announcing 'the death of English Cricket'.

I missed it all. At the moment Nasser Hussain was getting booed on the balcony by his own supporters, I was on my way to the Grand Canyon. I had gone on a road trip across America with Ben and Tom and our university friends, a final adventure before the real world came calling. In those pre-wifi years, a trip to the US could still isolate you from home – a half-hour at an internet café was an unaffordable luxury, and we sent postcards, not emails – so I couldn't keep up with the cricket. The truth was, I didn't even want to.

Since cutting the cord on the World Cup, I had enjoyed the freedom from the tyranny of fandom, of no longer needing to care how England were doing. For years I had lived with feelings I'd long ceased to consider peculiar. One was the heavy responsibility I felt to know the state of any ongoing match. My body used to spike with dread if someone asked me the latest score and I didn't know. Was it a fear of being disgraced, of being told I wasn't a *proper* fan? Or was it existential shock, the terror of discovering that my team existed independently of me? Either way, that summer, the habit was broken. For a while I felt the need to justify myself with defensive tirades – 'who cares who they're playing, they won't bloody win!' – but I eventually came to understand that no one cared that I was ignorant of England's first-innings performance.

As for the team themselves – and this was stranger – I didn't miss them at all. I let them drop, these men who had been both idols and imaginary friends, without a second thought. Like the callous child who stops believing in fairies, I didn't even notice as their Tinker Bell light began to die. My summer was just as fun without them: arguably more so, since I didn't have to drag their failures around with me like a purgatorial rite. Life was good: I had a degree; I had the best friends in the world; and I had enough money to get me from New York to LA, so long as I slept in a tent and ate nothing but Taco Bell. I was a grown-up in a grown-up world, and I didn't need the proxies of my childhood any more.

Revelling in this revolutionary state of independence, I moved back in with my parents. I had big plans – a place at drama school, a life on stage – that could only be pursued from the security of a rent-free bedroom. My mother wasn't known for her indulgent parenting and had always boasted of her hardline position on adult children in the family home ('when they're 21, they're gone!') but it turned out it was all bluff. Now she had lost Kate to university she was in less of a hurry to fling her fledglings out of the nest and see if they survived the drop.

In the summer, my parents had relocated from Luton to Bath, and while Dad had grown up in Bristol, Mum and I knew nothing of the West Country. Life was suddenly very different, but not necessarily in a bad way. I applied for drama schools, and went to auditions, and wondered how long it would take me to get an agent. In the meantime I worked behind the counter at Thornton's and subconsciously adopted the local burr. I dated a nice man who lived in London, worked for a bank, loved the opera and knew how to julienne a carrot, all of which I considered the most heavenly sophistication. I had lost all my friends to the post-uni diaspora, but I discovered for the first time that my dad was really excellent company. We became cinema buddies, went to pubs together, had dinner dates. In the course of a few months I got to know him better than I had in the first 21 years of my life.

The novelty of my situation was enough to keep me happy. Within a couple of months I was convinced that the boyfriend, with his bachelor pad and his beautiful manners, was my future husband; I didn't notice that he was less excited to visit me than he was to see my parents. I remained equally blind about my acting ambitions: the letters of rejection should have hinted that my talents lay elsewhere, instead they convinced me that my greatest gift was being thwarted. All those years of watching Atherton had left their imprint – a stubborn refusal to admit defeat.

I did envy my friends, however. The organised ones were already installed in grown-up-sounding positions in the civil service, accountancy firms or the BBC; Tom and the rest of the medical students were enjoying a second student life in training hospitals. Even Ben, who I could normally rely on to be even less ambitious than me, had got a job in London and forgone his mum's incredible cooking to kip on a friend's floor.

So I found a more sedentary job in the offices of a greetings card company, doing something that involved sending faxes and processing orders. I still couldn't tell you exactly what I was achieving, but I know that when I got it wrong one day – I accidentally shipped several thousand teddy bears to the wrong country – I was forgiven (but the unlucky teddies were incinerated as soon as they reached land). That incident aside, it was a pretty undramatic environment. Our data-entry computers were the kind where green numbers blinked at you from a black screen, so we didn't have the internet, although back then there wouldn't have been anything to buy on it anyway.

All this quickly reinstated my need for cricket. Maybe I could be blasé about the game while the Grand Canyon and the Empire State Building were in my eyeline, but with nothing to occupy my brain but basic administration, I started sneaking my pocket radio into work. It sat hidden in my desk drawer like an alcoholic's stash of vodka miniatures, waiting for the quiet moments I could take a guilty draw through my earphones. My colleagues were understanding and created an early warning system for when the boss walked by. In some ways, it was no surprise those poor bears met a fiery doom.

England's results were not showing notable improvement under the new coach and captain. The team won a single Test on their winter tour, thanks to the South Africa captain's strange and surprising offer to manufacture a run-chase on its final day. Forfeiting an innings was the kind of old-school custom that just didn't happen in the modern era – I had only read about it in books – and I was thrilled to see it put into practice. (My nerdy side had always loved the more arcane laws of the game and I secretly longed to see more people being 'timed out' on their way to the crease.) Since Hansie Cronje, the South Africa captain, was well known to be a Christian, I interpreted his gesture as both generous and gentlemanly. He clearly had a great sense of perspective about the game, and a strong moral core.

As for Nasser Hussain, I didn't know much about him at all. He had been a senior member of the side and Atherton's vice-captain for several series, but I never paid much attention to him until he became captain. Perhaps it's because I was so fond of Graham Thorpe, England's number four; Hussain, whose position switched between three and five, seemed merely an adjunct to him in my mind. When I did think of Hussain, the first image that came to me was a spiky piece of quartz that my dad kept in his study as a paperweight; he had a kind of jagged energy when he batted, and a large pointy nose.

In fact, of all the cricketers I've planned to meet Hussain is the one that I'm still, as an adult, a bit wary of. He has never made a secret of his impatient temper, or his inability to suffer fools. On my bookshelf sit the autobiographies of my three England captains of the 1990s. Alec Stewart's is called *Playing for Keeps*, a jaunty schoolboy term redolent of a life of locker-room promises and old-fashioned values. Michael Atherton named his *Opening Up*, an admission of the stubbornly standoffish front he always presented. Hussain's book is called *Playing with Fire*.

These days Hussain runs with the pack of former England captains in the Sky commentary box, where he's an excellent analyst and an acerbic wit. When he started, his combative streak was obvious in his regular on-air arguments with Ian Botham, although he seems to have mellowed into the role and laughs more easily now. Still, his life has been spent dissecting the game with some of the best cricketers in the world. My teenage interpretation of it might not be one he has a lot of time for.

As I disembark the train at Chelmsford, a large banner welcomes me to the home of Essex County Cricket Club, and a stern-faced Alastair Cook eyeballs me as I descend the stairs to the taxi rank. Hussain has picked an inn on the outskirts of his village for our encounter, and it's clearly one where he's known well. On my arrival the receptionist politely tells me they're not open, but when Hussain gets there he simply sweeps through to a corner table and we're soon presented with steaming cups of coffee. I send up a silent prayer that one day I will have such a decisive manner. That assertiveness notwithstanding, he's less intimidating in the flesh than I had expected: tall but not imposing, and the baseball cap he's wearing seems to soften his features. I tell him I've been reading his book and he says that's probably a good move: 'It's more likely to be factually correct than my wine-damaged brain cells,' he laughs.

Hussain is wearing training gear – he's doing some coaching this afternoon and it has got him thinking about when he was a kid. His younger son has a trial for the county under-13s tomorrow and he can remember going through the same: the peer pressure, the way you always knew exactly how well your friends and rivals were doing. 'Everyone says, "You must have known you were going to play for England,"' he says. 'But when you're young all you're worried about is getting into the next side.' From the age of ten the young Hussain was constantly comparing himself with the country's top schoolboy cricketers: Mark Ramprakash, Michael Atherton. 'Ramps was the one we all wanted to be: good looking, talented, smashed it everywhere, had the dance moves, everything.'

Atherton, meanwhile, was both a hero and a friend: 'I always admired Ath, even at a young age. Very straightforward, honest sort of guy. I tend to look at people and wonder, "Will they go off and stab you in the back? Are they a bit two-faced?" Ath never had a bad side in him.' He does find Atherton's reputation for seriousness amusing: 'Crikey, we had fun. Me, him and Brian Lara used to get on pretty well together, because we'd played against each other since we were boys. I remember, after an England game, Ath wrestling Lara in a pub in Trinidad, a good, alcohol-fuelled, rolling round the floor.'

I wonder whether knowing that at the time would have dashed my belief in the awesome dignity that accompanied the England captaincy. Hussain is full of stories that reveal just how limited my concept of the England dressing-room really was. He talks candidly of strops and sulks, and foolish things said in the heat of battle that caused furious stand-up rows. I had always pictured the England dressing-room as one becalmed by failure, a place of quiet gloom and the occasional eruptive celebration. The place Hussain describes is closer to a room full of 13-year-olds stuck inside one rainy break-time. Here's Gough, showing off again, while Caddick complains loudly that people don't like him; in the corner, Atherton is giggling irrepressibly at someone else's misfortune, and Thorpe storms out, slamming the door in a huff.

Hussain notices my goggle-eyes. 'Don't be surprised,' he says. 'You want to do well for your family, yourself, your fans, and you're losing, people are niggling each other, the papers are slagging you off, Shane Warne's giving you a little dig in the field . . . every little thing becomes so huge, and people react.' Himself as much as anyone, he admits. He once got his hand stuck in a locker door after punching his fist through it.

By the time the England captaincy reached him it was, if not a poisoned chalice, then one that had been passed around so much you knew you might pick up some nasty germs. It had diminished the reputations of previous incumbents Gooch and Atherton, while Stewart, who had actually won a series against a major Test nation while in charge, had been summarily dismissed after losing in Australia. I ask Nasser if he was nervous about accepting the job. 'I think they were more fearful than I was,' he replies. 'You speak to someone like Gus Fraser. He thought: "What the hell are they giving him the captaincy for? Nutter! Short fuse! Quite a selfish player as well . . ." and I was, I was worried about my game.' It was his way, he says, of coping with the overwhelming number of defeats. 'There's a siege mentality sets in, a bit of self-preservation.'

Atherton has written of his old friend that Hussain became a nicer person after he assumed the captaincy, because it finally dealt with his personal ambition. Still, their styles could not have been more different. Where Atherton had been doughty, self-contained, impassive, Hussain was a geyser of emotion. Gimlet-eyed and hawk-nosed, his very physiognomy announced a ruthless intensity, and you needed no degree in body language to read his mood in the field. After the stiff-lipped brigade of Atherton and Stewart it was strangely comforting to see a captain look as furious as I felt at a bowler's costly spell. Atherton's coolness was something I admired, but could never emulate; Hussain, however, seemed to feel things as keenly as I did. When other England players looked glum or resigned in defeat, Hussain just looked angry.

'Partly that's the person I am,' Hussain agrees, 'and partly, at the beginning of the captaincy, I had to be.' He's a sports fan, he says; he knows how infuriating it is to watch your football team – in his case, Arsenal – do a bad job. It was important to him that no one took defeat with anything other than bad grace. 'We should be angry if we're not performing. We *should* be angry with each other. I'm not looking for matey-matey. Speak to Michael Holding: the great West Indies side were all arguing with each other. And that Australian side that used to beat us all the time – Shane Warne can tell you who hated who. You'd think they were all very friendly. They weren't.'

Still, he says, the rage wasn't the whole story. Hussain's captaincy was no one-man show; it was a well-scripted double act with England's new coach Duncan Fletcher. Sitting silently on the balcony, his mouth folded down by the soft curvature of his jowls, the Zimbabwean always looked to me like a man on the verge of falling asleep. Occupying the same spot where David Lloyd could manufacture more static energy than a Van de Graaff generator, Fletcher maintained the stillness of a stone Buddha.

And it worked: while Hussain was, in his own words, 'effing and blinding and kicking and doing the Alex Ferguson' the coach was preserving the yin to his yang. 'The actual harsh words went out in Fletch's room over a quiet cup of tea.'

In the summer of 2000, Hussain's men lost their opening match against West Indies, but finished the Test series 3–1 winners, England's first victory over them in 31 years. In the official history of that summer, as set down in *Wisden* and the like, you will read about the opposition's fragility, and the hugely advantageous bowling conditions. They are not what I remember. What I recall is England's verve in the field, and the sweet sense of revenge as their bowlers humiliated the West Indies batsmen, bowling them out for 54 at Lord's, and for 61 at Headingley. It was the first time I had seen an England team do to others what had so long been done to them: make the foe look completely inept. And there were other firsts, miracles I could never have imagined: Andrew Caddick taking four wickets in a single over; England winning a Test in two days; Brian Lara averaging under 27.

While England's fortunes were improving, mine were not. I lost the sophisticated boyfriend after a disastrous house party where I drank a considerable quantity of absinthe and had to be put to bed in tears. The drunken scene itself was not what caused the end of our brief relationship, but the fact that I'd hiccupped through my sobs that I wanted to marry him. I woke up the next morning with the awful realisation that I'd blown it; for the next few weeks he treated me with the kind of extreme courtesy you normally reserve for the elderly and the unwell. He was too courteous to actually dump me, but he did stop visiting shortly after.

My hopes for drama school had also been dealt a blow by the fact that I had failed to get into any. My enthusiastic appeals to agents continued to receive polite form-letter replies. I landed a couple of auditions for touring theatre companies, and built entire imaginary careers around each before I was turned down. Thanks to the miracle of human optimism, each new failure remained both surprising and disappointing. Growing up, I had been taught I was capable of anything; becoming a grown-up meant learning I wasn't.

I had been so convinced that I was going to act for a living that it hadn't occurred to me to *want* to do anything else. Now my mother brought home books from the careers section of the local bookshop, promising to identify your strengths and reveal your vocation. The Bath life that had seemed thrillingly novel as a stopgap now felt lonely and miserable. A home-cooked meal could make me wince with sorrow – who was this girl, still living with parents who were, apparently, her only friends? I still went to the cinema with Dad, but now each movie we saw had become a poignant reminder of just how lost and alone I was. Happy films taunted me with a life I wasn't living, a wider world I was excluded from; sad ones seemed to show me my future. I cried at the end of them all.

The theatre was an equally painful experience. We'd often go, the three of us together; I'd generally be fine until the curtain calls, but the sight of the actors breaking from character and beaming with pleasure was too much to bear. I pretended I was moved by the performances – 'Silly sausage,' Mum would say when she saw me wiping my eyes with my sleeves – but I knew this pain wasn't fictional, it was mine.

One Saturday evening, we were all watching *Gladiator* on DVD; ten minutes from the end, tears already streaming, I realised there was no way I could hold in or explain away the sobs that were about to burst from my chest. I slipped away to my room before the final scene, and muffled the sound in a pillow. A cloud of panic descended on me. I was sure, at the age of 21, that I was going to be unhappy for ever.

I didn't want my parents to see me upset, but it became impossible to hide. The slightest thing was triggering tears: a TV romance, a burnt piece of toast, the well-meaning smile of a stranger. I sobbed on the sofa, I sobbed on the phone, I sobbed in my room. I sobbed when I discovered that Hansie Cronje was a match-fixer who had sold that Test match against England for a leather jacket. When my mother became worried, I sobbed in a doctor's surgery. It wasn't depression, said the doctor, just unhappiness. I nodded through the tears and, facial muscles straining and quivering, tried to summon up a hopeful smile. Then she and my mum cried too.

At the end of one grim week, my mother bundled me into the car and wedged a picnic basket at my feet. With a blanket tucked over my legs like a war veteran, and my eyes still puffy from the night before, she drove me to the county cricket ground at Bristol. I can't remember the opposition or the result, but I remember the sun, the breeze and the black cloth covering up the sightscreens. The bright green of the oval, the smell of ice cream – the familiar elements seemed to calm my anxious mind.

After that, the county ground and its gentle rhythms became a kind of therapy. I didn't go to the cricket with any interest in the outcome; sometimes I didn't pretend to watch the game at all. I just stretched out across the plastic seats, face to the sky, letting the indistinct chatter of the players and the murmur of the spectators swirl around my head. Who knows if it was really the cricket, or just the loving presence of my mum, but somehow at that ground I found some moments free of all the fears – of failure, of folly, and of the future in general – that were making me so wretched.

And while I claimed no real attachment to Gloucestershire, I developed a fondness for their sprightly, spirited band. They were outsiders, and revelled in it, unfashionable, unfancied, unstoppable.

With no star in their ranks (their sole overseas player, Ian Harvey, had played a handful of one-dayers for Australia) they joyously mingled inexperienced youth and wily, tenacious old men. Jack Russell would regularly park himself under the batsman's backside, then bark off-puttingly at his fielders. This was the home of W. G. Grace, after all, a place where tricks and schemes were tacitly smiled upon; 'Gloster' were a team who used what they had, and didn't worry about what they hadn't. With their pragmatic approach they had overtaken my own Lancashire as the country's leading one-day team, and Mum and I followed them to two Cup finals that summer. We learned the words to the local chants, and met their lunatic crew of supporters, who brought along a frozen supermarket chicken to every game for luck. 'We've got the whole chicken in our hands,' they sang, and we'd belt along then fall about in giggles. The team won all three one-day titles that year, but that meant little to me. I just felt grateful for the experience.

Looking back on that torturous time, from the safety of a fairly content life, I'm still sad and sorry for the young girl who felt so much anxiety about her future. On our squashy leather sofas at the inn, Hussain and I discuss our shared tendency to worry. He, too, suffered from the killer combination of being emotionally sensitive and desperate to succeed. As a result he was, he says, 'always nervy'. He puts it down to his upbringing, the approval he sought from a father who knew how to stretch him. 'He pushed me, in a nice way. But every innings was important, and it got over the top, really. I remember waking up, not wanting my alarm to go off because I was batting that day.'

Hussain says you can chart how the fears took hold through the evolution – or perhaps the deterioration – of his batting style. 'As a youngster, I was quite an attacking player, a strokeplayer, and towards the end I was just a blocker, because I was so afraid of getting out.' I tell him how one of my friends has a theory that you've only finally grown up when you realise that cricket is just a game. 'I don't think I ever did!' he says. 'That's what I enjoy most about my job now. I love it, walking through Lord's, I can turn up Thursday morning and I don't care. I don't care about the toss, the pitch; I don't care about the result. I don't have to practise, net, worry about my bat grips, my average, the papers . . . it's a great feeling.'

Even in the triumphant summer of 2000, Hussain was struggling with his own batting form. He made a highest score of 22, averaged ten, and missed the pivotal win at Lord's because of a cracked thumb. The honeymoon period that traditionally graces a new captain's efforts – the splurge of runs that accompanies the confidence and responsibility of leadership – had been a brief one. Hussain nods. 'You've had that high, and suddenly it comes down, and you have to look after 15 people!'

The England players were now his responsibility. At the start of the year it had been announced that the team would be given central contracts, the thing Atherton had so long been denied. I had read the news without excitement – financial particulars were of little interest to someone who still thought of her pay cheque as 'clothes money'. I had no idea how much impact that one piece of organisational progress could have on the England team – that they would finally *be* a team, training together, rooting for each other, accountable to one other.

As a young cricketer, Hussain had served his apprenticeship in a successful but outspoken Essex team, one full of belligerent characters. He had seen first-hand the dangers of team politics, and watched captains undermined by their own players. 'In any team you have one person who a lot of people listen to,' he says. In the England dressing-room, that person was Darren Gough: 'Mothers loved him, fans loved him, and any young player coming in looked up to him. He'd done great things in an England shirt and he was also was quite gobby.'

Gough's charisma wasn't just evident on the field, but in the late-night drinking sessions where complaints traditionally outed themselves and where the bowler frequently held court. 'If he was discontented, it would spread like a virus,' says Hussain. 'But I knew that if I had Gough I had the team.' Cue a number of positive pronouncements in Hussain's first months in charge. 'I made sure, any public statement about Gough: get him on your side. And the year I was averaging 12 and we were losing, I had his full support.'

Hussain is in his element now, talking keenly about the art of captaincy. His thoughts arrive fast and emphatic; I'm surprised how open he is about his methods, and how calculating they were. Not maliciously Machiavellian, perhaps, but ruthlessly effective. Gough and Caddick, the bowlers who transformed under his watch into a formidable opening pair, were treated to the same artful parenting he now practises on his children. 'I'd go to Gough and say, "That big-eared twit at the other end, you know what he's like, he doesn't want to bowl at the pavilion end," and Gough would say: "Give me the ball, skip, I'll bowl that end!" Then I'd go to Caddy and say, "You know what Gough's like, such a prima donna, the wind's in the wrong direction . . ." It's like my two boys: "Jacob, Joel's off the Xbox now, will you come off the Xbox?" It was just playing one against the other, really.'

Perhaps it was easier to employ those subtle arts under the central contract system, which fostered both an increased sense of team and a more general professionalism. 'These guys feel secure now, they're not threatened by the other guy,' says Hussain. 'So we tried to get people pushing each other, off the field. If you're not doing your job someone will quietly knock on your door: "Come on, we're better than this." Or it might be: "Let's go to the gym, let's go do some throwdowns."'

All this was happening behind the scenes, of course. Fans knew little of the changes, although we felt their effects in unlikely and tangential ways. For me, it was the rediscovery of a player I came to adore: Craig White. White – whose medium pace was so galumphing that he actually slowed down on his run-up – had not played a Test match in three years. His return to the England side had something mystic about it; White had suffered an unexplained blackout on a street in Scarborough the month previously and, the story went, was now a man reborn, living each day like his last.

The truth is more likely that the Hussain–Fletcher axis had done its work. 'Duncan would eventually lose patience with him – lovely lad, always injured – and it would be me knocking on his door saying, "I know Duncan's had a go at you, but I want you to do well, let's move on from this . . ."' It was an effective treatment. White was a key player in the summer against West Indies, and was in the squad to tour Pakistan that winter.

It was the first time I had followed a Test series on the subcontinent – England hadn't played in Pakistan in 14 years – and I knew it was important to set my expectations manageably low. Reading the history of past tours had taught me that they were a fractious business that often ended in defeat or, at best, long unsightly draws. The teams' first encounter fulfilled at least one of the stereotypes. At lunchtime on the final day, the game was still in its first innings. This was cricket as I'd never known it before: arid, attritional, and insanely dull. I was used to England failing, but not to this complete absence of action. I couldn't understand it – why not try, at least, to win a game?

Little did I know it was a cunning plan hatched by the two ardent pragmatists in charge. In Pakistan, where cricketers are treated like gods, victory is both expected and demanded by the cricket-crazed populace. Hussain says he had one goal on that tour: to 'stay in the game . . . I knew if we stayed in the game, stayed in the series, the pressure would shift from our side to their side. Because everyone expects them to win every single game.' Hussain and Fletcher picked teams that batted deep and long, and bowlers who could keep a tight line on unhelpful pitches. Their tactics were unashamed: 'Play boring, turgid cricket.'

Does anyone go to a football game hoping to see a lifeless goalless draw? I doubt it. But there does seem to be a divide between those who treasure the 'beauty' of their chosen sport, and those for whom the end justifies any means. I understand the football fans who railed against *catenaccio*, or boring, boring Arsenal; the union fans who would rather see their teams play free-flowing rugby and lose than suffer 80 minutes of kicking up and down the field for a three-point win. These days, I might even number myself among them. I've spent more than 20 years watching the game I love; the more I've seen, the more I've developed a taste for the good stuff.

Back then, however, my appreciation of cricket and wine shared a similar philosophy: I was pretty happy with whatever was available. Under the soul-sucking lights of Sainsbury's, you can admire the £30 bottles of Burgundy, knowing that they contain liquid that won't leave you with a blue tongue, a crashing headache and some funny scum in your mouth the next morning. But until the day you can afford them, you'll reach for the Blossom Hill, and you'll still enjoy drinking it, because you've nothing better to compare it to.

Personally, I was never going to turn down cheap wine if the alternative was no wine at all. My experience of watching England play cricket was one ruled by the supreme likelihood of defeat, which made anything other than a loss a cause for rejoicing. I was never going to balk at a positive result for my team, however ugly or unearned. Other people may find the prospect of a drawn Test frustrating, disappointing, second-rank. I used to love them.

It didn't matter what sort of draw, either. Sure, I loved the exciting kind, the one where a dogged rearguard action withstood the best that a mighty opposition could bring, and denied a team of infinitely more class an almost inevitable victory. But I didn't play favourites. I'd be just as happy if we dodged the bullet by bowling every ball out of reach down the leg-side, or a three-day monsoon blew in and ruined a Test at its midway point. When the Jamaica Test of January '98 was abandoned after only an hour because of the dangerous pitch in Sabina Park, I had celebrated the fact we had one fewer Test to lose, and felt cheated when officials added an extra match to the schedule.

Unlike the newspaper writers, who seemed to find it infuriating when England played poorly for four days then escaped their just punishment, I loved a draw we had no right to. I loved a draw that papered over the cracks of our incompetence and insufficiencies. They were still David and Goliath battles to me, just with an alternate ending. One where David's slingshot misses by a mile, Goliath laughs and picks David up by the collar, and David wriggles out of his tunic and legs it, naked but alive.

So while I didn't understand England's tactics in their first two Tests against Pakistan, I still enjoyed the results. Two draws meant two non-defeats. It also meant they went into the final game with the series still alive, a rare enough occurrence in my experience of watching England that I carried it round with me, occasionally bringing it out to pet and coo over. Craig White had played his part, ploughing steadily through Pakistan's batsmen, and batting just as stalwartly.

In the last Test, I looked forward to another stalemate. Pakistan had batted for most of two days, and Atherton had responded with a nine and a half hour century so free from frills that Michael Henderson of the *Telegraph* deemed it 'insufferable viewing'. But it had kept England in the game, and I hadn't had to watch it. On the final day Pakistan had a lead of 88 runs, and seven wickets in hand – a draw seemed the only possible result. Then Pakistan's lower order fell in a tangle. Hussain and Fletcher's waiting tactics had finally paid off.

England needed 176 in the three and a half remaining hours of daylight. Pakistan's captain Moin Khan responded by slowing the action down to the brink of actual inertia. This was a tactic I had rated highly in some of England's most heroic draws of the recent past. I would yell at our players to take more time tying their shoelaces in the middle of the pitch. Now I found myself taking a highly moralised stance on such behaviour, and labelling Moin a cheat, a cad and a coward.

The radio commentators in Karachi warned how quickly the sun goes down in that part of the world, and the creeping threat of darkness added a gothic element to the suspense. I sat listening tensely; as England edged closer to their target, the commentators were struggling to see the action. How long would the umpires let them play on? The batsmen's shots were becoming best guesses, and fielders in the deep stood unsighted, powerless to stop the ball racing past them to the boundary.

With 20 runs still needed, and the muezzin calling the faithful to evening prayer, a wicket fell. Hussain can still remember running out to join Graham Thorpe at the crease, the ground around them a smear of black: 'Waqar steamed in, I nicked one and Moin dropped it because he couldn't see it. *I* couldn't see it!' Moin remonstrated with the umpire – *we can't play on like this* – and umpire Steve Bucknor told him it was his own fault. 'Steve was stubborn, and once Moin had crossed him I *knew*,' recalls Hussain. 'I said to Thorpe, "We're going to finish this off, mate."'

After a fortnight of treacly gameplay, their success – England's first Test victory in Pakistan in 39 years – was urgent and dramatic. 'The whole thing about that tour was realising your strengths and your weaknesses,' says Hussain. 'It's like going to Chelsea, and you're Burnley. You're not going to go there and win 5–0. Your centre-forward's not going to score a hat-trick and make John Terry look very silly.'

Sometimes the only way forward is the slow way. A look at Hussain's captaincy record proves that, more often than not, his uncompromising methods proved effective. He didn't turn England into a great team. But he did make them a better one. They lost fewer matches and series than they had under Atherton, giving fans the sense that one day a corner might be turned. As for me – he taught me that sometimes pragmatism is more suited to the moment than ideals.

That winter, I escaped the torpidity of life in Bath. I let go of the acting dream; what came next, I had no idea, but it was clear I wasn't going to find it in the West Country, sending teddy bears across the high seas. Ben was looking for someone to share a flat with in London, and the prospect of moving in with my old college friend was more than enough to counter the terror of how I'd pay the rent.

We spent an afternoon in Green Park reading the flats-to-rent section of *Loot* like religious scholars studying an ancient text. Somewhere in its mystical script – *£450pcm exc, u/f, gch, n/s only* – we knew our destiny was hidden. Our destiny turned out to be an ex-council flat near Stockwell tube station. We moved in without owning a single piece of furniture between us; for our housewarming we bought sushi, wore dressing gowns, and told everyone we were aiming for a Japanese aesthetic. But the emptiness of the flat, our bank accounts, and our CVs, didn't frighten us. We were crouched in our new lives, listening for the starter's gun.

Chapter 12

Michael Atherton is haunting my dreams. Literally. He's been making the occasional cameo for a year now, since I started meeting the cricketers. But this week he's popping up most nights. Sometimes he's pally, sometimes cool and aloof. Occasionally he's angry with me, and I feel terrible, and desperate to make things better, but I just can't remember what I've done wrong.

It's been like this ever since we arranged a time and a place to meet. I have put it off as long as I could. Atherton was the first person to agree to talk to me, 12 months ago – cautiously, reticently, yet courteously and graciously. But I was too cowardly to follow up with dates. He's busy with his TV commitments, I reasoned; I'll come to him last. Now a new summer is about to start, and there's no more procrastinating. He has found a couple of hours in his diary for lunch, and I have found a smart restaurant near my office that I hope will induce in me a calm professionalism.

I will need it, as I've spent the days beforehand in a wretchedly nervous state. My mum's exhortation to 'just be yourself' is no help at all. It's the thought of being myself – excitable, over-eager, and prone to embarrassing scenes – that is powering the washing machine where my stomach used to be.

The problem isn't that I can't imagine talking to him. The problem is that I have imagined talking to him. Plenty. When I was 14, I used to talk through my troubles with him in my head, and make up his responses. It helped me to get things in perspective – best-friend traumas, school bullies, teachers giving me a hard time. He was always a good imaginary listener. So even though Atherton is the person I most want to sit down with, it's also the meeting I dread. He, I am sure, will be as straightforward and lucid as he is on the TV. But I have no idea what he'll make of me. Even if I were known for my ability to play it cool, which I am not, it feels like a rather dangerous thing to do, to let someone know that they were your hero. It's a one-way street, after all: an act of commitment that has meant so much to you, and absolutely zero to them.

My mum met her cricketing idol once. Her firm was receiving a corporate award and, by pure coincidence, David Gower was the man handing them out. He was so charming that she fell completely mute. It was, my dad maintains, the only time that had happened in her life. Gower had made his Test debut the year she had me. While I was still in a cot, she oohed along at his creamy cover drives – the way he didn't so much compile runs as conjure them – and joined in the groans when he got himself out to a nonchalant shot, his mind seemingly elsewhere.

It was fair to say that his Goldilocks looks were quite as attractive to her as his lissom batting. In the eighties, women like my mother admired Gower because he had the devil-may-care charisma of a gentleman playboy. Cricketers were still sex symbols back then – even the men developed feelings they couldn't quite understand for Ian Botham and his rampant machismo.

I became smitten with a man whose defining characteristic was being imperturbable.

Certainly, few others saw the attraction. After a short period at the start of his captaincy when he was, quite literally, the blue-eyed boy of English cricket, Atherton's northern reserve began to be considered uninspiring and uncharismatic. The more England lost, the worse it got. At the end of matches, he sat in front of the TV cameras with a grim expression and a sardonic turn of phrase. He had no interest in managing his public image, nor a particular pride in his personal appearance. When he took to the field unshaven, the short golden stubble on his cheeks did not look like a daring nod to youth culture, just lazy habits.

Once he was given the sobriquet 'Captain Grumpy' by a newspaper, it stuck; after that, even people who didn't follow the cricket felt they had the measure of the man. I suspected – no, I knew – that there was more to him than that. It wasn't just his intellectual side, either, although it warmed my heart whenever I heard he'd been spotted playing chess at a hotel, or reading Milan Kundera in an airport. There was, too, the man I pictured in my gentle daydreams: an Atherton with a softer side, an Atherton always ready to smile, kind and loyal to his friends and teammates in ways invisible to the outside world.

I was confident that this Atherton existed, and occasionally came across glimpses that seemed to support my claim. The wicketkeeper Steve Rhodes once told a journalist that the team would 'run through a brick wall' for their leader, and I carried that quote around with me long after Rhodes had left the scene. 'It is a shame,' wrote Michael Henderson in a 1996 match programme, 'that the private man, who is amusing, gregarious and intelligent, peeps out infrequently from behind the public carapace of indifference.' I couldn't prove that Atherton was a beloved captain or a good man, but I had an unshakeable faith that he was both, and I stood firm in my belief whether his team were winning or losing.

With the benefit of hindsight, and Atherton's newspaper columns, a vast number of fans have realised just what an incisive cricket brain he owns, and how good a captain he might, with the right team and the right circumstances, have been. He has been vastly more appreciated in retirement than he was during his career. And while his sportswriting regularly wins awards, it's on the telly that he has really won people over, projecting both an acute intelligence and a surprisingly lively personality.

I used to feel a certain amount of pride in how popular he became – *told you so* – but after a while I got pissed off at how many people were claiming him as their own. I wondered where all these people were back in the days when Atherton was constantly being called on to resign, when his name was a punchline on satirical news quizzes, and why it always felt, when England lost, that I was the only person in the country defending his tactics, his record, his moody persona. It felt, too, that something was being taken from me. Hero-worshipping a largely unsuccessful England captain was so unusual that it felt like part of my identity. Now that others liked him too, it was as if a piece of me was under threat.

I'm starting to sound like a crazy woman already.

I get to the restaurant at noon, and Atherton is already there, sitting behind a table in a capacious armchair. He is, of course, completely familiar. A hint more lined, perhaps, than he appears on the television, with a shade more colour too – he has just returned from two months in the Caribbean. A quietly striped shirt collar pokes above a navy blue jumper, smart-casual with an emphasis on the casual. The curled hair, cropped short to reveal elfin ears, looks exactly as it has done since he first assumed the captaincy, aside from a few silvery strands.

He greets me pleasantly although I sense a wariness. Atherton has been a journalist for over a decade now, and faced plenty of inquisitions in his years as captain. He knows better than anyone how an interview works. What to ask first? I pour some water with a slightly shaky hand. I look at my questions, and worry he'll find fault with them all.

I decide the only way is to ask the big one first. 'You're a historian,' I say. 'Do you think history has judged your team fairly or harshly?'

'The first thing I'd say,' he says, 'is I don't think about it very often.'

I look surprised. I am surprised. He continues, 'I do not look back on my career at all, unless I'm asked forcibly to.'

'Why not?' This is confusing. Does it upset him? Is he ashamed of it? Is the next two hours going to be torture for us both?

'Because it's just a time of life that has passed. And when I stopped playing, the great fear for me was that you could turn into somebody who's forever . . . harking back to what I did. I think it's quite a sad thing to constantly be boring about that.'

His speech is unhurried, almost languid. I wonder if it's a tactic, a form of occupying the crease. He tells me he has given all his memorabilia away – not that he had much to begin with. 'I was never someone who kept cricket stumps or got shirts signed, basically 'cos I couldn't be arsed.' The side of his mouth tweaks upwards, not quite a smile, but close. 'There's nothing to remind me of that time. If you walked into my house you wouldn't know that a cricketer lived there, and that's a very deliberate thing.'

'Anyway,' he continues. 'Is the team judged fairly? I don't know. How do you think it's judged?'

I flinch. I didn't expect to be questioned myself, and I don't want to say anything that will offend him. But I don't want to be a coward, either. So I say that it's probably remembered as one of the most unsuccessful England sides in history. Atherton agrees it was 'a low ebb'. But statistically, he says, the eighties were marginally worse. 'That wouldn't necessarily be a public perception, because the eighties was staffed by some fabulous cricketers and an Ashes-winning team.'

I feel foolish, both because I have apparently fallen for a common misconception, and because I have never once checked the stats. And it is, I realise, completely believable: even I've been surprised at some of the results as I've looked back, at matches I had completely forgotten England won, and series that were closer than I remembered. Atherton calls it 'narrative fallacy', which I suppose is what happens when you debate the past with a Cambridge history graduate.

There's common agreement, for instance, that England's Ashes campaign in 1994–95 was doomed the moment Australia's Michael Slater opened the match by smacking four off Phillip DeFreitas. 'We got beat 3–1 in that series, but we won the fourth Test and we would have won the third but for bad light,' he says. I detect a hint of annoyance – not directed at me, just at lazy assumptions. 'We could have been two-all going into the final Test. People looking back at that first ball saying it was a harbinger of things to come – that's what sports journalists do, see the end result and trace it back. But life's not like that.'

Maybe it's the English graduate in me, but when I look at Atherton's own narrative I see a tragic trajectory. At the start of his captaincy he picked a squad of young players he planned to nurture into future champions, the way Allan Border had rejuvenated Australia's demoralised team in the late eighties. Atherton respected Border because he was a 'straightforward character, not full of artifice', the very qualities Atherton's former teammates have told me they admired in him. But his vision quickly faded at the hands of boardroom figures – notably Ray Illingworth – whose power of selection outranked his own. 'I had a clear strategy,' says Atherton. 'I just couldn't make it happen. Probably my weakness as much as anything.'

I can't tell if that last observation is honesty or modesty, or both. It was, as he says himself, 'a chaotic time'. English cricket, though professional, still preferred to inhabit the comfort zone of old-fashioned amateurism. Players received invitations to play in the England team by post; preparations for a Test match comprised a mandatory three-course dinner (with wine and speeches) the night before. Atherton's frustrations as a young leader whose modern ideas were continually checked by hidebound authority must have been intense.

He seems extremely phlegmatic about it – after all, he says, you can't choose what period you live through. He also believes that the captaincy came to him too soon. 'But I'd say that about my career as an England player too. I wasn't good enough and didn't know enough about the game.'

Atherton made his international debut at 21, the summer he graduated university. Adulthood and success seemed to arrive together so quickly and naturally. To the teenage me, that fact had always been a source of hope and confidence. It's true that when you're 14, everyone in their twenties is sophisticated, but a cricket captain like Atherton, commanding his troops in the field, seemed particularly mature. Actually, he tells me, he did most of his growing up on the job: 'That is one of the beauties of cricket: when captains are 25, they're going to make all the mistakes, and that's what's fascinating. You've got this guy in charge of the team who is completely immature and short of experiences in life, learning about himself as much as anything.'

The restaurant is filling up, and a pair of older gents has taken the table next to us. It's obvious they've clocked Atherton and he instinctively lowers his voice a little, but he doesn't seem too bothered. I ask when he felt most out of his depth; he says he was probably out of his depth throughout: 'I look back and can't believe some of the things I did or said to players. But it's the narrative fallacy again. At the time, you can only do things from the point of view of a 25-year-old who's a bit wet behind the ears.' I guess it must be awkward, having to tell your friends they're not doing a good job. He shakes his head. 'At times it wasn't awkward enough. I just let rip instinctively.'

When Hussain was explaining the way he had gamed some of the players, saying this thing to Gough and that thing to Caddick, it occurred to me that I could not imagine Atherton doing the same. Not that Atherton would disapprove of the use of psychology – but his character was never an artful one. I suspected Atherton would resist anything that felt like puppeteering, or telling a player something other than the unvarnished truth.

When I ask if he can remember any of his team-talks, he replies bluntly, 'Nothing that would go down as the Gettysburg Address.' And his preference for honesty crops up in his conversation quite a bit. He says it's one of the things he enjoys about sport itself: 'You can walk off at the end of the day and you know if you've had a good day or a bad day because the scoreboard tells you so. It's a meritocracy more often than not. You can't bullshit people, you can't go round telling people how good you are if you've got three noughts in a row.'

There was one occasion when his hardboiled approach had tested my loyalty. I was 16 as Graeme Hick crept, tortoise-like, towards his first ever Ashes century, during a period of the Sydney Test when England needed quick runs. Atherton sent a message to the middle telling Hick to hurry up; Hick did not. He was on 98 when Atherton ran out of patience and declared. The dressing-room was, by all accounts, a sizzling silence of anger and reproach.

I wrestled with this piece of utilitarian ethics and felt awful for Hick, the kind, gentle soul who really, really deserved to catch a break. I never admitted it to anyone, not even my mum, but for the first time I truly doubted Atherton. His behaviour just seemed so mean. For a few days I had winced every time I remembered what he'd done, and I wonder how long it took for Hick to forgive him. 'Well, he was a little upset at the time, which is probably an understatement. He was rightly sore for a couple of weeks. And then he was fine.'

It was one of those mistakes of youth, he says, one he regrets. I ask how he thinks a management expert would evaluate him, how they would rate his 'soft skills'? 'Empathy, you mean? I think I was empathetic of players' difficulties because I was an average player myself. You'd have to ask other people . . . well, you have asked other people.' Caddick did call him a poor man-manager, I say. 'He's absolutely entitled to his views,' Atherton shrugs. I get the impression that he didn't see why his own creed of personal accountability shouldn't apply to all. 'You need to give players a sense of responsibility. You can't be nannying them all the time.'

At this stage, I realise, he could be reading from my mother's parenting notes (if my mum had ever written a self-help book, it would have been titled *Buck Up*). It makes me wonder what his parents were like. He says his mum was gregarious, and his dad quiet; I resist the urge to shout, 'Snap.' Did he get his ambition from them? 'My dad had a strong work ethic, but that's different. I don't think I've ever been ambitious. Ambition makes it sounds a deliberate thing, doesn't it? To say you're ambitious means you've set out in a certain timeline achievements that you want to have made. I've never really been like that. I've just thrown myself into what I'm doing and assumed that life would pan out in one way or another . . . I wouldn't say I'm ambitious, I'd say I'm hard-working.'

When I ask how he fell in love with the game, he looks genuinely stumped. 'I don't know, really. My father played for a village club in north Manchester called Woodhouses, and I remember always going to watch him as a five- or six-year-old.

I would go with my little packed lunch and I would watch intently. And I was always just good at cricket. As a kid, you're attracted to the thing you're good at, 'cos that gives you status and confidence.'

Atherton is a thoroughly Lancastrian name. It signifies that at some stage your ancestors came from the place itself – an industrial town between Manchester and Wigan which had been making nails and mining coal since the 13th century. I don't know how far Michael Andrew Atherton can trace back his family tree, but I like the idea that it probably contains coal miners. The work seems a good metaphor for the way Atherton came about his runs: digging away at the face, minute after painstaking minute, knowing that hard work alone would bring his reward. It may not have been a rich seam of gold, or flash of silver, but the runs he delivered were always a precious and welcome commodity.

His hero, funnily enough, was Gower too. Presumably the young Atherton – a teenager when Gower was at his peak – watched him with a more technical appreciation, paying attention to the effortless use of the wrists, the way he picked the gaps in the field. Atherton always had natural talent – by 11, he was too good for his peers, and played in teams two years ahead of him – but he also had that work ethic, and as a boy he practised constantly; every hour not spent on schoolwork was devoted to his cricket.

He didn't try to copy Gower – he was too pragmatic a child to think he could replicate such a carefree style – so he concentrated instead on what he could do. Atherton had patience; he had technique. He had a contentedness in his own company that long, solitary bus rides to school had only encouraged. In time, concentration became his greatest strength. At the crease, he could shut himself off, give every delivery his complete focus.

His childhood sounds strangely familiar to mine: an academic school, a blissfully undramatic home life, 'pretty studious' as a teenager. 'I wasn't particularly rebellious, or into the usual things teenagers would be into.' I picture his parents watching him grow, delighted at his enthusiasm, proud of his dedication. No doubt at some stage, real-world anxieties began to mingle – could he make it, and would he be happy if he didn't? Was he investing too much of himself?

I think of my parents, and all the times they ferried me to drama classes and rehearsals and shows, even though, after the debacle in Bath, my hopes of going pro were over. I had headed to London still entirely unsure of what career might suit me, yet with a strangely baseless confidence that someone in the big city would eventually hire me to do something. On the day my parents helped me move in, Mum hugged me and told me if I ever felt sad or lonely, I could always come home for the weekend. She then predicted that I wouldn't need to.

As usual, my mother proved right. London's endless possibilities – not to mention the expense – left no time for moping. Within a few weeks, and without even noticing, I had been assimilated into the life of the city. I found a job at a recruitment company: the dotcom bubble was fully inflated, businesses were investing wildly in online ventures, and my task was to produce spurious articles about career advancement for their spurious website. In the year I worked there, the website only placed one candidate in a job, and that was to fill a position on our own team. But the City firm that owned us kept funnelling in cash. As long as they did, I made the most of working in an office near the Bank of England, and drinking alongside rainmakers in wine bars where I could barely afford a Coca-Cola. My colleagues were fun to be around; the writing work was curiously easy. The pay was good enough to allow nights out at trendy-yet-budget eating places, and even a few theatre tickets, if I sat far enough from the stage.

My funds also stretched to a season ticket to Surrey County Cricket Club. Living a 15-minute walk from The Oval, I had decided it would be a scandal not to buy one. The 'Gardens Estate' where Ben and I lived had been named in hope rather than observation, and the only places to pause and reflect were the traffic islands in the middle of the murderously busy roads that shuttled Londoners between more fashionable postcodes. So, on match days, the empty stands of a 20,000-seat stadium provided the closest thing to a private retreat I could manage. From the benches in front of the pavilion I could feel ownership of The Oval's vast green lawn, and the sounds of the south London traffic were, if not stilled, then at least a bit blurred.

It was another Ashes summer. Mum brought our usual picnic to the Lord's Test but, in a departure from tradition that symbolised my coming of age, this year I had bought the tickets. England were one-down in the series and Hussain had broken his finger, which meant that Atherton was resuming the field as England captain. It was not going well. When we arrived on the third day, Australia were already well past England's feeble first-innings total. We watched in disbelief as the England fielders dropped four catches off the same batsman. Atherton spilled the last one himself. By the time Australia were all out, they had a crushing lead. It was time for one of Atherton's trademark captain's innings. I watched him take up his familiar role as human anchor. His defence looked as solid as ever, but something was different. Was it the way he stood – a bit cramped, a bit crabbier, perhaps? Or was it the way his bat seemed to arrive a fraction later at the ball than usual, so that each new delivery caused me a millisecond of unexpressed panic?

He ran little, but made runs anyhow. The welcome the fast bowlers had reserved for him – fast, short deliveries that cannoned off the ground towards his eyebrows – was nothing new. But he seemed less inclined to duck out of their way, and there was no sign of his sinuous sway, the one he used to execute like the bend of a flame at a birthday child's breath. Instead, he swiped at them with his bat, a helicopter blade slapping the ball to the boundary. A warm round of applause caught us off guard, and we glanced at the electronic screen: Atherton had surpassed Colin Cowdrey's total of Test runs. He was now the fourth-highest England run-scorer of all time.

After an hour, Steve Waugh threw the ball to Shane Warne. Atherton had always enjoyed the mind games that facing Warne involved. Duelling with the greatest leg-spinner of his age – heck, of all time – was a far more cerebral pursuit than avoiding the slings and arrows of outrageous pace. But that day there was no Fischer v Kasparov marathon. Warne slung the ball to the leg-side; Atherton knelt instinctively to sweep it away, and missed completely. The ball boomeranged back behind his legs, hitting middle stump. It was a good delivery, but it was not the kind of mistake Atherton often made. He had scored 20.

I'm not sure whether I registered that Atherton's powers were waning. Not in my conscious mind at least. Graham Gooch had played for England until he was 40; Atherton was only 33 and I believed I had years of watching him left. But I couldn't ignore the struggles he was having that summer, or the weariness in his face when the camera caught him in close-up. I winced when newspapers wrote about his weakness against Glenn McGrath, the Australia bowler who had tormented him in the two previous Ashes series. And then there was his bad back. It had been an open secret for a few years, but it had never kept him out of a game, not until 1998, when he was forced to sit out a Test in Australia. Every now and then, you would hear that he'd been given an injection of cortisone, the magical substance that could return a bedbound sportsman to instant life. Back problems are among the regular currency of sports injuries. Atherton had never claimed it as an excuse for poor performance, so neither had I.

It was only after his retirement that he admitted he suffered from something called ankylosing spondylitis, a hereditary rheumatism that had curved his father's spine so badly it had ended his professional footballing career. When Atherton was diagnosed with it in his early twenties, he pulled a Jed Bartlet – like *The West Wing*'s bloody-minded president, he didn't want his degenerative condition to be public knowledge in case it affected people's perception of his career, or what he was capable of. Atherton didn't want to give the selectors any excuse to leave him out of the England team, so he lived silently with the pain, which he later admitted was semi-permanent.

Nasser Hussain told me that even his teammates knew little about the state of his health: 'I only put two and two together later and realised that his grumpy days generally coincided with how bad his back was.' Atherton often had to literally drag himself out of bed, and he managed the creeping immobility with twice-daily doses of anti-inflammatories that slowly stripped the lining of his stomach. All those times he had to arch quickly out of the path of a bouncer, he did it with a bad back. All those six-hour days he spent crouched at slip, or bent over his bat, were spent in pain. No wonder his batting was cussed.

It seems strange to me that his dad never warned him off a career in sport, but Atherton says his father played at a time when very little was known about the condition, and they 'never really talked about it too much'. At the start of his career, Atherton was told by a surgeon that his own problems were caused by a stress fracture, and even had an unnecessary operation to fix it. 'I had a screw put in there,' he says, suddenly remembering, and reaching to feel for it through his shirt. 'I've still got it, actually. Yeah, it's still there.'

The problems with his back were a defining element of his career: 'a constant, constant weariness, really'. The England captaincy, for all its privileged status, was also enervating. Everything came to his door: player problems, yes, but also financial decisions, logistical details, when, where and how to train. When Ray Illingworth became coach in 1994, he adopted such a hands-off approach that Atherton was required to source practice equipment and run fielding drills and net sessions. He considers the support staff today's team travels with – dozens of specialist coaches, analysts, doctors, masseurs and psychologists – and raises an eyebrow. His aides were a single coach and a physio (and, for games abroad, a tour manager and scorer).

In between his England commitments, Atherton was still a Lancashire player, required to play for his county whenever and wherever they needed him. 'And, as a single bloke, you're trying to get three bags of laundry done on your day off,' he adds. He was too self-contained to make a fuss, either in public or private. Perhaps he didn't think it was appropriate. He had that code of personal responsibility; he also had a strong sense of duty, one he suspects was 'drummed into' him under Graham Gooch's leadership. I imagine a certain pride too, in both the struggle and the self-sufficiency; the kind that might stop you seeking help, or at least admitting vulnerability.

Certainly, when I ask him to name his best moments as an England player, he skirts quickly past 'the obvious ones' – Johannesburg, the Donald duel – to focus on his leanest periods as a batsman. He remembers the early season of '98 '. . . when I just could not buy a run for Lancashire. I went into the first Test against South Africa thinking, "Jesus, how am I going to get another run?"' Battling back from those kind of lows – he scored a century in that opening game – is what stands out in his memory. 'Being able to raise your game somehow, I don't know how . . . they would be the moments that other people wouldn't recognise.'

It surprises Atherton that he had a reputation as a technically sound batsman. 'I always thought of myself as technically very poor, actually. I got runs in spite of my weaknesses.' But unlike for Ramprakash, say, or Hussain, batting never felt like life or death. 'I was never desperate. I never got overly nervous. I genuinely always felt that it was just like the game I played at school.' He had a laidback attitude, a naturally low heart rate and a sense, at the back of his mind, that his job was ultimately pretty trivial; to play his best, he says, he had to kid himself that it was important.

That chimes with what his teammates have told me of the man who was the first to giggle when things went wrong. Crawley told me of a time the pair had been batting together against Australia when a throw had deflected off Atherton's bat and he had called Crawley through for a run. Cricket etiquette deems this very poor form indeed and Crawley – unaware of what had happened – found himself receiving a heap of abuse from the fielders as he stood up to bat. Safe at the non-striker's end, Atherton had found the situation incredibly funny.

Atherton argues he was equally quick to laugh at himself. But, even so, the demands of the captaincy took their toll. 'If you speak to my friends from university they would say that they found me more difficult, I think, during the time that I was captain,' he admits. He recalls a friend's thirtieth birthday: 'I spoke to him a couple of days later and he said, "The person I put you next to, you didn't say one word to him all night." And that wasn't a deliberate thing, it's just you'd go out and you'd be sat there thinking cricket thoughts, thinking about how to do the job better. It was something I found very difficult to get out of my head.'

I used to worry, as a teenager, that Atherton might be lonely. Unlike most of his teammates, he didn't have a family, though he was sometimes pictured in the papers with a girlfriend. 'With all positions of responsibility there is a slight sense of loneliness,' he says, emphasising the word 'slight'. He talks about the past as phlegmatically and unemotionally as I would expect from him – and I respond with a demeanour so professional and composed I barely recognise myself. Somewhere deep inside, there's a mini-me rattling her cage furiously, disgusted at how ordinary the whole encounter seems. Who is this serene impostor, talking to her hero as if he's just a regular guy?

He eats while we chat, and when he's finished, he leans back, resting his arm on the top of his chair. He's not unwilling to answer questions, but he looks back through the lens of analysis not anecdote, an assessor rather than a storyteller. A couple of times I disagree with him, just to see what happens, but my arguments are too predictable and my questions not oblique enough to test him. His expression rarely strays beyond the range of neutral and serious. I feel I'm meeting Atherton the captain – careful, reasoning, loyal to his teammates, wary of outsiders. Of his other sides – the silliness that Hussain describes, or whatever it was that would cause Steve Rhodes to head-butt a wall – there is no sign.

Early in 2001, Atherton's doctor told him that he was not prepared to administer any more cortisone injections. His playing career had an expiration date: one more summer, one last chance to wrest back the Ashes. But Australia were sending one of their greatest teams in history to defend them: Shane Warne, the Waugh twins, Ian Healy, Justin Langer and Matthew Hayden, Brett Lee and Jason Gillespie – every department of the team was stacked with uncompromising, merciless talent.

The standard of international cricket has come up a lot as I've talked to players of the nineties. Every one of them has pointed out how extremely high the quality of opposition teams was during the era they played: the devastating power of the pace bowling that dominated the arena, from Ambrose and Walsh to Donald and Pollock to Wasim and Waqar; the once-in-a-lifetime batting talents of Sachin Tendulkar and Brian Lara. It has only been possible to appreciate what a special time it was in hindsight. It sets a context for all those England defeats.

No team was as ruthless or dominant as Australia at the turn of the century. For 18 months, between 1999 and 2001, they won every Test they played, home and abroad. By the midpoint of the Ashes series England were 2–0 down and still without their injured captain, Hussain. Atherton was forced to take the reins once more, in the decisive Test at Trent Bridge, a situation that seemed needlessly cruel. Especially so when he was out, off the second ball of the game, to his nemesis Glenn McGrath. It brought Atherton a new record: he now had more Test ducks than anyone in England's history.

The game was lively and brief: 17 wickets fell on the first day, and nine more on the second. England managed to keep themselves level on first-innings scores, then fell apart to Warne, and Atherton's half-century barely slowed the inevitable slide to defeat. The Ashes had been retained in just over seven days of play, and I found I had a grudging respect for an Australian team. To be clear, I still hated each individual player with the force of a thousand furies, but there was something about their utter ruthlessness I couldn't help but appreciate. Australians always wore their aggression well. Snarling or swearing or throwing a ball just a little too close to the opposition looked cool on them, in a way that it never did on Englishmen. Our attempts to match it tended to look clumsy and tacky.

I mention this to Atherton. 'Glenn McGrath was a terrible sledger,' he replies. 'Really gauche. So not all Australians could carry it off.' Unfortunately, McGrath didn't need to use words to get Atherton out. He haunted his favourite victim for the rest of the series. The sharp-angled bounce he got on the ball – the kind of vertical take-off deserving of its own *Top Gun* soundtrack – seemed primed for the shoulder of Atherton's bat. In the penultimate Test at Headingley, he had him caught behind twice with identical deliveries that reared and cut back at Atherton's waist, the second so fast it barely had time to graze his thumb along the way.

As a Surrey member, I could have bought a ticket to the final Test at The Oval for peanuts if I'd only been organised enough to apply for one. But I was hopeless at admin, and the deadline came and went without me noticing. Now, I realised, instead of spending the August bank holiday sitting in the pavilion, holding a Mr Whippy and a bottle of factor 25, I was going to be sitting on an uncomfortably low Ikea futon less than a mile down the road.

I had other reasons for feeling sore. For the past two months, I had been seeing a guy who worked as a computer programmer, and things had been going well. When I'd gone away on holiday for a few days, he insisted on spending the day before helping me pack. When I returned, he never called at all. After a week of wondering why he was suddenly too busy to see me I read his blog, and discovered he'd met someone he liked better while I was away.

So my mood was a downbeat, distracted one. There had been suggestions, all week, that Atherton could be about to retire, but he had refused to confirm anything; there was far more anticipation around whether Shane Warne would take his 400th Test wicket. Australia responded to an unexpected defeat at Headingley vengefully, and massacred England's bowling. By the time I sat down to watch the match on Saturday, their score of 641 for 4 loomed like a monolith over the remainder of the Test.

And still there was no news on Atherton's decision. The commentators stopped speculating, and started to wonder instead whether this would be Steve Waugh's last match in England. I was fractious and faintly annoyed. If Atherton was going to retire, I felt that I had a right to know. On Sunday evening, England were asked to follow on. Only a rearguard of Johannesburg proportions could save the game, but no one really had the faith for that. Not even me.

The opening pair had been out in the dimming light less than half an hour when it happened. McGrath slid a ball along the invisible channel he seemed to keep to Atherton's off stump. The batsman responded too late. The ball carried to a man standing just behind his right shoulder. Atherton had scored nine.

As he walked away from the celebrating fielders, pulling angrily at the Velcro straps on his gloves, the camera caught his face in close-up. His head gave a small, disbelieving shake; his face broadcast his disappointment. The Australia players stopped congratulating each other and turned to applaud him, but Atherton kept his eyes fixed on the ground a few paces ahead of him. Even as the sound of 20,000 plastic seats tipping up was drowned out by the sound of 40,000 hands beating together, he barely looked round at the standing ovation he was receiving. He didn't even slow down.

It all seemed to be happening too fast: I didn't feel sad at his departure, so much as unprepared. As I realised that this was really it – that all these people couldn't be wrong – I cursed myself for not being at the ground. I stood up from the futon, needing to make some gesture, and a few moments later Ben came out of his bedroom to find me clapping at the television screen, and raising a ridiculous but sincere salute as Atherton reached the pavilion steps. He sped past his two friends, Hussain and Stewart, who were applauding him into the dressing-room, and disappeared behind the dark reflection of the window.

Only Atherton, I think, could have finished his last game with such a stubborn refusal for ceremony. Perhaps that was the greatest difference between him and his fans: even lovers of Atherton's no-frills approach to cricket and to life could still be sentimental about the man himself. Atherton spared himself not a single tear.

Sitting opposite him 14 years after that low-key conclusion, I ask if he can remember what he was feeling. 'Relief, I think,' he says. 'There comes a point where you know you're done. I'd already mentally finished and gone. All the ways that you're one-eyed as a player – you think the umpire's against you, you think the luck's not with you, you view the opposition a different way – in the last couple of days, when I knew that I was finishing, I started to see things in a different light.'

It was, Atherton says, a kind of dawning maturity that only comes to sportsmen when they leave the field of play. To be successful in sport you must think and act like a child, with a selfish objective and a limited perspective. It's why, as a Manchester United fan, he was amazed that Alex Ferguson could still be a football manager so late in his life. 'For a 70-year-old man to still be snarling at referees and thinking that every foul should be a penalty is a bizarre, curious thing. By the time I finished I realised I couldn't be like that.'

And he acknowledges that retirement changed people's perceptions of him too. Yes, he admits, people have warmed to him a bit more. 'My experience has generally been that when you stop playing, people think more kindly of you. I think they think highly of you if those basic fundamentals are there: you gave the team your all and you showed pride in playing for England. And I don't think anyone could argue that we didn't try our best.' He finds it amusing that, when the England team are doing badly now, his name will suddenly be on the tongues of fans who should know better. 'They forget that you were useless or led a losing team or got out for nought so many times. The supporters say, "Oh, we could do with you out there," as if I'm a player who averaged 60! People have slightly selective memories,' he chuckles.

It's not the only irony of his retirement, of course. The big one is his choice of post-playing career: a high-profile job in the media, the industry he saw as 'utterly irrelevant' when he was captain. I say he must feel a bit sheepish now he's on the other side of the microphone. He maintains that, some obstreperous performances in press conferences aside, he was 'pretty helpful' to journalists. He finds it hard to believe he was tailed through the Lake District by a couple of tabloid reporters in the wake of the dirt-in-the-pocket-affair – 'it just seems so nonsensical now' – but suspects that he escaped lightly. 'I'd hate to think what the reaction on social media would have been today.'

He certainly must love it, his second career. The Sky rota is punishing enough on its own – Hussain told me that his time was now accounted for for the next two years – and Atherton also writes every week. You would have thought, having held one of the most high-pressure roles in English sport, you'd allow yourself to take it slightly easy. He has a family now and could, presumably, enjoy a pretty good lifestyle without working as hard as he does. He looks back as if the thought wouldn't occur to him. He likes to be busy, he says. He wants to be busy.

And he is busy. He's going straight from here to a meeting in St John's Wood. I'm running out of time; if I'm going to tell him what his career meant to me, I have to do it now. But I'm struck dumb. What should I say to him? Can I articulate his legacy with the kind of scrupulous honesty he would demand? After all, his sporting career gave me pleasure, but an equal-to-greater measure of pain. I can't remember any scenario when I ever consciously drew on his feats as inspiration, or wondered, when faced with a dilemma, 'What Would Athers Do?'

He has told me he never considered himself a role model. He didn't think, he says, about the ten-year-old boy watching television, watching him ('maybe I ought to have done, a bit more'). But anyone could see that. His bloody-minded shaving rebellions, his 'so-what' performances in press conferences – these were all the acts of a man who wanted people to leave him be. He was an anti-Beckham, a proto-Murray, his eyes focused upward on the next objective, his mind dwelling for less than a few seconds on what others thought of him. How hard, then, to imagine that somewhere in another town or another country his actions shaped people he didn't know existed.

Perhaps 'shaped' is too strong. My character, after all, remains very different from his: I am not stubbornly defiant; I avoid conflict at all costs; I am one of the most suggestible people I know. There is nothing self-contained or introverted about me. And those traits we do share existed in me long before I encountered him. I admired Atherton's work ethic precisely because I had always been someone who tried their hardest. I liked his determination because I, too, was driven to achieve.

But being a teenager isn't always about achieving – sometimes it's just about surviving. The grinding business of growing up could be lonely, and there were long spells where it felt like it was just me against the world. Atherton showed me how glorious those solitary stands could be. He was the physical embodiment of St Paul's exhortation to the Ephesians: that, 'when the day of evil comes, you may be able to stand your ground, and, after you have done everything, to stand.'

In *Beyond a Boundary*, C. L. R. James quotes Philip Lindsay, an Australian who wrote in 1951 of the effect watching Don Bradman had on him. 'Most of us need an ideal,' wrote Lindsay. 'Nor is it necessary for that ideal to symbolise one's particular ambition . . . and to me Don Bradman became that symbol of achievement, of mastery over fate.' Bradman, he wrote, 'helped me to keep my faith alight, and this association of myself with him as nearly of an age and of the same country made me feel somehow that I must not let him down as he had not let me down.' It is the most perfect description of my own hero-worship that I have read.

But I don't think I'll ever be able to explain that to Atherton, who is not, in the flesh, a man who invites intimacies. He is Jack Russell's Mr Obsidian. It's not just that I strongly suspect he would find my admission embarrassing (though I do), or that I don't want an awkward exchange to be my abiding memory of this lunchtime (I don't), or that the conversation of the two gents next to us has faded out and it's getting harder to pretend they're not listening to every word we say. It's also that I realise that such information is simply irrelevant to him.

That's the real fantasy at the heart of fandom. It's not just that we convince ourselves that we know and understand the object of our affection. We believe that they are someone who would understand us, too. After all, who spends their time following a hero who they think *wouldn't* get them? If we met, we think, that person would see us for who we were. And they would approve.

It's only after I leave that I realise what I was secretly hoping for: a moment of connection, some kind of validation from the person I've put on a pedestal for most of my life. But that's impossible. I doubt I've met the true Atherton, just as I know he hasn't met the real me. So as I wander back to my office, I am subdued. Something has happened here that feels incredibly final: even more so, perhaps, than the moment he walked off a pitch for the last time.

In 2001, when Atherton quietly left the sporting stage, it didn't hurt; in fact, it made a sort of sense. My life had found a balance, and a hope, and a future. I was crossing the threshold of adulthood, and it felt time to say goodbye. Now all that's left to say is thank you.

Chapter 13

Mum and I are at Lord's. Our tradition hasn't changed much in 20 years. We still arrive at the ground in a state of garrulous anticipation, as if the next six hours of sporting action were capable of changing our lives for ever.

Our tickets direct us to the very middle of a row. 'Why do you always get seats so far from the aisle?' Mum grumbles. 'Can't you say you've got a disability?'

'No, but next time I'll tell them I've got an elderly mother.'

At 11.40 a.m., an England bowler takes a wicket and Mum takes it as a cue to celebrate with a bottle of prosecco. Within an hour she is groaning loudly every time a ball passes a fielder, then adds, 'I'm getting too loud, aren't I?'

We gossip and giggle and speculate about the spectators sitting around us. A few rows in front a man is wearing a pith helmet and leather waistcoat. A little to the left, a sun-coloured older gentleman is sitting with a rather glamorous blonde in her twenties. They are filling in a scorecard together. 'It's my daughter's first time at the cricket,' he tells us. 'I'm just trying to teach her the ropes.'

As the lunch hour approaches, my mother delivers military-style directions: 'We'll get the food and I'll leave your coat over the seats so they don't get wet and we'll go down to the Nursery End and we'll nab a spot and I'll go for a wee and you'll guard the bags . . .' Our picnic is one of Mum's Marks and Spencer's specials, and spread out on a blanket it looks like a king's feast, a ridiculously generous array of antipasti, salads, quesadillas, chicken legs, rolls, puddings and pork pie. Close by a group of men sit in a small circle around two packets of crisps and four pints of lager. 'That makes me sad,' my mother says. 'Don't they have mummies?'

We reminisce about our lives, and talk about what's happening in them today, and decide that we are both pretty happy. We even miss the first 20 minutes after the game resumes, just sitting there, talking. In the old days, I would never have countenanced us missing a single ball, but these days coming to the cricket is as much about enjoying Mum's company as it is about the action.

The way I watch cricket has changed plenty. When I first started following England, if they began to show some promise I would get excited far too quickly. I hadn't yet learned to be sceptical, and I didn't understand how rapidly a match could turn against you. 'Mum, Mum, they've got three wickets! They're *bound* to win now, aren't they?' 'There's still a long way to go,' she'd reply, trying to temper my hopes. I could never understand why she wanted to be such a killjoy and I suspected that she just didn't care as much as me. Now I have the same ingrained pessimism that comes to all England cricket fans who love not wisely but too well.

In the winter of 2013 I was in Sydney for the final match of the Ashes series. England were 4–0 down, and the home crowd were in a festive mood; by contrast, England's players looked like the walking dead. Zombie batsmen took to the crease, and shortly returned to the pavilion with glassy eyes. Among the vibrant ranks of earthy Aussie fans, I felt like a shaman, the only one who could see the spirits haunting the team, and discern the ghosts of batting collapses past. You could have transported the entire stadium back to the nineties without raising a murmur.

There was, however, one difference: I was enjoying myself. England were consistently hopeless – my eyes ached from rolling – but I could still find pleasure in Australia's performance. Their opening bowlers, Mitchell Johnson and Ryan Harris, were a duo of aggressive, ruthless speed that hadn't been seen since the days of Donald and Pollock, Ambrose and Walsh. My teenage self would have agonised for the batsmen and wished for any event – bowling change, sudden injury, freak rainstorm – to end the terror threat. Instead, I was riveted, awestruck. I didn't want to be anywhere else.

I know now that I will never feel as committed to another sporting team as I was to England in the nineties, and that's OK. That's probably healthy. As Michael Atherton pointed out, it takes a certain immaturity to remain so passionately partisan about the game, and to believe in the supreme importance of its trivial outcomes. One thing that meeting my heroes has taught me is that, while they might have been different from the people I imagined, my adolescent self was closer to them in spirit than I ever realised. They may have been ten years older than me but the way that sport made them think and behave wasn't so very far removed from a teenager.

On the other hand, I don't think the decade of defeats affected us in quite the same way. I had always assumed that the nineties must have been even more painful for those who played through them. I felt extremely sorry for the players, not just as a teenager but also in the years that followed. I thought it must be tough that they not only had to experience first-hand the sharp end of defeat, but live with the bitterness of those memories too. And yet few of the players I've met remembered being especially unhappy, or described great regrets since. They were professional sportsmen: losing games was always part of the deal.

It was probably a far happier experience for them than for me. They were doing the thing they loved and being paid for it. And they were having plenty of fun as they did. For the fans, an England tour could make winter all the grimmer. Waking up on a dark December morning to news of an overnight batting collapse and an innings defeat, I would head to double maths in misery; but the players would be heading to the bars and the beach. A few said they wished they had played in a climate where sportsmen were better treated, better equipped, prepared and rested. But largely, they are proud of being nineties cricketers. Most were gratified to have played during what they considered a golden period of world cricket. No players of the current day, they believe, can bear comparison with those who menaced England so repeatedly – the pace bowlers of West Indies and South Africa, the swing bowlers of Pakistan, and the two deadliest spinners in Test history, Shane Warne and Muttiah Muralitharan.

Perhaps one day people will revise England's most embarrassing period of history, and rate its captain and its players a little higher. The stats do prove, after all, that Atherton's team wasn't quite as consistently awful as our memories tell us. Cricket nostalgics get warm fuzzies at the eighties talents of Botham, Gower, Gooch and Gatting, but wince at the still-tender bruises of the nineties, despite the fact that the decades can barely be separated in terms of results. Unlike in the eighties, the nineties team was never in an overall decline. But nor did it establish a pattern of improvement. And Hollywood doesn't make movies about sports teams that are as terrible at the end of the film as they were at the beginning.

Back at Lord's, the afternoon session is in its classic post-lunch lull. Mum hands round snacks to our neighbours, firing up little conversations with strangers all around her. Lots are fathers with their sons; Mum has always cut a dash among the mostly male crowd with her gregarious nature and her brightly coloured wardrobe. The booze is drugging me into a semi-somnolent state, and I'm vaguely aware that Mum is talking enthusiastically about me. It sounds very much like she is trying to pimp me out.

I once saw a father and his teenage daughter at a rugby match wearing T-shirts that pronounced them a 'Dream Team!', the kind of sentiment and fashion choice you could only get away with in a sporting stadium. It's not cool to be that close to your parents, especially when you're young. But I've always liked how near I feel to my mum when we watch cricket, even if we're not sitting in the same row, or the same house, or the same city. I like knowing we have the same allies, and we're feeling the same emotions. I love how, in those moments, she understands me, and I understand her. So, whatever else they achieved, the men who made that happen are heroes.

The more I think about it, the more grateful I am to England's team of losers. They may not have given much satisfaction, but they were, as Atherton put it himself, always triers. And that wasn't a bad quality for a young girl to aspire to. I watched them give their best through the enduring tough times, the constant lows, when there wasn't a redemptive arc in sight. Following them taught me to expect, and to deal with, disappointment. I'd had a pretty blessed upbringing: loving parents, happy home life, good schooling. Supporting a perennially losing team was probably a decent way to learn that things weren't always going to go well.

Disappointment wasn't the only emotion that the England cricket team helped me to handle, either. Envy, love, anger, joy: feelings rush through a 15-year-old raw and unfiltered by wisdom or experience, and cricket was a proxy for them all. I didn't have boyfriends, or rows with my parents, so my sports team was a surrogate. Here was the relationship where I could let it all out. This was where I could express and release the heartache and the thousand natural shocks that teenage flesh is heir to, whose intensity was entirely out of proportion with the stable, comfortable nature of my daily life.

There are other places for a middle-class British girl to achieve catharsis: I could have headed to the mosh pit, or become an opera buff. But I was neither trendy nor sophisticated, and sport is a rare arena where an over-excitable nature can camouflage itself, and yelp at will. Since I had never been interested in vigorous exercise, cricket, as cerebral as it was physical, suited me perfectly. Jogging with little urgency around the field, or watching a ball fall out of their reach, its players were easier to relate to than an athlete gliding effortlessly through water or running a marathon.

I remember asking my dad, once, whether my parents were never concerned that my cricket obsession was out of hand. Dad didn't see the point in following sport, after all. Didn't it worry him that his daughter's happiness depended so heavily on the actions of 11 men who weren't him, or that she spent her spare hours obsessively cutting out pictures of them for her walls? 'No,' he said mildly. 'Little girls get passions about things. It could have been a lot worse.'

The game became many things for me before I could finally learn, once more, that it was just a game. It was a proving ground, a marker of personal identity, a bonding mechanism, a channeller of adolescent energies and a toxic waste area for dumping nuclear angst. The players themselves – the men I had constructed from the two-dimensional plane of the pictures on my walls – were substitute older brothers, annoying, infuriating, delighting, inspiring. But in real life, it turns out they rarely felt in control of their futures. Their sporting lives were exhilarating but erratic, and they were constantly encountering invisible forces they found frustrating, demoralising, exhausting.

The nineties were the foundation of a modern era to come – a grim old time without which change would never happen, and whose protagonists could do nothing other than endure, believing that better was on its way. No wonder, as I underwent my own messy transition to adulthood, I identified with England's cricketers. They travelled life's highway a little way ahead of me and I watched on – with nervous fascination and an eagerness to follow.

Acknowledgments

People say you should never meet your heroes, but that's only true if your heroes are idiots. I am so grateful to the 11 fascinating, funny, patient and thoughtful men who agreed to meet me to talk about their England days. Thank you also to team physio Dave Roberts for the stories he shared. I'm especially indebted to Mike Atherton – if it wasn't for him, I would never have written this book at all. Of course, he may have preferred it that way.

Here are some of my other heroes. Rob Biddulph: you pushed me to come up with this idea, you nagged me to get an agent, you spent a year listening to me whinge about how hard writing is. Oh, and you designed the book cover too. You really have to stop being such a nice guy. (Thank you very much for being my friend.)

Other friends have also gone above and beyond the call of duty. Philip Cornwall, you have saved me from so many a factual error in my life, thanks for minesweeping once again. Nick Coleman, I turned up on your doorstep, and you found yourself mentoring a first-time author. You were brilliant at it and I'm very grateful.

Charlotte, my editor at Bloomsbury, and Stan, my agent at Jenny Brown Associates, know that this book wouldn't have happened without them. I'm also grateful to Giles Clarke for helping put me in touch with players and to Ruaridh Nicoll for being a pretty understanding boss. Others don't know the contribution they've made: Rob Moody, whose

YouTube channel robelinda2 is a geek's delight and has been invaluable in prodding my memory, and the *Guardian*'s sports writers, whose wit and warmth regularly inspire me.

Rob Smyth, Steven Lynch, Travis Basevi are statistical geniuses and kind, generous men who I am lucky to know. Ed Cumming is a very funny writer who will sulk if I don't tell people that he came up with the title for this book. Eva Wiseman read and advised on passages even though she hates cricket. Andy Bull and Lawrence Booth gave calm encouragement, Ben Horslen complemented it with rousing rhetoric, and Alex Davison completed the job by taking me out, getting me drunk, and making me believe I could do anything.

Matthew Hancock is my sports editor at the *Observer* and this book is the first thing I've written in a decade I've not forced him to edit. It only exists because he helped me find my voice. I must also thank Stephen Fay and John Stern for teaching me to write about cricket and Tim Lewis for modelling how to be a real editor, writer, and grown-up.

I've always known I'm lucky in my friends, but in the course of writing this book I have been overwhelmed by their support. I'm grateful to many people at KXC – to Hub, to the Eagles – who have looked out for me, cooked for me, prayed for me. Thanks to the Shoulers and to Cathy Aizlewood for providing me with escapes when I needed somewhere quiet to write.

When I was going back through old boxes of keepsakes from my student years I found a short note in my dad's handwriting that he had sent alongside a cheque, for whatever sum I had managed to talk out of him. It said, 'Love also enclosed'. Mum, Dad, Kate, Justin, I hope you enjoy the contents of these pages. Love also enclosed.